And You Thought There Were Only Four

400 Questions
to Make Your Seder
Enlightening, Educational
and Enjoyable

Joe Bobker

gefen גפן
publishing house בית הוצאה לאור
JERUSALEM ♦ NEW YORK

Typesetting and Cover Design by S. Kim Glassman

1   3   5   7   9   8   6   4   2

Gefen Publishing House, LTD.
6 Hatzvi Street
Jerusalem 94386, Israel
972-2-538-0247
orders@gefenpublishing.com

Gefen Books
600 Broadway
Lynbrook, NY 11563, USA
1-800-477-5257
orders@gefenpublishing.com

www. israelbooks.com

Printed in Israel   Send for our free catalogue

ISBN 965-229-366-0

To my wife Miriam
who *always* "sets"
the table just right,

and to my four sons
who *always*
add to the Seder
the Pesach symbols of
curiosity and questioning,
wit and intelligence...

CONTENTS

ACKNOWLEDGMENTS

After explaining the laws of Pesach, the cheder Rebbe asks his young class to use the word *matza* in a sentence.

"Matzas are eaten at the Seder," says seven-year-old Yaakov.

"Very good," the Rebbe smiles. "How about you, David?"

"Matzas are made without salt," says young eight-year-old David.

"Excellent," replies the Rebbe when suddenly six-year-old Izzy, who has only been in the country a few months, raises his hand and triumphantly declares, "Time matzas on!"

Leshana haba b'Yerushalayim,
next year in Jerusalem,

and *Chag kasher vesameach,*
a joyous and kosher Pesach,
to everybody!

vii

When asked what his most important contribution is to the Jewish people, Mr. Bobker, who currently lives in New York with his wife Miriam, a barrister from Melbourne, replied, "Eli, Avi, Benny, Dovi, Hadassa, Baylie, Layella, Devorah, Dalia, Toby, Chesky, Yoni, Baruch, Ze'evi, Mattie, Mordechai, Henny, and David – my four sons, four daughters-in-law, four granddaughters and six grandsons (as of Rosh Hashana, 2005)."

FOREWORD

Strange, isn't it? Weeks before the Seder, we meticulously prepare all the holiday symbols, except one. The most important one. The most precious one.

The one elementary Pesach requisite that no one prepares for in advance, yet whose absence is conspicuous at the Seder, is the presence of a child, any child, for only Jewish children, with their imaginative interaction, can accelerate the recounting of the tale of the Exodus.

In spring of 1946, one year after the liberation of Adolf's death camps, some of the U.S. Jewish military personnel stationed throughout the world found themselves in Germany over Pesach. A thoughtful U.S. government had provided everything for their Seder – everything except for a Jewish child. Realizing that they had no one to ask the *Ma Nishtana* foursome, a frantic and agitated search for Jewish children was conducted throughout all of Berlin.

It failed.

Adolf had been thorough, systematic, determined. Whilst stalking the land of Europe, he had gratuitously slaughtered millions of God's first, second and third born so there was not a single solitary Jewish child to be found. That missing

Jewish-Germanic child (the "Fifth Child") had disappeared alongside one-and-a-half million other tortured European Jewish children into the deep black hole of history.

At that particular time and place, the presence of any child would have sufficed. Wise, wicked, simple, inexperienced – no matter.

In the end, the military personnel settled on an American bar mitzva boy who had just arrived to Germany with his father, a chaplain.

Pesach without children is like a cantor without a song, like an actor without any lines, or a storyteller without an audience. Why? Because Jewish children embody the ultimate symbol of chag. They represent victory over disaster, triumph over tragedy; their presence shouts endurance over destruction. Children make Pesach both whole and wholesome, enjoyable and everlasting.

I remember, as a child, that the best part of my father's Seder *tisch* was not the melodious tunes, the abundance of delicious dishes, the four brimming cups of wine, nor the reclining. Not even the search for the hidden *afikomen*. The part of the Seder that fascinated my sister Chanala and I the most, year in, year out, came just before the thanksgiving prayer of *Hallel*.

Our childish imaginations were awed and stirred by the mystery of that omnipresent Fifth Cup, a goblet of wine, known as the *koso shel Eliyahu*, that just sat there all night, untouched by human lips. The cup belonged to Eliyahu HaNavi (Eliyahu means "my God is God"), the invisible Prophet Elijah, a man of great mystery, a phenomenon *sui generis*, defender of God and champion of monotheism, who lived during the seventh century BCE in the northern kingdom of Israel.

Elijah's name appears neither in the Torah nor in the Book of Prophets. We only find mention of him in the Grace after Meals. (Elijah, Elisha and Nathan don't have their own "books" because as "pre-classical" prophets they did not write down nor have their words recorded.) Chronologically, Elijah has nothing to do with the Exodus since he lived some 600 years after the time of Moses. What then does he have to do with Passover?

When the rabbis of the Talmud couldn't agree whether Jews should drink four or five cups of wine, they decided to pour a fifth cup that would remain full – and defer the answer until the future when, according to tradition, Elijah, expecting to return before the Messiah, would prepare his way by settling all of history's open-ended rabbinic disputes and Talmudic stalemates, and shed light on the difficult recesses and inconsistencies of Scripture. (I imagine that his first answer will be whether his own cup should be drunk or not.)

Whenever these "hard questions" arise, the Torah text concludes with the word *teyku*, which is derived from the Hebrew root *kum*, which denotes, "let it stand," or from *tik*, a "file." Thus the term *teyku* suggests, "File it away." Jewish mystics see *teyku* as an acronym for *Tishbi y'taretz kushiyot veba'ayot*, "Elijah the Tishbite will resolve all problems and difficulties" (Tishbite referring to Elijah's birthplace, the village of Tishbe in Gil'ad, north of the River Yabbok).

In the meantime, Jewish tradition has assigned to Elijah a larger-than-life presence: a wise Jew and dispenser of special insights whose sheer presence was the ultimate invitation to redemption and reconciliation. Elijah is the Messiah's front-runner with a message that better days were a'coming for us; he is the unseen prophet-guardian of the people of Israel whose miraculous presence attests to this time being *Leil Shimurim*, the "night of Divine watchfulness."

Elijah was the enigma of Pesach, the conundrum of the wine-stained pages of the Haggada. My father would strain his ears in the hope of hearing this prophet's footsteps. My mother would hold back tears of hope that Judaic redemption was, finally, about to enter her home. One could cut the tension with a knife when I was sent to open the front door (a task I rightfully claimed as mine each year), and then rushed back to the dining room to watch the rim of the wine glass. It had to move. That was like Halacha in my home. It was predestined, inevitable, a foregone conclusion.

And Elijah never failed to oblige; each year he would slip in and out, taste the wine, participate with us in our annual celebratory evening of freedom and birth as a holy nation. Yep. The wine always moved. I saw it with my own eyes.

During his Seder, Rabbi Menahem Mendel Morgenstern of Kotzk once opened the door to welcome Elijah. As he left the room, one of his thirsty guests drank the wine from Elijah's cup. When the Rebbe returned and saw the cup empty, he turned to his guest and, not wanting to embarrass him, said, "My dear friend, both you and Elijah are welcome guests in my home. As the prophet did not appear to drink his wine, you are certainly entitled to it."

Not in our home: the punctual prophet always showed up, honoring our humbled family with his imbibing habits, with his majestic and mysterious presence, just as he had honored thousands of other Jewish homes for the past 3,000 years; invisibly passing over Auschwitz arches and through Gulag gates, blood libels, Christian stakes, task masters and slave lords all.

The predominant emotion that I felt during the Seder night was relief; relief that Elijah was consistent in his zealousness to visit my family, my home, to sip from my, sorry, his goblet. His silent presence stirred my childish imaginations. His stubborn insistence at showing up each year, just at the right time, was reassuring. That is why so many yiddishe folk songs have been composed in his honor as the harbinger of unity, salvation and consolation, expressing love and longing, sung when the Pesach doors are flung open or at the closing of the Shabbat.

When the prophet exited our home, he may have exited incognito but he left behind something very tangible: hope, a quality that if "deferred maketh the heart sick."[1]

The hope that springs eternal in the human breast is why Elijah's annual comings 'n goings leave in their wake a contagious symbol of enthusiasm and expectations for a better world, for the light of liberty, for an indomitable Judaic optimism.

Hope, in the home of Holocaust survivors, was better than life; and it was "hope" that began our Sedarim with *hashata avdei, leshana haba bnei chorin* ("currently we are subservient, but we can envision our liberation"), and also ended them, at around midnight, via the soft lyrics of *Nirtza* that expressed yearning for the swift arrival of "*Mashiach tzidkenu.*"

I have a confession to make: sometimes, when I watch my four sons' eyes fixed on the full goblet of Elijah, I knock the table ever so slightly to make the wine move. I'm sure my father, my father's father and his father never resorted to such cheap trickery – and the wine *still* moved.

I feel guilty. I'll try not to do it next year.

---

1. Proverbs 13, 12.

THE EXODUS STORY
AND ITS MESSAGE

Question 1

Who was Moses?

Although Moses' birth marked a major event in Jewish history, signifying the birth of the future leader of the Jewish people, it is described with no fanfare, no lengthy family lineage, just a simple sparse announcement, "The woman conceived and bore a son," accompanied by an understatement, *ki tov*, "this is good" (the same words used by God during Creation).

Moses' biography would have to include "The Missing Years," since several decades of his life, from maturity until he returns as God's elected emissary, are squeezed into three short verses. The Torah is strangely silent about this sixty-year gap, a disappearance literally in mid-narrative, leaving us clueless as to Moses' character or spiritual development. Consider his near invisibility: As a baby, Moses begins his life in a temporary wicker basket (*tevat gomeh*); the Pesach Haggada ignores him totally in his own adventure; he becomes nationally homeless (poignantly expressed when he names his first son, Gershon, from *ger sham*, which means, "I am a stranger in a strange land"); the daughters of Reuel (Yitro) including his future wife Tzipora simply describe him as "a man of Egypt" (in contrast to Joseph who is contemptuously called "the Hebrew slave"); he spends the last forty years of his life "hiding" behind a facial veil so that the Divine radiance does not frighten the folk; and finally, God ensures that the site of his grave remains unknown to history. The Torah fast-forwards through the birth of Moses, skips over the crucial moment when he first discovers that he is Jewish, ignores his formative teenage years, devotes only twenty-two verses to his young adult life, and condenses eight of his remarkable decades into five terse, concise chapters.

Yes, the Torah also applies this policy of obscurity to Abraham ben Terach, the father of Judaism, whom we meet only as a fully integrated adult already endowed with deep spirituality. However, in sharp contrast to Moses, the Midrashim expound at length on Abraham's early life, helping us recreate a detailed profile. Why such telegraphic brevity with Moses? By speeding through Moses' early and middle years, the Torah is making the statement that beginnings are less important than endings; that judgment must be reserved for what one ultimately achieves in life. Many redeemers of Israel enter the most significant chapter of their lives in adulthood; Moses at eighty, Aaron at eighty-three, and the great Rabbi Akiva only began to study Torah at the age of forty. The lesson? That one must never give up or despair; that despite life's bumps, detours and frustrations one must persevere, for sometimes ailments are only imaginary barriers to determination and resolve.

Is Moses a *born* leader? No, but Moses is prolific in leader-ship, blessed with the ability to be *nosei be'ol im chaveiro*, to share his fellow's burden and fate; to empathize with the suffering of his fellow Jews. A slew of events transforms him from a shepherd of flocks to the leading shepherd of the whole House of Israel; even as he reluctantly, with disarming honesty, demands of God, "Who am I, that I should bring the Israelites out of Egypt?" This question "Who am I?" is directed at himself, a senior citizen entering into the final trimester of his life, estranged from the Jewish people for eight decades. When ordered to return and rescue "his brothers," he instantly declines *shlichut* (from the Hebrew verb *shlach*, "to send") to serve as God's agent. "Send someone else," he begs. Why? "I am not a man of words, but slow of speech and tongue." Moses' objections are to no avail; the Heavens are unswayed and assign to him a "spokesman," none other than his older brother (Aaron).

The Midrash is however unconvinced: it sees no physi-cal impediment in Moses other than a concern that he is no longer fluent in the language of his people, and thus lacks the capacity to move their hearts and minds. This is true: as his life progresses, we witness an articulate Moses giving speeches, rulings, warnings – even arguing with God with not a trace of a stammer nor stutter, as the ever-confident messenger expands his lexicon with ease.

Question 2

Given the primitive means of travel available, how did the Jews of Judea, scattered across the holy land, manage the back-and-forth trek to Jerusalem for Pesach sacrifices?

They didn't. The rabbis divided the country into twenty-four districts (*ma'amadot*), and assigned a special week to each district in which local delegations would go up to Jerusalem. Once there, these emissaries saw to it that their morning and evening sacrifices took place at the same time as prayers were being said back home in their synagogues (a model for the future practice of daily *shul* prayers). And to ensure that there were no second-class Israelites, offerings were "equalized" (*each* being "a satisfying aroma to God") by way of sliding-scale dues. For example: the Jew who could not afford the choicest of a sheep or goat could use a pigeon; and if one was too indigent to even afford a pigeon, then a tenth (*epha*) of plain ground wheat would do just fine.

Question 3

What was "Operation Matzah Ball Express?"

In order to fulfill the desires of the Holocaust survivors to have their first Pesach Seder in Occupied Germany (April 15, 1946), the u.s. Army worked hard to provide a massive influx of Pesach-related ingredients. The u.s. Army dubbed this operation "Matzah Ball Express." They provided tons of matza, gallons of wine, two-and-a-half-ton truckloads of gefilte fish, bushels of nuts and apples, and cases of candles and Haggadot, and thanks to the efforts of Rabbi Mayer Abramowitz, Jewish chaplain to the u.s. 3ʳᵈ Infantry Division, and General Frank T. Schmidt (under orders from European Theater of Operations, headed then by Dwight D. Eisenhower), the scarred and scared several hundred Jews in the bombed-out cities of Kassel, Fulda and Marburg were miraculously able to celebrate the Festival of Freedom in an underground bunker in the shadow of the ashes of Auschwitz. When General Schmidt sat at the head of the Seder *tisch*, the Jews sang, *Lo mir aleh aleh in eimen dem general mechabed ponim zein*, "Let us all greet the general!" together with a *Shehechiyanu*, "Blessed are you, God, who kept us alive to reach this season!"

Question 4

Are there any similarities between the Exodus of the Jews from Egypt and the "other" exodus, that of the Ethiopian Jews' flight to Israel?

Yes. After millennia of suffering in an oppressive society, Ethiopian Jewry (thought to be either descendants of the tribe of Dan or the progeny of King Solomon and the Ethiopian Queen of Sheba) crossed the Sudanese desert for the holy land, *twice*, in secret airlifts known as Operation Moses (1984) and Operation Solomon (1991). Like the slaves in Egypt, they left at a moment's notice, fleeing a hostile society that accused them of dual loyalty because of their preferred language (Hebrew) and their intense love not of Ethiopia but of Israel. The Ethiopian government forbade Jews to own land, thus further exacerbating their transient status and ephemeral relationship to a homeland.

Pesach was always *the* festive chag for Ethiopian Jews who practiced a pre-Talmudic form of Judaism: they do not use a Hagadda nor do they drink four cups of wine, a custom introduced later at the time of the Mishna. Instead the head of the household or the *kes*, "rabbi," would tell the Torah tales of the slaughtering of the paschal lamb, the ten plagues, the Exodus itself. In Ethiopia, the Jews would scour every corner of their one-room thatched mud huts to remove any crumb of chametz. Some families, on erev Pesach, would destroy all of their dishes and cooking vessels and craft new ones, a symbolic start to a new (and kosher) year that they hoped would lead to their redemption. Since there were no local kosher stores, each family made their own matza, either from wheat or legume flour, water and salt, and ate it almost immediately. Why? To avoid even the remotest possibility of leavening.

Question 5

What happened in Bnei Brak?

Bnei Brak is the location where five of the ten Sages from the tannaitic period (Eliezer, Joshua, Elazar ben Azariah, Akiba and Tarfon), all wanted men on the Roman hit list, gather on Pesach to "recline" and discuss the Exodus from Egypt. Bnei

Brak, a city near Jaffa that belonged to the Tribe of Dan, is where Rabbi Akiva established his yeshiva and held court. It is also the place where Rami bar Yechezkel finally understood the Torah's description of *Eretz Yisrael* as a "land flowing with milk and honey"; whilst observing goats grazing beneath fig trees, the rabbi literally witnessed honey oozing from the ripe figs into milk dripping from the goats, to form a stream of milk and honey.[1]

The question is this: How could it possibly be that the greatest Sages of the time, who stayed up all night in Bnei Brak discussing the Haggada, didn't know when it was time to say the *Shema*? These five rabbis were the then leaders of the rebellion against the Romans, and had hidden themselves in a cave with no windows from Hadrian's ruthless armed forces who were patrolling everywhere in search for the "Most Wanted." Thus, they had to be told by their students (who were in fact "guards" keeping an eye out for the enemy) when daylight came, not just to say the Shema but also to be more cautious.

Question 6

What's Nero got to do with Pesach?

In his Jewish wars, the turncoat Jewish historian Flavious Josephus recalls how the emperor Nero, determined to count how many Jews were in Jerusalem, had his troops count how many paschal lambs were killed. The number? Two hundred fifty-six thousand, five hundred. The Talmud describes a similar "count" conducted by the High Priest that came to 600,000 pairs of

---

1. *Yehoshua* 19:45; *Sanhedrin* 32b; *Ketuvot* 111b.

lamb kidneys. The masses that descended to Jerusalem for Pesach were so numerous that the Talmud labeled one year the "Pesach of the crushed one," after an old man died from suffocation.

Question 7

Why is Freud's name sometimes associated with Moses?

When fascist Germans first started displaying a bloody lust towards Jews, Sigmund Freud, a confused self-hating Jew who was considered the father of psychoanalysis, decided not to question the Jew-haters but delve into the question of, "Why do Jews attract this undying hatred?" In the same year that the SS started their rape and murder of Polish Jewry, Sigmund Freud decided to publish his final book (knowing he was dying of cancer) called *Der mann Moses und die monotheistiche Religion, Moses and Monotheism*. Sigmund described his work as a "historical novel," but it's simply unpleasant fiction, nothing but a crude, anti-traditional reconstruction of Judaism, in sharp contrast to, for example, the first-century Philo of Alexandria's *De vita mosis, The Life of Moses*.

Freud's reinvention of Jewish history reflects his inner conflicts with his own Jewishness ("We do not believe that one great god exists today," wrote Sigmund, "but that in primeval times there was one single person [i.e., Moses] who at that time had to appear gigantic"). Unlike Schiller (*Die Sendung Moses*) or Warburton (*Divine Legation of Moses*), who at least acknowledged that Moses was a Jew, Freud tells the story of Moses the

Egyptian in the same way that he would describe Hercules or Prometheus, or Spartacus in Rome or Nat Turner in the American South, a slave uprising void of any theological underpinnings (*ta hiera grammata*). Freud was correct, however, on one issue: anti-Semitism was fueled by a fear of monotheism; but his misplaced goal to redefine Moses as an Egyptian and not a Jew, in his fantasy attempt to shift the world's anti-Jewish vitriol away from the Jews, was a failure. In his revisionism, he claims that the ritual of *brit mila* was Egyptian, that Moses "invented God (*finxisse*)" as the legal authority behind his man-made laws; and that he chose Aaron as a spokesman – not because of his stutter but because he couldn't speak Hebrew!

Question 8

Has there ever been the charge of blood libel in the United States?

A contemptible ritual murder charge was made on September 23, 1928, erev Yom Kippur, against the Jewish community of Massena, northern New York, near the border with Canada. The local mayor (Gilbert Hawes) and "enlightened" state police joined the Ku Klux Klan, superstitious locals and ignorant officials to investigate whether the Jewish community had kidnapped Barbara Griffiths, a four-year-old girl, for use in Yom Kippur rituals. The ignorance and religious bigotry of these white, Anglo-Saxon Protestants was such that they got their Jewish festivals mixed up: the European Catholics made the evil blood libel charge on Pesach, around Easter time, and never on Yom Kippur).

The Jews of Massena, immigrants from Russia and Poland,

consisted of only twenty families who congregated around the town's shul (*Adas Yisrael*), the courageous Orthodox rabbi-*shochet-ba'al tefilla* (Berel Brennglass), and the president (Yaakov Shulkin). After they were brought in and questioned as "suspects" in ritual murder, the little girl, an hour before *Kol Nidrei*, wandered out of the local wood about half a mile away from her home, after having gotten innocently lost – and so it was that the first potential blood-ritual pogrom in the United States was averted.

Question 9

What's the connection between Pesach and the blood libel?

Pesach, because of its proximity to Easter, became synonymous with the frightening blood libel, an absurd yet deadly ritual murder accusation that Jews eat and drink the human flesh and blood of Christians (even the fourteenth-century English poet Chaucer referred to it in his *Canterbury Tales*). Who started this hideous lie? The perverted Antiochus. The King of Syria spread it as part of a propaganda blitz to discredit Judaism during the Maccabean struggle. It then lay dormant for several centuries until 1144, when it reappeared in Norwich, England and quickly spread to Germany (where it was known as *alilat dam*) and Blois, France, where immoral anti-Semites (and treasonous Jewish converts, such as Peter Schwartz and the notorious John Pfefferkorn) used it as a convenient justification for pogroms and theft of Jewish property. This led to the Jewish custom of opening the front door during the Seder meal to "show" the *goyim* that Jews had nothing to hide.

"God! I ask you to hasten the redemption of your people, Israel," cried the Maggid of Koznitz, "and if You do not wish to do so – then redeem the gentiles!" The rabbis insisted on gentile bystanders watching them bake matza in order to dispel any doubts. Each year Rabbi Shmelke of Nikolsburg invited a prominent non-Jew to his Seder, and translated every word in the Haggada. One year, when he sang out, *Leshana Haba b'Yerushalayim*, he added, in Hebrew with no translation, "God! Enough! The time has arrived for You to redeem us from this exile. I am already ashamed in front of this non-Jew!" The six-teenth–seventeenth-century Rabbi David ben Samuel Halevi, author of the *Turei Zahav*, was against red wine because of the fear that its color would incite the charge of blood libel. He knew what it was to be afraid, since he was a victim himself of the Chmielnicki pogroms in 1648–49.

Question 10

Who wrote the *Brah Dodi* poems?

These three morning Pesach prayer-poems, known as the *geula piyyutim*, were written by three poets of Israel: the tenth-century prolific liturgist Rabbi Shelomeh ben Yehuda haBavli (who pleads for the liberation of Israel), eleventh-century Italian Rabbi Meshullam ben Kalonymus (who cries for the restoration of Jerusalem), and the prodigious politically connected eleventh-century Rabbi Simeon ben Isaac ben Abun of Mayence (who beseeches that the redemption be "prompt and complete").

Each prayer begins with the phrase *brah dodi*, which means "Make haste, my friend!" On the last day of Pesach, we also recite a *geula* ode from Rabbi Yehuda haLevi, the "Sweet Singer of Zion" poet-philosopher, Toledo-born author of over three hundred poems who died in Egypt, attempting to reach the land of Israel.

Question 11

What is the Pesach of *Yom Hahesger*?

It literally means, the "Day of Shutting In," and refers to the laws of Avignon and the Comtat Venaissin that for many generations prohibited Jews from leaving their homes during Pesach (which usually clashed with their Easter). The Jews wrote special hymns for the occasion, such as...

> Like a princess set away
> In her palace on this day;
> Hidden, like a lovely maid
> Thus her prayer 'fore God she laid
> (He Whose spirit, wondrous-wise,
> All that liveth vivifies):
> "Rouse Thee, at this spring-tide feast
> Till our servitude ceased!"

Question 12

Where in the Torah do we first read about the Exodus saga?

The groundwork for the Exodus story is laid even *before* a handful of Jews arrive in Egypt. In His earlier Covenant with Abraham, God makes a promise, "I will also judge the nation whom they serve, after which they will leave with great wealth."[2] Thus, even before the long period of enslavement, it was known that the Jews would be rescued and would depart "with great wealth" (which is why God reminds Moses to "Tell the people that each man should ask his neighbor and each woman should ask her neighbor for silver and gold articles").[3]

Question 13

Which term is more correct – Israelites or Hebrews?

I don't know, but perhaps Moses gives us an inkling. When he addresses Pharaoh (a foreigner), he refers to his people as "Hebrews," but when he speaks to his folk directly, he fondly calls them "Israel."

---

2. Genesis 15:14.
3. Exodus 11:2.

Question 14

What were the *orei miskenot?*

When the Torah searches for a term to describe the sweat, toil and labor of the Jewish slaves in Egypt, it uses *avodat perach*, a term for meaningless work that is designed to "break a person." According to a Midrash, the Jews built *orei miskenot*, "pitiful cities" (Pitom and Ramses), structures built brick-on-meaning-less-brick on wet, sandy swamplands, designed to collapse immediately upon completion.[4] What was Pharaoh's purpose? To break a person's spirit, to imbue futility amongst Jews, to cause a state of inescapable anguish, despair, hopelessness. The saltwater into which we dip raw vegetables represents tears of torment and torture, anguish and angst, despair and depression.

Question 15

How many Jews originally went to Egypt?

Jewish history records seventy (souls) from Jacob's family who go "down to Egypt" as guests under Joseph's protection. The oldest? Serach, daughter of Asher, whose great longevity makes her *the* only known eyewitness to the entire Egyptian-Judeo experience. The question is obvious: that a "great and populous nation" emerges from only seventy people is an extraordinary demographic harvest, but were there *exactly* seventy of them

---

4.   Exodus 1:11.

or does the Torah merely use the number seventy to signify a large number?

The Torah itself lists *only* sixty-nine, a number that excludes daughters-in-law but includes one wife, Rachel (which is proof of her unique status in the family). Since seventy *is* recognized as a precise count, who is missing? I don't know, but rabbinic speculation focuses on three possibilities: Jacob; Yocheved, daughter of Levi (born "between the Egyptian entrance walls"); or God Himself ("I will go down *with you* to Egypt").

Question 16

What happened to Moses' two sons, Gershon and Eliezer?

As the yiddishists say, "Small children, small joys; big children, big annoys!" One of the great sources of mystery in the Torah is its near total silence regarding Gershon and Eliezer. Is there any father-son relationship here? We don't know; there's no hint of one. And worse, in an ominous sign, we hear absolutely nothing about their descendants, Moses' grandchildren (if any). Obviously, Moses had a problem of estrangement on his hands and, like a lot of parents, preferred to keep it "in house." This was a true Judeo-tragedy. Why? Because sons usually assume the mantle of leadership unless they are incapable, or, worse, unsuitable.

So what went wrong? Some suggest that since the boys were absent at Sinai they were deprived of any firsthand experience of God, of the "shock 'n awe" of His thunder and lightning. The Torah is mute on the possibility of shortcomings, but not the blunt Midrash: "Your sons sat around and did not engage in Torah!" It seems that the ultimate teacher of all teachers, Moses, responsible for bringing Torah to the entire nation, derived no *nachas* from his own sons. This family heartbreak surfaces in many generations, when leaders are unable to strike the balance between their communal and personal obligations.

Question 17

Why is the Shabbat before Pesach called *Shabbat Hagadol*, the "Great Shabbat"?

I'm not sure: there are several possible explanations. One is obvious. This was the Shabbat when Jews with faith, in the first major act of Judaic slave defiance, took lambs to sacrifice, which they knew would enrage their Egyptian neighbors who worshiped the animal. That they were not harmed is miraculous, and calling it the "Great Shabbat" reflects the greatness of this miracle.[5] The other reason to call this Shabbat "great" is because this Pesach sacrifice order (*korban Pesach*) is the first mitzva of the Torah. The Midrash links the dedication to mitzvot directly to freedom, since one can only keep mitzvot in a climate of freedom, and, likewise, only one who keeps Torah can be considered truly free.[6]

The term *Shabbat Hagadol* is definitely old (ancient Hebrew manuscripts contain the expression, *Rava Yoma de'Shabata*, which means "*Shabbat Hagadol*"). But what does the term refer

5.   *Tosafot*, Exodus 12:3.
6.   *Deuteronomy Rabba* 10:8.

to? Rabbi Shneur Zalman of Liadi, author of the Tanya, offers a pragmatic explanation: "It is because we remain longer in shul on that Shabbat to hear the laws of Pesach and to tell the wonders and miracles that occurred in Egypt; and because of the long time people spend in the synagogue, they feel the day is longer (*gadol*), and therefore it became known as *Shabbat Hagadol.*" Perhaps it is so-called because the length of the rabbi's special biannual sermon was "long and great (*gadol*)"?

Why did the rabbi speak on this particular Shabbat? To take advantage of when the masses were in town, visiting family for chag. This custom is linked to a Midrash that describes how Moses delivered to the Jews a major *dvar Torah* on the laws of Pesach on the eve of their Exodus. Some Jews, immediately after *Shabbat Hagadol mincha*, prepare for Pesach by reading the Haggada. Is there a special *Shabbat Hagadol Haftora?* Yes.[7] The one that discusses "bringing the entire tithe to God's storehouse," a reference by Malachi, the last of the prophets (whose focus was ensuring that Jewish society be built on the foundations of justice, morality and equality), to the law that on erev Pesach of the third and sixth year of *shmitta* (the seven-year sabbatical cycle), Jews were required to declare that they did not have certain tithes in their possession (ranging from those dedicated to *Kohanim, Leviim,* the poor, or allocated to be eaten in Jerusalem). And if they did? These tithes were either distributed or destroyed.

Why do we need a *Shabbat Hagadol* if the miracle occurred on the tenth of Nissan? Because Miriam, sister of Moses, prophetess and leader in her own right, died on that day. Thus

---

7. *Malachi* 3:4–24.

a celebratory day would be inappropriate.[8] Are we supposed to do anything special on *Shabbat Hagadol?* No, except listen to the rabbi's *Shabbat Hagadol drasha* (which is not a halachic requirement).

Question 18

Why did God need two messengers, Moses and Aaron? Wasn't one enough?

"One was needed to take the Jews out of Egypt," explains Rav Shmuel Mohliver, "and another to take Egypt out of the Jews, because the Exile had sunk into their hearts and had become part of their innermost being." This theme echoes redemption of the future which also requires "two messengers": a descendant of Joseph (the first Messiah) to take Israel out of Exile, followed by a descendant of David (the second Messiah) who will take the Exile out of the Jews.

Question 19

What is Moses' real birth name?

The Midrash gives Moses no less than thirteen names, but God, and thus Jewish history and tradition, uses the name given to him by Pharaoh's daughter who "drew him [*meshitihu*] from the water."[9] This name represents mercy and compassion, which

8.   *Magen Avraham, Orach Chayim,* 430:1; *Likutei Sichot* 12:36–37.
9.   Exodus 2:10.

are both such hallmarks of Judaism that even God's Torah is known as *Torat Moshe*. The Malbim, the preeminent nineteenth-century Russian Torah commentator, combines two Egyptian words, *mo* (water) and *sheh* ("to exit," or "escape"), to arrive at *Moses*.

Considering the fact that, according to a Midrash, the Jews were saved from perpetual servitude because they preserved their Jewish names, it is ironic that God continues to call Moses by his Egyptian name (even after liberation). In contrast, according to Frankfurt Rabbi Shimon Hadarshan (Shimon the Biblical Orator), his father called him *Chaver*, his mother called him *Yekusiel*, his sister called him *Yered*, his brother called him *Avi Zandach*, and his nurse called him *Avi Socho*. These multiple names perplexed some scholars, who suggest that the diversity results from the nonconformity of *mo*, since water, with no identity of its own, always adjusts to any container into which it is poured.

Question 20

When we sing Pesach songs, are we singing the original tunes?

Alas, no. Although the words remain the same, the original melodies and accurate musicology are long lost, especially those from the Temple era and even the folk songs of the destroyed Eastern Jewish communities, courtesy of Adolf. The simple chant of the post-Red Sea crossing, *The Song of Moses*, is still one of triumph, of springtime joy (the tune we sing to the *Song of Songs* was discovered by Lazare Saminsky in the Caucasian

Mountain regions of Georgia; he arranged the modern version so that it showcased the skill for solo voices). The *niggun* of the Prayer for Dew on the first morning of Pesach is not that old and can be traced to the prayers of the Jewish troubadours and minnesingers of Western Europe; whereas the melody for the blessing of the *omer*, which we chant on the second eve of Pesach, is one of great dignity.

By the time we leave *shul* and return home, the Seder songs become more robust, lively, joyous – childlike, even! And the *Ma Nishtana?* The tune is an echo of the one traditionally used in Ashkenazi yeshiva study halls during the time of the Mishna. The Chassidim have contributed a lot to our array of tunes: thanks to them, we have the fabulous rhythmic Slavic form of *Vehi She'amda*; and even the ominous Ten Plagues follows the *Haftora* style of the High Holidays. Meanwhile, *Echad Mi Yodea* ("Who Knows One") is sung in the vernacular of Bukharan Jews as well as in Ladino (Judeo-Spanish), Hebrew and in Yiddish parodies (that begin, *Mah adabbera, mah assappera oteka*, "What shall I say, what shall I speak unto thee?") that sing about the expensive matza bakers, the harrowed housewives, even "The Rabbi and the Teamster on Seder Night!" And then we have the cumulative delight of *Chad Gadya*, a "chain reaction" German folksong (how do we know? it appears in no Sephard Haggadot) that is so popular that its methodology has been "borrowed" by many – e.g., the English, "I Know an Old Lady Who Swallowed a Fly," whose final "accumulated" stanza goes like this:

> *I know an old lady who swallowed a cow,*
> *I don't know how she swallowed the cow.*
> *She swallowed the cow to catch the goat,*
> *She swallowed the goat to catch the dog,*

She swallowed the dog to catch the cat,
She swallowed the cat to catch the bird,
She swallowed the bird to catch the spider,
That wriggled and jiggled and tickled inside her.
She swallowed the spider to catch the fly,
But I don't know why she swallowed that fly.
Perhaps she'll die.

Question 21

Was Pharaoh really the father of the *ba'al teshuva* movement?

Commenting on the Torah verse, "And Pharaoh drew near, and the Israelites lifted their eyes, and there were the Egyptians marching after them, and they were very frightened, and the Israelites cried out to the Lord,"[10] the *Midrash Rabba* addresses the obvious grammatical problem. *U'Faroh hikriv* is usually translated as, "And Pharaoh drew near (or approached)," but its literal translation is, "And Pharaoh made [someone] approach." Does this mean that Pharaoh was involved in *kiruv* work (bringing people closer to Judaism)? Yes, apparently he was. The Midrash recalls how thanks to Pharaoh, the Jews, caught between the Red Sea and Egyptian army, suddenly rediscovered God (they "lifted their eyes [and] cried out to the Lord!").

---

10. Ibid., 4:10.

Question 22

Wasn't it risky for the Jews to slaughter the lamb, the symbol of Egyptian deity?

One can only imagine the risk! What would have happened to the Jews if, after slaughtering the Egyptian god lambs, the tenth plague *hadn't* materialized? They would have had to contend with their neighbors' hostile retribution. And yet, despite the fact that this generation abandoned the "old life," swapping "leeks and cucumbers" for manna, they were never glorified by our Sages as a superior generation or praised by Jewish history. In fact, Jewish tradition blames this insecure and unprepared-for-freedom generation for mistakes and catastrophes of such depth that we have a day of mourning (Tisha b'Av)[11] in the Jewish calendar because of them.

Question 23

Are the "Red Sea" and the "Sea of Reeds" one and the same?

No. The former is an inlet separating the western Arabian Peninsula from the east coast of Egypt, while the latter is one of the lakes between Egypt and Sinai and is the one referred to in the Exodus. How, then, did the "Red Sea" enter the Hebrew texts? In the third century, Ptolemy Philadelphus decided that his Great Library of Alexandria should contain a Greek version

---

11.   Numbers 13–14.

of the Hebrew Torah, and ordered the Alexandrian rabbinate to comply. The rabbis immediately declared a day of mourning, in the belief that any version other than the original Hebrew of God was blasphemous (unlike today when new versions of the Torah and Talmud are lauded as celebratory events; the Church, however, agreed with the Jews – when William Tyndale translated the Bible into vernacular English, he was burned at the stake!).

Ptolemy's Greek-Hebrew, the oldest Torah translation in the world (*Septuagint*), is a tortured mistranslation with a trickle-down effect. It ended up in Vulgate's Latin (*Mare Rubrum*) and in the popular King James's seventeenth-century English Bible. Despite the vastly different contexts of the two seas, the original translators extracted the same term (*yam suf*) from the Tanach (1 Kings 9:26) and misapplied it to the *yam suf* in the Torah (Exodus 13:18).[12] The sea mentioned in the Tanach is described in reference to King Solomon's navy at Ezion Geber, near Eilat on the shore of the Red Sea [*yam suf*],[13] while the sea mentioned in the Torah refers to the shores "in the land of Edom."

The confusion is compounded by the often-idiosyncratic use of the *yam suf* expression. The Torah[14] uses the term to define the borders of the promised land – "stretching from *yam suf* to the Sea of Philistia" – which identifies it with the modern Red Sea. The Torah also refers to *yam sof*, "sea of land's end" (which places it at the Gulf of Aqaba, Eilat, the southern tip of the Sinai Peninsula). Meanwhile, to further complicate

---

12.   1 Kings 9:26; Exodus 13:18.
13.   1 Kings 9:26.
14.   Exodus 23:31; Numbers 21:4.

the problem, Jeremiah[15] uses the same term in other geographic contexts (Teman, Bozra). The mistake was based on an assumption that *Edom* (a geographic location on the west side of the Aravah,[16] known today as the central Negev Highlands, northeast Sinai) and *adom* (the color "red") were one and the same. It didn't help matters that the coral colors and eastern shorelines of these waters appear reddish.[17]

In Hebrew, the word *suf* is derived from the Egyptian *twf*, "papyrus, reed thickets," which do not even grow in the Red Sea (they are found amongst the freshwater marshes of the northern Delta region, or amidst a long narrow strip of eastward bound water from Suez to the straits of Bab el-Mandeb, the demarcation line between North Africa and the Arabian Peninsula).

By the way, if you want clarification, don't bother looking up Egyptian records: they call both the Red Sea and the Sea of Reeds, "the Green Sea"!

Question 24

Is it true that the Exodus story contains the first recorded act of civil disobedience?

The midwife saga is the first recorded example of the heroic act of civil disobedience, which is why the Torah specifically mentions the two Hebrew midwives, Shifra and Puah, no less than seven times by name (Shifra, which means, "to be beautiful," and

---

15.   Jeremiah 49:21.
16.   Numbers 34:3; Joshua 15:1.
17.   *Encyclopedia Britannica.*

Puah, which simply means, "a girl"),[18] in contrast to Pharaoh who, despite his power and presence, is left anonymous. (The largest maternity hospital in Tel Aviv is located on the corner of Shifra and Puah streets!)

Why, out of a huge population, does the Torah only mention two midwives? I don't know. How important were the midwives to Israel's survival? Very. Shifra means to "make better," whilst Puah is akin to a mother's comforting sounds (*"poo, poo…"*) to calm crying babies.

Midwifery was one of the few "female" professions;[19] the Torah even has a Hebrew expression for "birth stool" (*ovnayim*, although no one knows exactly what this word means). The midwife also had a halachic duty; in the case of twins she had to testify who was the firstborn.[20] Were the midwives Jews or gentiles? We're not sure; the translation could either read "Hebrew midwives" or "midwives of the Hebrew women" – although it seems highly doubtful that Pharaoh would have trusted Jewish midwives to deliver and then immediately kill Jewish babies, and yet they disobeyed their king "and let the boys live [because] they feared God."[21] That the power of morality over evil is based on "fear of God" is a theme that runs supreme through Jewish texts: the Amalekites were evil because they "had no fear of God"; Job was righteous because he "feared God"; etc.[22]

---

18.   Genesis 49:21; 16:6; Job 26:13; Daniel 3:32, 4:24.
19.   Genesis 35:17, 38:28.
20.   Ibid., 38:28–29.
21.   Exodus 1:17.
22.   Genesis 42:18; Deuteronomy 25:18; Job 1:1, 8; Leviticus 19:14, 32.

Question 25

What was so important about the Nile that God told Moses to meet Pharaoh there?

Since Egyptian gods didn't have bodily needs, and knowing that the sight of their ruling deity going to the bathroom (a "human, earthly" act that acknowledges dependence and a lack of control) would shatter any illusion of godlikeness ("Pharaoh would rise early in the morning, and go out to the Nile to perform his bodily needs there"),[23] God tells Moses to confront his adversary at this moment of the day, in the morning. The Midrash describes Pharaoh as standing there in *kalon*, "shame," an embarrassing surrender to any claim of immortality, for in his attempt to appear godlike, Pharaoh knows he can't fool those who see him go to the bathroom like any other human being.

Jews, on the other hand, have no problem in thanking God for their complex, natural physical needs. In fact, they even make a blessing after going to the bathroom (*Asher Yatsar*),[24] attributed to the late fourth-century Abbaye, rosh yeshiva of Pumbeditha, a scholar who thought Jews should be more aware of the complexity of the human body ("Blessed art thou who has created in man a system of veins and arteries"), and thus included it in the morning prayers as a daily wish for *gezundt* ("physical health").

---

23.   Rashi, Exodus 7:15.
24.   *Brachot* 60b.

Question 26

Other than its conclusion of death, does the last plague differ from the others?

Yes. It is the only one where the Jews don't sit around, waiting passively for God's next move. At this point, the entire Jewish community suddenly becomes busy, hectic, involved. What consumes their energy? Preparing for the paschal lamb, as ordered ("The whole community of Israel shall take a lamb to a family, a lamb to a household, slaughter and eat it hurriedly"), knowing full well what to expect: "For that night, I will go through the land of Egypt and strike down every firstborn in the land of Egypt, both man and beast."[25]

Question 27

How does matza reflect freedom? Is freedom absolute?

When Franz Kafka muttered, "you are free and that is why you are lost," he was halfright, for when God said to Moses, "Let My people go," the sentence ended with, "that they should *serve Me* on this mountain." Freedom had a post-Exodus plan: fifty days after liberation, the Jews would be asked to serve another Master (God), be given a new set of orders (Torah), and directions to a new home (*Eretz Yisrael*). It's inevitable: everyone must serve someone! Be it kings of flesh or humans of fallibil-

---

25. Exodus 12:3–13, 21–23.

ity, freedom from slavery means a new form of subjugation to a new Master.

Matza serves as a reminder that freedom is *not* absolute, but far better a Just God than an unjust Pharaoh, better Torah than enslavement, better One God of compassion and humility than many gods of pleasure, pride, hubris. How does matza reflect these concepts? Matza is bare food, nothing but flour and water, a "bread of affliction" (*lechem oni*), a simple symbol of simple freedom that is purposely not enhanced with any great catering fanfare (i.e., no side ice sculptures or chopped liver mountains molded in the shape of Pharaoh or a lamb).

Question 28

If four is such an important number, why don't we have four matzot instead of three?

Of the four expressions of redemption that God uses in describing the Exodus[26] (which explains why we drink *four* cups of wine), only the first three ("I will take you out...save you...redeem you") refer to the Exodus itself. The last expression of redemption ("I will take you as a nation...") was only fulfilled fifty days and forty years *later* when the Torah was given at Mt. Sinai and the Jewish nation entered the holy land.

Defined as "flat, tasteless, the poor man's bread," matza is suggestive of the deteriorated spiritual state of the Jews prior to the giving of the Torah, and it is for this reason that we only have three matzot. By the time the "tasty," more matured, spiritual

---

26.   Exodus 6:6–7.

relationship with God materialized at Sinai, as represented by a fourth cup of wine, the matza was a symbol of the *past* serfdom, not the *future* redemption.[27]

Question 29

I get confused: what's the difference between the mountains at Moriah and Sinai?

Charles Dickens had his tale of two cities but Jewish history is a tale of two mountains. Mount Sinai was the locale for the "giving and receiving" of Jewish Law (Torah), whereas the mount at Moriah, in Jerusalem, was the site of the first and second Holy Temples. However, their lasting importance is not the same. At the end of the Seder, we don't say, "Next Year at Sinai," but "Next Year in Jerusalem," because Sinai was just a fleeting, nostalgic moment of glory and sanctity, whilst Jerusalem is the permanent home of God's Presence (*Shechina*), and thus still imbued with enough holiness (*kedusha*) to act as the future site of the third Temple ("The land of Israel sits at the center of the world; Jerusalem is in the center of the land of Israel; the sanctuary [*Beit Hamikdash*] is in the center of Jerusalem").[28]

---

27.   *Exodus Rabba* 6.
28.   *Kedoshim* 10; *Sifrei Deuteronomy* 152.

Question 30

On Shavuot and Succot, Jews are told to "rejoice!" Why not on Pesach?

Although the Egyptian military was a dangerous and cruel enemy, God frowned on any rejoicing whilst "His handiwork" was drowning.

What's more, Pesach is the day when God "sits in judgment" for the crops; thus it was premature to "rejoice" when the verdict of a good harvest was not evident yet. This is why Malachi was chosen for the *Shabbat Pesach Haftora*. The prophet makes a connection between those farmers who are blessed with a good harvest and those who are honest in donating (tithing) their products according to the laws of Moses. Hopes for finding favor in God's eyes and receiving a bountiful harvest are the basis for the pre-chag act of distributing charity to the needy ("wheat money," known as *maot chittim*).

The final reason why we don't rejoice on this *chag* is because Pesach symbolizes our existence in exile, while Succot and Shavuot are intrinsically tied to the holy land itself.

Question 31

What was the point of choosing a lamb on the "tenth" day and then waiting *four days* before slaughtering it? Why not do it all on the same day?

There's that number *four* again! The waiting period had a clear purpose, and it had to do with the nature of the lamb, chosen because it was a deity to the Egyptians who worshipped Aries (the Zodiac sign of a lamb, in Hebrew, is *T'leh*). "They [not only] abstained from killing sheep," wrote the Rambam, but also "held shepherds in contempt!"[29] Thus, the average Egyptian man-in-the-street was forced to observe, helplessly and shamefully, the rounding up of his precious gods, who were then tied outside the homes of their slaves for four full days.

This is why, explains Chizkiya ben Manoach (*Chizkuni*), thirteenth-century French rabbi, God timed their deity's sacrifice "towards evening," in full view, during "rush hour," when "Egyptian laborers returning from work" couldn't help but witness the power of the Jewish God roasting their gods.

Question 32

Why did God mark the Jews' doorposts with blood? Surely God knew which households His own people occupied?

You are reading it wrong. The blood on the house was *not* a

29.   *Guide for the Perplexed*, Book 3, 46; Exodus 8:26; Genesis 46:34.

designation direction for God but, according to Rabbi Natan and the Rambam, either a symbol for the Jews ("The blood on the houses shall be a sign for *you*...but not a sign for others"), or, according to Rabbi Isaac and Chizkiya ben Manoach (*Chizkuni*), a sign for the Egyptians to keep them in a state of fear and panic.[30] Why the disagreement between the rabbis? It stems from *where* the blood was sprinkled; if on the doorpost's inside, then it was intended for the Jews; if on the outside, then it was for the Egyptians.

Question 33

Is there any reason why the Egyptians met their end through drowning?

Yes. When Pharaoh realizes his extermination plan to co-opt midwives into Jewish infanticide isn't working, he conscripts "all his people" in a national effort to drown all Jewish male firstborns in the Nile. Since Pharaoh chose water as his murder weapon, God repaid him in kind by drowning the Egyptians.[31]

Question 34

Is freedom a Jewish concept?

Why is this insurrection different from all other insurrections? The dramatic *mano a mano* Moses-Pharaoh confrontation represented an unprecedented revolt for liberty, since all earlier

---

30.   *Mechilta* of Rabbi Yishmael; Exodus 12:13.
31.   Exodus 1:22.

rebellions had been selfishly motivated by the ruthless goals of one self-absorbed man, or one country's urge for power, plunder, prestige. But "Let My People Go!" kickstarted a revolutionary new theology of liberation that became a legendary force in history, powerfully captivating the hearts of all mankind (*coram deo*), and stirring a solution to Rousseau's lament, "Man is born free, yet everywhere he is in chains."

This early Judaic demand for emancipation has inspired hope, optimism and buoyancy for countless Freedom Days – from Bastille's *Liberté, egalité et fraternité*, "liberty, equality, and brotherhood," through English Puritans and Soviet Jewry, to the Fourth of July, echoed by Emma Lazarus's poetry of freedom etched into the Statue of Liberty.

Remember, despite being *the* centerpiece of Jewish history, the Exodus story alone has not made the Pesach Seder *tisch* the most observed family ritual in Jewish life. It was the means to an end, not an end in itself. Later descendants and generations are still benefitting and celebrating its more permanent accomplishment: the ideology of deliverance from evil, a ceaseless triumph for all folks, and fidelity to a value system (Torah) given just three months after the Exodus from Egypt.

Question 35

What sin were the enslaved Jews guilty of that God made them suffer in the first place?

We're not entirely sure, although the Jews were definitely punished because of the sins of their forebears, *ma'aseh avot siman lebanim*. The Ramban claims that they were punished because of Abraham's lack of faith in going to Egypt in the famine, and/or mistreating Sarai;[32] the Talmud states that the Jews were being punished for Abraham's lack of faith at the *Brit Ben Habetarim*, when Abraham asked how sure was his inheritance of the land;[33] and Jewish mystics believe that they were being punished for Abraham's poor treatment of Hagar. Their basis for this belief is that the word for affliction, "*innui*," appears thrice in relation to Hagar, but appears in only one other place in the Torah, when talking about the future servitude of the Jews.[34] Abravanel believes that the Jews were enslaved as a punishment for Joseph's ten brothers selling him as a slave to Egypt. In the same way that Joseph was enslaved, *midda keneged midda*, so were the Jews in Egypt. Midrash and the Netziv, Volozhin's nineteenth-century rosh yeshiva, blame the abolition of *brit mila* after the death of Joseph and his brothers.[35]

There are some scholars who don't agree that there was any sin to begin with! According to them, God genuinely believed

---

32. Ramban, Genesis 12:10.
33. *Nedarim* 32a.
34. Genesis 16:6, 9, 11; 15:13.
35. *Exodus Rabba* 1:8; *Netziv, Ha'amek Davar* 1:7.

that years of slavery were simply a necessary educational prerequisite for freedom and nationhood, shared fate and unity, sensitivity to others (*ki gerim hayitem be'eretz Mitzrayim*). In other words: you cannot appreciate what you have until it is gone!

Question 36

So, how do I recognize a miracle as a miracle?

It's often hard. If asked, "What's a greater miracle? Bread coming from the earth or bread coming from Heaven?" most would answer the latter. Why? Because manna falling each day from the sky is so unusual, so infrequent, so abnormal, that it *must* be greater! But it's also a miracle that a tiny seed can be placed in the ground and, through a complex equation of sun and soil, rain and temperature, it grows into grain. It is then harvested, packed, shipped, unloaded, unpacked, displayed, chosen, rung up by a cashier and finally ends up on your table as bread. We all take this process for granted, but the bread that ends up on our table is a life-sustaining nutrient. Now that's a miracle!

The word for miracle in Hebrew is *nes*, derived from the Latin *mirari*, "to wonder," or "to marvel at, be amazed by;" but *nes* can also mean a "sign" (*ot*) or a "test" (*nissa*).[36] A *nes* is simply seeing the common in an uncommon way, or as the Rambam puts it, "A miracle does not prove what is impossible; rather it is an affirmation of what is possible!"[37] That a "miracle" must contain some virtuoso supernatural component

---

36. Genesis 22:1.
37. Guide to the Perplexed 3:24.

is a common myth. So what turns a natural event into a *nes?* Timing and consequence. That a waterway in Egypt parted is *not* a miracle in and of itself; that it parted just in time to save Jewish lives transformed it into a miracle. This is based on the belief that God, through the forces of nature and history, still actively directs the world. Thus, faith (*emuna*) is a prerequisite to recognizing miracles; or as Mendel of Rymanov put it so succinctly: "If 1,000 believing Chassidim were to gather around a block of wood, it too would work miracles!" Jews who wonder why there are no Biblical miracles today miss the most obvious and amazing miracle of all: the very survival of *Am Yisrael*, the people of Israel, after Auschwitz, and the reestablishment of a Hebrew-speaking Third Jewish Commonwealth after centuries of attempts to destroy us. (When David Ben-Gurion asked Rav Isaac Herzog, the chief rabbi, why God did not send a miracle to preserve the new State of Israel, the rabbi replied, "Ben-Gurion, I regard *you* as one of God's miracles!")

Question 37

If man can split the atom and invent the Internet, what's the big deal about God splitting a sea?

Oscar Wilde expressed how desensitized we are to the wonders of nature, when he commented, "Niagara Falls is nice. But the real excitement would be to see it flowing backwards."

Question 38

Does Egypt give us a preview of the Achilles heel of Jewish history?

Yes. Disunity! Even after siblings (Jacob and Esau) are reunited, there is not a single future reference to them ever getting together again. It is as though God knew that, despite having achieved *shalom*, sibling rivalry would be a continual struggle within the House of Jacob. In a tantalizing preview of the future, the Torah describes how Moses, after killing an Egyptian, bumps into two Hebrews fighting each other, rather than those who enslaved them.[38] Moses' bewildered question, "Why are you hitting your fellow Hebrew?" and the argumentative response, "Who made *you* ruler and judge over us?" is a sad indication of the internal fighting that becomes the Jews' Achilles heel. God was aware of the danger of fragmentation among the Jewish people, and therefore held back from giving the Torah until all the Jews camped "as one" (*ata echad veshimcha echad*), an unambiguous Heavenly cry for the *sine qua non* of Judaism: unity.

It is for this reason that our greatest Sages always sprinkled their texts with a gentle nudge to fellow Jews and Jewish leaders to choose the path of tolerance, compromise and moderation, to learn not to condemn or alienate but to embrace and accept (a lesson of the four sons and their wildly disparate characters), "to reason together," "to seek the good in everyone," and "to see to your own sins before criticizing others."[39]

---

38.   Genesis 33; Exodus 2:11–14.
39.   Isaiah 1:18; Nachman of Breslov; *Bava Metzia* 107.

Question 39

Does the Exodus story prove that Jews are chronic complainers?

You mean perpetual *kvetchers?* It would seem so. The word *kvetch* comes from the German word *quetschen*, which means, "to squeeze," as in the reflexive Yiddish phrase, *kvetshn zakh*, or *gebn a kvetch*, as in, "exert yourself!" Just imagine! Despite their awe-inspiring brush with God at Mount Sinai, and their stunning leap from abject servitude in Egypt to miraculous freedom, the Jews, cantankerous and querulous, are simply unable to appreciate their history and destiny (*Vayehi ha'am kemitonenim*, "The people took to complaining bitterly").

It's embarrassing, *especially* when the French comment on this character trait ("The Jews have always been malcontents!" roars the nineteenth-century Bernard Lazare). After His unruly folk loudly accuse Him of "bringing us out into this wilderness to starve to death!" God responds with a shower of manna. When they whine about thirst, God responds with water gushing from a rock. When they complain that the water is bitter and undrinkable, God makes it sweet and potable.

So, what do the Jews have to *kvetch* about? They're bored and unhappy with their limited culinary pickings, having suddenly developed a "gluttonous craving" for such delicacies as Egyptian "cucumbers, melons, leeks, onions, garlic, meat, fish." They conveniently forgot that for dessert they and their families were given hundreds of years of lashes and oppression served on trays of humiliation. No wonder the Torah portrays the Jewish people in such a negative light. The final word belongs to Ben Zoma: "Who is rich? He who is content with his lot!"[40]

Question 40

Shouldn't the verse, "Now, we are here; next year we should be in the land of Israel. This year we are slaves; next year, free people," be written in reverse order – the second sentence appearing first?

The structure might appear out of order – surely freedom should come first, regardless of the geographical location. Only then, once you are free, can you move to Israel! If you're not free, how can you go anywhere? The Haggada does not relate to the concept of freedom as the ability to physically move from one place to another, but rather the ability to use your mind and think. In order to achieve this freedom, you need an "environment of Israel," a culture of Judaic values, ethics, morality whereby the Jew is free to express his Judaism. Whether that is Cairo or Berlin, Spain or Leningrad, freedom can only surface when one's self-expression can reign and roam free.

---

40. *Avot* 4:1.

Question 41

Was there an exact moment when the Jews went from being enslaved Jews to being free Jews?

Yes. There was a precise moment when Independence Day officially came to the Jews, transforming them *at that very moment* into a people and holy nation. This moment actually served as a precedent for Jewish law regarding the subject of when an owner legally acquires a servant: the moment the servant performs his first service. What was the "first service" of the Jews, as a collective nation? The offering of the paschal lamb. In fact, the word *avoda*, "service," appears for the first time in reference to the Pesach offering.[41] And because the lamb offering marks the precise moment of Jewish nationhood, the practice was not discontinued when the Jews, now a nation ensconced in its own land, later offer sacrifices at the Temple.

Question 42

When, and by whom, was the *Song of the Sea* sung?

Known as *Shirat Hayam*, the song was sung by Jews who were privileged to have experienced and witnessed firsthand the awesome and unexpected miracle of a sea parting as well as the dramatic defeat of their enemy oppressor. And so the Jews broke out in song and praised God. Jewish tradition reveals that in one

---

41.   Exodus 12:26.

single moment, those Jews reached a higher level of spirituality than that attained by the greatest of Hebrew prophets.

Who were the first to start singing? The handmaidens. Why? Because they knew on a personal level what slavery was and thus were the first to recognize the nature of liberation ("A handmaiden saw at the Red Sea what Ezekiel, son of Buzi, did not see in his prophecy [in *Ma'aseh Merkava*, "The Work of the Chariot"]").[42] After the handmaidens came the infants, nurslings and even the fetuses! Why? Because they were dependent on others and thus they too instinctively understood, and appreciated, the meaning of independence. "Out of the mouth of babes and sucklings hast thou ordained strength!"[43]

Question 43

Why do we assign such importance to the *Song of the Sea* when it seems to challenge the concept of monotheism?

The idea that the *Song of the Sea* challenges the concept of monotheism is a common myth. Jews, uninterested in eternal competitiveness, and secure in their knowledge of truth (*emet*), are believers in ontological monotheism which proclaims the existence of only one unique, universal God (*Shema Yisrael Hashem Elokenu Hashem Echad*, "Hear O Israel, the Lord our God, the Lord is One").[44] There are others, however, who believe that while there is only one all-powerful, all-omniscient

---

42. *Mechilta Shira* 83.
43. Psalms 8:3.
44. Deuteronomy 6:4.

God, there still exist other gods. The disturbing words are: *Mi kamocha ba'elim Hashem, mi kamocha nehedar bakodesh*, "Who is like Thee among the gods, O Lord, Who is like Thee, Majestic in Holiness."[45] The expression "Who is like" seems to indicate that God is being compared to other gods, and therefore supports the claim that other gods exist.

Rashi, the fundamental Torah commentator and teacher *par excellence* of the Jewish people, tackles this problem head-on by first acknowledging the reality that others (Pharaoh) do accept the existence of gods, and interprets *elim* to mean "strength." Thus, any "comparison" exists only in the human imagination ("Pharaoh called himself a god, Sancherib called himself a god, Nebuchadnezar called himself a god!" writes Mechilta of Reb Ishmael). However, Abraham ibn Ezra and the Ramban go much further than Rashi. They argue that God is being compared to the angels (called *elim*), and that a battle rages between them.[46]

Question 44

Why did ordinary Egyptians have to suffer because of Pharaoh?

Rabbinic commentary is full of concern for the average man-in-the-street Egyptian, even the enemy soldier! When the angels were about to rejoice at the sight of the Egyptian army drowning, the Midrash relates the harsh Godly rebuke, "The works of

45. Exodus 15:11.
46. Ibid., 15:2; Genesis 14:18; Ramban, Commentary on the Torah, Exodus 15:11.

My hands are drowning in the sea, and you want to sing?" Our rabbis adopted this message ("Rejoice not when your enemy falls; be not glad when he stumbles"),[47] and were careful not to gloat at the discomfiture of the ordinary populace, stressing that the majority of plagues were directed at the Egyptian gods. Remember: the Nile was worshiped as the source of life and prosperity (and so its waters were turned to blood); the frogs were regarded as sacred (so they were turned into a vehicle of devastation when allowed to run amuck); the earth was worshiped, as were its crops (hence locusts were sent to consume all of its vegetation); the sun was a god (so it was checked by a plague of darkness). And since the firstborn son of Pharaoh was idolized as divine, he too was fair game.

Question 45

How could God take our ancestors out of Egypt "on the wings of eagles," but allow their holy European descendants to be agonizingly reduced to crematoria ashes?

Our rabbis clearly understand the enigma of theodicy, the potentially devastating overdose of "too much suffering,"[48] and the generations of martyred Jews who had perfect faith in the coming of a Messiah who had, indeed, tarried! The paradox has been around since an innocent Job was punitively tested by God

---

47. Proverbs 24:17.
48. Ethics of the Fathers 1:7.

to counter a Satan challenge. His friends, limited by man's ignorance of the Divine plan, seek, but cannot offer, solace. When
Job pleads (unsuccessfully) for an explanation for his suffering,
the reply is: *Don't ask, I won't tell!* Job then does what all victims
do: he plunges into a self-examination that shifts the question
from "Why, God?" to an inward "Why me? What possible sin
have I committed to deserve this grim destiny?" And it is Job
who provides Jewish history's traditional answer, "Though
He may slay me, yet will I believe in Him, but I will argue my
ways before Him"[49] – in the same spirit of Abraham's "*J'Accuse,*"
haShofet kol ha'aretz lo ya'aseh mishpat? "Shall the Judge of all
the earth not act justly?"[50]

Question 46

How many enslaved Egyptian Jews actually left for Israel?

Excluding Levites, women and children, 603,550 males.[51] Is this
a guess? No. The Book of Numbers owes its very name to a God-
ordered "counting," via the donation of *shekalim* ("coins"), which
serves as a basis for the future division of Israel.[52] Six hundred
thousand is also the (approximate) number of Holocaust survivors who left Europe for the same holy land, and six hundred
thousand (approximately) is the number of Jews who initially
left the Soviet Union (*Operation Exodus 1*, the proportional

49.   Job 13:15.
50.   Genesis 18:25.
51.   Numbers 1:46.
52.   Exodus 1–4, 26, 30:11–16, 38:26; Numbers 26:53.

equivalent of moving the entire population of France to the United States!). A coincidence? Six hundred thousand is also the (approximate) number of Hebrew letters in the Torah; the word *Yisrael* being an acrostic for *yesh shishim riboah l'Torah* ("There are 600,000 letters in the Torah"), or *yesh shishim riboah anashim l'Yisrael* ("There are six hundred thousand Jews"). The 603,550 Jews who left Egypt ("not counting dependants")[53] were defined as "able-bodied infantry men [of fighting age, over twenty]." This extrapolates into a staggering 2.5 million men, women and children, an enormous mass (more even than the Egyptian population, which is why Pharaoh moans to Moses that "they [the Jews] are now more numerous than the [native] people of the land").

Question 47

The Pesach melody from the Haggada, Dayenu, consists of fifteen lines. What does the number fifteen symbolize?

Answers range from the fifteen steps that led up to the Temple to King David's fifteen Psalms of Ascent to the fifteen stages that lead the righteous to perfection.

When the melody was first discovered in its present form in the early Middle Ages (written either by Rashi or Rabbi Shmuel of Falaise, one of the *baalei Tosafot*), *Dayenu* was not intended to be an expression of exclamation but a question: if God had only given us one good fortune, would it have been sufficient? Our answer is a resounding yes! Why? Because even

---

53.   Exodus 12:37; Leviticus 1:46.

if we do not witness ongoing, sensational miracles, we still have to be thankful. In other words, we are grateful for each small miracle, thankful for small mercies, and accept "more" not as a right – but as an added bonus!

Question 48

What's the basis of the multiplication of plagues being "five-fold"?

Rabbi Yossi the Galilean asks the same question! "How do you know that the Egyptians were struck by ten plagues in Egypt and fifty at the sea?" He answers his own question by saying: "In Egypt the magicians said to Pharaoh, 'this is the finger of God,'[54] whilst at the sea the Jews 'saw the great hand which God had used in Egypt.'"[55] Rabbi Yossi then extrapolates that if ten plagues arose from only one "finger" then an entire "hand" at the sea was surely five times as much (i.e., fifty plagues). Rabbi Akiva agrees, and notes that this "five-fold" matches the five letters of the Name of God (*Elokim*) which represents strict justice. Is this a unanimous rabbinical mathematical conclusion? In concept, yes, but in conclusion, no.

Rabbi Elazar prefers the Name of God that represents attributes of kindness and mercy, and it only has four letters (*Yud, Heh, Vav, Heh*), and thus argues for a "four-fold" increase in the number of plagues (forty plagues at the sea). The differences relate to the purpose of a plague. Rabbi Elazar was convinced the Heaven's intent in creating the plagues was to sensitize the

---

54.   Exodus 8:15.
55.   Ibid., 14:31.

Jews to their love and care by God, whilst Rabbis Akiva and Yossi saw the plagues primarily as punishment for the enemy.

Question 49

If the Jews were that numerous, why did they not just overwhelm their oppressors and take over Egypt?

This was a goal that God would not support. Taking control of a corrupt society was an anathema. Breaking free from the past, however, wholeheartedly rejecting the old culture (paganism) for a more ethical religion (Torah) in a new land (*Eretz Yisrael*) under one moral Master (God) with a final end game in mind (messianism) was the aim.

Question 50

Is it true that the Jews were in a state of disbelief as they witnessed the the splitting of the sea?

Yes. At the sight of drowning Egyptians ("our oppressors"), the Jews were struck by the fact that Mother Nature in the wilderness had become not an enemy, but a "friend" – and yet, says the Midrash, they were so nervous and insecure that they believed the Egyptians might still "come out of the water a mile downstream and attack us." So the Heavens produced the evidence that the job was finally finished by washing the dead bodies ashore for all to see. It took a miracle to restore and refresh the Jews' faith.

The Chernobyler Rebbe knew this more than anyone: during the year he kept a notebook and duly recorded all the miracles *he* had witnessed or of which he had been the beneficiary. When it came to Pesach, he would rush through the Haggada and then take out his notebook and spend the rest of the night recalling his year of personal miracles to his family and guests.

Question 51

I've heard that the way the four sons are ordered in the Hagadda represents a warning of generational proportions. What does that mean?

Even an irreligious Jew will be able to recall a grandfather or great-grandfather who was pious. The order in which the sons appear in the Haggada signifies the disconnection from the Judaic heritage throughout the generations. The generation of the *chacham* are the "wise" immigrants, the "first" generation as in the "first" of the four sons – those who refuse to let their new surroundings and culture interfere with their portable luggage of Sinai values. These Jews are "committed" Jews; they pray in Hebrew, perform mitzvot, study Torah.

What happens to their children, the "second" generation in exile? The "second" of the four sons, the generation of the "wicked" (*rasha*) are so-named because, despite the fresh memories of their parents' value system, they actively choose to walk away from this "old, primitive" world. They embody the "wickedness" of those who would turn their backs on their own parents, opting instead for the excitement of rebellion.

As for the third generation, symbolic of the "third" son, these children don't even have any Torah-based parents to rebel against; they are deprived even of the art of protest, and, being the "simplest" of the sons, are reduced, even as they harbor faint memories of pious grandparents, to superficiality. ("What is this?" they mumble out of sheer boredom.) The odds are that this generation has a lukewarm Torah education, if any at all.

That is why his offspring, the "fourth" generation, comprising those who know not even what to ask, have tragically no concept of what it means to be Jewish. The father is ignorant, the grandfather is embarrassingly old-fashioned, and the great-grandparents have been reduced to fading yellow photos on the living room wall. This, the Haggada cautions, is the "last" generation, the one that does not hesitate to marry out, who embraces assimilation with eagerness and ease. The warning that can be derived from the four sons is that after this, there is no "fifth" son.

Question 52

What's the Torah's view of slavery?

Rav Avraham Pam, twentieth-century yeshiva dean of *Torah Vadaas*, notes that the only quality that differentiated a slave from a free human being was the ability to control one's free time. Italian Rabbi Ovadiah Sforno, a major commentator of the Middle Ages, goes one step further: the significance of the "day," as a unit of Jewish Time, was meaningless until after the Exodus. Why? Because a day meant nothing to a slave who was deprived of any power to shape it. When Ludwig Boerne cried out, "Because I was born a slave, I love liberty more than you," he was confirming that only the liberated, emancipated from tyranny, could appreciate Time as a precious gift; a Divine boon to be used wisely, judiciously, meaningfully. The noble eighteenth-century words on the Liberty Bell in Philadelphia, "Proclaim liberty in the land to all its inhabitants" is first found in Leviticus. A good employer must be concerned not just with himself but with his workers' and their families' wellbeing (unlike early American life, when twenty percent of the populace was enslaved, and one slave was counted as only "three-fifths" of a person for purposes of representation in Congress).

Question 53

What good did the Egyptian booty do for the Jews in the desert?

A Midrash takes the unusual Torah phrase, "Moses *caused* Israel to set out from the Sea of Reeds,"[56] and paints for us a startling image: Moses had to drag the reluctant Jews away against their wishes. Why? The slang saying, "All that's gold glitters!" was in full force that day, which is why some families still bring out all their gold and silver utensils for the Seder *tisch*, to recall the gold and silver that the Jews took with them out of Egypt.[57] The horses and chariots of the massive Egyptian military were

---

56.   Ibid., 15:22.
57.   Ibid., 3:22; 11:2; 12:35, 36.

adorned and decorated with jewels and precious stones that had been washed up on the seabed. The Jews, now free to go treasure hunting, went down daily to the water and collected the wealth of Egypt (*bizat hayam*, the "collection of spoils from the sea"). Moses had no choice but to "force them to depart."

At first, the Jews react to the sight of the washed-up gold and jewelry of the drowned enemy in materialistic ecstasy; but then, within three days, it suddenly dawns on the Jews that although they now possess an abundance of "precious stones, gems and pearls," they have no water to drink! Their matza lasted thirty-one days but the first spring water they taste in Shur was named *Mara*, after its taste of "bitterness," akin to the name the rabbis give Pharaoh, *Meror*, "the Bitter One," and the herbs we eat at the Seder, called maror, a symbol of "bitter" oppression. Even the Jews were bitter, and ask, "What shall we drink?" to which Moses has no ready answer, turning immediately to God with a plaintive, "What should I do now?"

God responds with another miracle: a tree was cast into the waters which immediately turned "sweet."[58] What sort of tree? Is this a flora that's sweet by nature? The Torah is mute, but the Midrash describes it as a laurel tree, with God's Name written on it, that "purified the tainted waters [and] made them drinkable." By the time they reach their next stopping place (Elim), God is ready: He has prepared twelve springs of waters (representing the number of Tribes) and "three score and ten" palm trees (i.e., seventy, representing the number of Jews who went to Egypt with Jacob and the number of nations in the world).[59]

---

58. Ibid., 15:23; 4; 5.
59. Ibid., 15:27.

Question 54

Why did Moses and Aaron ask Pharaoh for a three-day "break"[60] instead of demanding immediate freedom?

Moses and Aaron asked for a break because this was what they were instructed to to do at the Burning Bush.[61] This was God's first, initial test of Pharaoh. The brothers were to make a relatively straightforward request – just "three days off, for religious reasons" – the denial of which would reveal to all how stubborn this king was. In fact, during the entire confrontation, summarized in four contiguous Torah portions (*Shemot* to *Beshalach*), this was the *only* request made in front of Pharaoh, a monarch who argued just for the sake of being argumentative.

First Pharaoh agrees that the Jews *can* "go and offer sacrifices to your God"[62] – but then stipulates *ba'aretz*, "only locally, in Egypt," not "in the desert." He then agrees to the desert, but adds "not too far"! But Moses never intended to just go for three days: doesn't that make his request deceitful in nature? Yes: but deception as a tool against an enemy is justified according to Don Isaac Abravanel, the statesman of Spanish Jewry, whose "proof" is God's "ambush" advice to Joshua in his war against Ai, intended solely to hoodwink the adversary. [63]

---

60. Ibid., 5:3.
61. Ibid., 3:18.
62. Ibid., 8:21.
63. Joshua 8:3.

Question 55

No matter how hard I try, I find it impossible to envision that I myself am leaving Egypt. What am I doing wrong?

On the surface, it seems totally unfeasible for each generation to imagine themselves enduring the horror of Egyptian slavery; we cannot smell the bricks, hear the screams, feel the wounds, see the baby bodies floating in the Nile. On the flip side, we cannot personally experience the "shock 'n awe" of miracles. So why does the Haggada ask of us the impossible? It doesn't. Jews *do* have the ability to transport themselves back in time and reflect upon the grandeur of Jewish nationalism and identity, and the spiritual inspiration of our ancestors' flight. We are capable of reliving the intense feelings of relief at being rescued from horrific generational suffering, pain and oppression.

If you look carefully at the text, you will find that in several places Egypt is not referred to as "the land of" Egypt, but just "Egypt." The difference is subtle but deep. Fleeing the land was a physical act, while fleeing "Egypt" represented an escape from an immoral environment, a system and pattern of values totally alien to those the Jews discovered three months later at Mount Sinai. It *is* possible, say our Sages, for each generation to close their eyes, and at least go back to "Egypt," to enter a mindset in which we are shaking off an alien culture of idolatry, sorcery and black magic and are donning the ideological wardrobe of spiritual well-being. Pesach, in its overt educational format, presents us with a direct challenge: using our memory as a tool, we shake off the slavery of contemporary Judaic ignorance and complacency and replace it with the knowledge necessary to give every Jewish child the foundation of Jewish identity.

Question 56

Did the Jews of the desert keep Pesach?

Initially, Pesach was to be observed as a remembrance commemoration "in every generation," but then the Torah adds, "when you shall come into the land [of Israel]...you shall keep this service." We do know that the first anniversary ("in the first month of the second year") was kept by the Jews in the wilderness, "in accordance with all the laws [received during that past year at Sinai]."[64] However, there is no further mention of Pesach in the next thirty-nine years of wandering, until Joshua "encamped at Gilgal and kept the Passover in the plains of Jericho."[65] Rav Levi Ben Gershon (Ralbag, also known as Gershonides), the famous thirteenth-fourteenth-century French Torah commentator, claims that this was the first opportunity the Jews had to observe Pesach. To prove his point, he points to the first thing that Joshua does when he crosses the River Jordan – he circumcises the folk. If that generation were unable, because of the treachery and hazards of desert travel, to perform the mitzva of *brit mila*, they would have been equally unable to keep the mitzva of Pesach.

When was the next Pesach kept? Although we have no

---

64. Numbers 9; Deuteronomy 16:1–8.
65. Joshua 5:10.

reason to doubt that the Jews kept this chag faithfully, Pesach is not mentioned again until King Hezekiah ascends to the Jewish throne,[66] rededicates the Temple, and sends out invitations to "all Israel and Judah, Ephraim and Menasseh [to come to] Jerusalem to keep the Passover."[67] When the King died, so did Pesach, temporarily. Both his son (Menasseh) and grandson (Amon) were an embarrassment to Torah and Judaism, defiling the holy Temple with idolatrous practices. Pesach had to wait until his great-grandson (Josiah) took over[68] and reversed the disastrous policies of his predecessors.

Question 57

Why, when listing all the "abundances" that God gave the Jews, does the melody Dayenu declare the Temple in Jerusalem as the last and thus "greatest" gift of them all?

According to Jewish tradition, a river ran out of the Garden of Eden and split into four directions, in order to spread the intensive presence of God to all four corners of the globe. The Temple, being the inspiring umbrella of "God's Presence" (*Shechina*), represents and incorporates it all, which is why it is still the focus of Jewish hopes and prayers after three thousand years. Its mount is called Mount Moriah, which literally means the mount

---

66.   726 BCE.
67.   II Chronicles 30:1.
68.   621 BCE.

of "teaching," for from Jerusalem, everything flows ("From Zion goes forth Torah, and the word of God from Jerusalem").[69]

Question 58

What's the basis for the name Miriam?

The name "Miriam" is derived from the Hebrew word *mar* ("bitter," as in *maror*), chosen because it related to the bitter times of Jewish suffering during which she was born and raised.

Question 59

What exactly is matza?

The term matza, which the Zohar calls "the bread of faith" (based on the similarity between *mitzva* and *matza*), is derived from the Babylonian *ma-as-sa-ar-tum*, which means barley, the first grain harvested in the Mideast, replaced centuries later by wheat. It is crisp, flat and unleavened, made of flour and water, and baked before the dough has had time to rise.

When I was a child, matza was round; today it is square. Why? Because machine-made matza is easier to bake and pack if it is square. Which is better? It's preferable to eat the traditional round shape,[70] a custom based on the Torah's description for cakes of unleavened bread (*uggot matzot*),[71] whose Hebrew root (*ug*) means "round" or "circular," and thus indicates that round

---

69.   Isaiah 2:3.
70.   Rashi, *Moed Katan* 4b.
71.   Exodus 12:39.

matzot, symbolic of our forefather's "bread of affliction," are probably what our ancestors ate when they left Egypt.[72]

When Rabbi Israel Spira led seventy Bergen-Belsen Jews to demand flour for baking matza, it was a demand so audacious in the SS Valley of Death that a stunned Adolf Haas, concentration camp commandant, acquiesced. Before the Iron Curtain collapsed, it was matza that physically symbolized an individual's involvement in Judaism at a time when one dared not mention the word "matza" out of fear and instead referred to it as "diet bread." (In those days, nearly all matza produced in the Soviet Union was non-kosher because it was made with regular flour, however the rabbinate approved it as "kosher" because it was the only matza available.)

Question 60

Was the plague of the firstborn (*makat bechorot*) the only one that resulted in Egyptian fatalities?

Yes. The tenth and final plague slays the country's firstborn males (*makat bechorot*) and animals, including Pharaoh's son as he sits by the side of his father's throne. This final blow, no more than one stroke, unleashed "at midnight,"[73] caused total panic. Pharaoh finally gave in, and his terror-stricken populace gave their Jewish neighbors, slaves for 210 years,[74] their gold, silver and garments to get rid of them ("and you shall take the spoil

---

72. Deuteronomy 16:3.
73. Rashi, Exodus 12:12.
74. Rashi, *Targum Jonathan*, Exodus 12:40, 41.

from the Egyptians").[75] Thus a nation was born, and the future of mankind would never be the same in the face of "the soldiers of God."[76] The Jews fled so fast from Ramses to a place called Succot,[77] that not even their dough had time to rise into bread. And even God couldn't wait: new Torah laws were given to them on that same day, while they were still on Egyptian soil.[78]

The Midrash and Ibn Ezra both claim that that the plague of the firstborn ("there was no house where there was not someone dead") was the *only* real form of severe retribution, noting that none of the other plagues caused Egyptian fatalities. The other plagues were merely a reaction to Pharaoh's insolence; a requital in kind (*midda keneged midda*) for the pains the Egyptians caused the Jews (the first plague of blood, for example, struck the Nile because the Egyptians "cast the Israelites' children into the sea").

Pharaoh himself had derived his power by birthright, being the firstborn of the firstborn of the firstborn. Without firstborns and slaves, the entire Egyptian society would crumble, thus the final plague struck at the very epicenter of Pharaoh and his civilization, paving the way for the liberation of the Jews.

---

75.   Exodus 3:22.
76.   Ibid., 12:41; Numbers 1; Isaiah 40:2.
77.   Exodus 12:29–37.
78.   Rav Hertz on Exodus 13:3.

Question 61

Is it true that God only helps those who help themselves?

Whenever Reb Mendel of Kotzk would hear other nineteenth-century rabbis cry to God to bring the Messiah he would chastise them: Cry to Jews, not God, to bring the Messiah! "When there is a possibility of danger," advises the Talmud, "do not depend upon a miracle." It is for this reason that the Redeemer will eventually show up on a donkey,[79] signifying a non-miraculous, earthy arrival.

This "Miracle-or-not-here-I-come!" lesson was first taught in a place called Pi-hahirot when Moses, in the face of Pharaoh's army, decides to pray for *siyata dishmaya*, "assistance from Heaven." The Heavens respond quickly, but not in the way that Moses expects. "Now is not the time for prayer. Tell the people to go forward and I'll help them."[80] This heavenly reaction proves that not only do actions speak louder than words, but that the Heavens only help those who help themselves.

Question 62

Why is there a connection made between God pairing couples and the splitting of the Red Sea?

It was the parting of the waters in front of the Egyptians that

---

79.   Daniel 7:13; *Sanhedrin* 98a.
80.   Exodus 14:15.

motivated the rabbis of the Talmud to make a startling comparison: *Kashe lezavgam kekriyat yam suf*, "It is as difficult for God to pair couples as it was for Him to split the Red Sea!" The question is obvious. Why is it difficult for an All-powerful God to split some waters? What was so challenging for God at *kriyat yam suf*? And even if it *was* difficult for God to split the waters, how could this possibly be analogous to the pairing of couples?

The similarity lies in initiative: God had to restrain himself from immediately helping His people under siege at the Red Sea. He waited until the Jews helped themselves before He came to their aid. Likewise, coupling (*lezavgam*) cannot occur unless a man and a woman take life into their own hands, as did Nachshon by stepping out into the raging waters, by actively seeking, maintaining and enhancing a relationship. It is only *after* this human effort that God helps couples to find their *bashert* (predestined mate).

Question 63

Why was Moses, an Egyptian prince, chosen to rescue the Jews?

Having grown up in Pharaoh's palace, Moses was unfazed by the aura of royalty. No Jewish slave, explains Rabbi Zevi Hirsch Chajes, "would ever have dared to demand total emancipation from Pharaoh." Only Moses, a free man all his life, could imagine freedom for his people and confront authority to demand it.

Question 64

Did all the Jews willingly participate in the Exodus from Egypt?

No. Incredibly, even the lure of liberty was not enough to move the entire Jewish community out of Egypt. The Torah truthfully admits: only one in five Jews were sufficiently adventurous and imbued with faith to take up the challenge of emancipation. Such is the beauty and mystery of the *am segula* ("chosen folk") that only a handful, a bare minority, an insignificant statistic, dramatically changed the course of Jewish and world history.

Question 65

What is the Torah's intention when it says, "This" is my God (*Hashem yimloch le'olam va'ed*)?

The answer lies in an ancient and fascinating Midrash…

When an Israelite woman in Egypt felt that she was about to give birth, she would go out to the fields, have her children and leave them there, saying to God: "Lord of the World! I have done mine, now You do yours!" God Himself would immediately come down to cut the umbilical cord, wash and anoint the infant… He would place two stones in the child's hand. From one he could suckle oil, and from the other honey…and so the children would grow up in the fields… When they were asked:

"Who took care of you?" they replied: "A certain beautiful and
praiseworthy young man came down and took care of all our
needs," as is written: "My beloved is fair and ruddy, a paragon
among ten thousands" [a reference to the *Song of Songs*].

When Israel reached the sea, these same children were
among them. They saw God and said to their parents, "This
is the one who did all those things for us when we were in
Egypt!" Thus, Scripture says: "*This* is my God and I will glorify
Him!"[81]

Question 66

When exactly was the *Song of Songs* sung, and by whom?

I don't know. When a Midrash asks the same question,[82] it gives
us multiple choices – but no definitive answer! The *Song of Songs*
was either sung at the splitting of the sea (according to Rabbi
Eliezer ben Hyrcanus, who can only visualize this outburst of
song as a result of *seeing* something miraculous);[83] at the "Tent
of Meeting" (Rabbi Meir was convinced that intimate love songs
were only appropriate at a holy site); at Sinai (Rabbi Akiva accepts this locale on the basis that the term *given* [in that *Shir
Hashirim* was "given to the Jews"] is the same expression used
for the receipt of the Torah at Sinai);[84] or when the Jews built

---

81.   *Exodus Rabba* 23:8; Rabbis Judah and Yohanan, *Targum Jonathan*,
      Exodus 15:2.
82.   *Canticles Rabba* 1:2.
83.   *Mechilta deRashbi*; *Canticles Rabba* 2:14.
84.   *Yadayim* 3:5.

their Temple (since the author is Solomon, the king who built the Temple).

Did all scholars approve of this song? No. Saadia Gaon of Sura, Babylon, didn't "get it" ("It's like a lock whose key is lost"), and the thirteenth-century Meir of Narbonne warned against it ("it deserves to be destroyed in order to prevent simple souls from being ensnarled by it!").

So, who sang it? We don't know. Again, it's a choice: the Midrash narrows it down to God and/or the angels. But all agree on one thing: in this slim collection, the Torah's most sacrosanct emotional love poem, an amorous yet anonymous dark-skinned Shulamite ("I am black but comely!")[85] directs her bleak warnings of love, thrice, to the "daughters of Israel" in a gripping, emotional love story that gushes and blushes about "comely cheeks, eyes like doves, lips like a thread of scarlet." Such expressions, notes Rav Nosson Finkel, the Alter from Slabodka, are simply an acknowledgement of the spiritual value of the human form, created in God's image (*Betzelem Elokim*), and are thus nothing to be ashamed of.

Question 67

What has more primacy – the Exodus or the splitting of the sea?

The Midrash[86] assigns the top halachic slot to the Exodus, on the basis that it must be mentioned daily in the *Shema*, an obligation more stringent than recalling the splitting of the sea.

---

85. Song of Songs 1:5.
86. *Exodus Rabba* 22:3.

More importantly, *only* the Exodus is mentioned in God's first command; in contrast, the splitting and crossing of the sea is credited with instilling faith in the Jews.[87]

Question 68

What was Pharaoh's relationship to Joseph?

When Joseph made his first appearance before the ruler of Egypt, he explained Pharaoh's dreams, credited them to God, and laid out an economic plan so that "the land not perish through the famine."[88] This Pharaoh (not the one of the Exodus who follows and "knows not Joseph")[89] was impressed and, despite his policy of brutal oppression, he still gave the God of the Jews credit for making Joseph "wise and discreet,"[90] and rewarded Jacob's son with a high position in governmental affairs.

Question 69

How exactly did God "speak" to Moses?

The Torah uses the terms *kol* or *davar*, "voice" or "word," when God's acts in the world do not involve any intermediaries (angels, messengers, etc.). The seeming infinity of meanings in His

---

87. Exodus 14:41.
88. Genesis 41:33, 41:36.
89. Exodus 1:8.
90. Genesis 41:39.

Word, explain the Sages, results from the sheer awe and power in God's "thunderous" *kol*;[91] thus when God tells Moses in Midian to go back, He does so in one word ("Go," *lech*, return to Egypt"), which is also heard by Aaron in Egypt who hears something totally different ("Go [*lech*] into the wilderness to meet Moses").[92] This inspired the Psalms to sing, "God has spoken once; two things have we heard!"[93]

The double interpretation of God's words also occurred during the fourth of the Ten Commandments; the Jews heard both *zachor* ("Remember") and *shamor* ("Keep" the Shabbat…"), even though it was "one utterance" which, according to a Midrash, was so powerful that the Jews actually *saw* what was being said![94] Each person present understood what they heard based on their own level of human comprehension, and, adds Rabbi Yochanan, to ensure the seventy nations of the world also got the message, God's *kol* split into seventy voices.[95]

Faced with a plurality of acceptable interpretations and sincerely opposing rulings, Jewish law thus concludes that, "Both these and those are the words of the living God," as articulated by the Talmud, based on a famous Jeremiah quote, "Just as the hammer breaks up into many sparks, so, too, may one passage give rise to several meanings."[96]

91.   Job 37:5.
92.   Exodus 4:19, 27.
93.   Psalms 62:11.
94.   Exodus 20:8; Deuteronomy 5:12; Exodus 20:15; *Exodus Rabba* 5:9.
95.   *Tanchuma*, Exodus 4:27.
96.   Jeremiah 23:39; *Eruvin* 14; *Sanhedrin* 34b.

Question 70

What comes first: faith or miracles?

A woman once asked the Belzer Rebbe to pray for her. "But," he asked her, "do you have faith in my prayer's efficacy?" She reminded him that the Jews at the Red Sea were "first saved and then believed!" The Rebbe smiled, and prayed on her behalf. In order for a miracle to occur, a reminder that God is still involved in the affairs of man and nature, human beings need to first be receptive to God's intervention. Once they witness a Divine miracle, their faith is reignited and what was mundane is now transformed into something sacred (which is why we thank God, thrice daily, "for the miracles that are with us every day"). The Baal Shem Tov, who communed with nature, believed that only a person with faith can see and appreciate a miracle, and so his great-grandson, Reb Nachman of Breslov, declared that, "A man should believe in God by virtue of faith rather than miracles."

The question is obvious: why were there more miracles in the times of the Torah than there are now? First, miracles still occur today on a daily basis, but we may not be aware of them. But more importantly, the miracles that God performed during, and after, the Exodus took place at a time when He was guiding an enslaved and scared folk back to freedom, and to a brave new world of "Chosen People" spirituality. It seems that miracles, lots of them, were essential in order to get the job done.

Question 71

What exactly happened during the ninety days between the Exodus and Mount Sinai?

The Torah describes seven episodes: the Red Sea deliverance, the alkaline waters of Mara, the manna, another water episode (at Massa and Meriba), the fight with Amalek, the arrival of Jethro, and the appointment of Judges. Do these seven episodes have anything in common? Yes. They basically, and embarrassingly, all illustrate the nature of an insecure, anxious, weak and apprehensive folk that sometimes, but only sometimes, followed Moses as their undisputed leader. At the Red Sea, they reacted with fright ("It is better for us to serve the Egyptians than to die in the wilderness!");[97] and when they were hungry and thirsty, the "free" people suddenly preferred slavery to emancipation ("Why did you bring us up from Egypt to kill us and our children and livestock?").[98]

---

97.   Exodus 14:11–12.
98.   Ibid., 16:3, 17:3.

Question 72

Why thank God for taking us out of a place of evil (Egypt) when He elected to put us there in the first place? And what took Him so long?

Yes, God put us in Egypt, but at the same time He also warned the folk to stay away from the immorality, depravations and abominations ("Like the actions of the land of Egypt you should not practice!"); a plea that was ignored as the Jews complicated matters by slowly sinking into the depths of impurity. God decided to save his people when He heard Israel's bitter cries, but, according to the Midrash, the Jews were incapable of hearing the call of liberty because they had become accustomed to the local idolatries.[99]

Kabbalists claim that the Jews, now willing serfs (which is why, initially, they "did not listen [to Moses]"),[100] had plummeted to the penultimate (49th) level of impurity, and that the 50th was the "point of no return."

99.　Ibid., 2:23–25, 6:9; *Mechilta Pisha* 5.
100.　Exodus 6:10.

Question 73

How many years were the Jews in Egypt? Four hundred thirty? Four hundred? Two hundred ten?

"Your seed will be strangers in a land that is not theirs," God tells Abraham, "and they will enslave and oppress them for four hundred years."[101] So the answer is four hundred years, right? Wrong! The eleventh-century master Rabbi Solomon ben Isaac of Troyes of France (better known as Rashi), explains that this is a mathematical impossibility.[102] God's time capsule that spans from Abraham's promise to the Exodus (a period of psychological enslavement, since Abraham had to live with the knowledge that his descendants would be slaves in Egypt), includes years that were *not* spent in Egypt. Remember: Isaac was sixty when Jacob was born, and Jacob was a hundred thirty years old when he arrived in Egypt. If you add a hundred ninety to the two hundred – and ten years the Jews were in Egypt, you get four hundred years.[103]

So where does the number four hundred thirty come from? Add thirty years until Abraham's son (Isaac) is born to the four hundred years from the birth to the Exodus! The Torah's use of the word *vayagar* ("temporary dwelling") seems an odd choice to describe a period of two hundred ten (or four hundred thirty) years, but the transitory expression reflects the fact that the Jews never considered themselves Egyptians, maintaining hope for a future permanence in their own homeland.

101. Genesis 15:13.
102. Rashi, Exodus 12:40.
103. Genesis 25:27, 47:9.

Question 74

Why does God stress the importance of keeping Pesach in the spring season?

As the Chafetz Chaim said: "The trip is never too hard, if you are going home." The spring season embodies the idea of freedom; it follows a winter in which mankind is forced against its wishes to stay indoors for shelter, trapped as in a cage by the fierce elements, depressed by the darkness of long nights. Even Mother Nature suffers mercifully: there is no bounty, no harvest, no nutritional signs of life. Freedom goes where freedom grows. Spring and its new brightness liberate us (emotionally) from our unwelcome and unpleasant (physical) winter lairs; the sunshine nudges a reluctant winter barley crop, and as the vegetation buds, the ancient fear of starvation joyfully recedes. Move over anxiety, welcome to the excitement of a new pulse of life! Reminds one of *zeman cherutenu*, "the Season of our Freedom," which sounds like Pesach to me!

Question 75

Why do we have to make our Seder appear to be "noble"?

The major theme of Pesach is that of freedom (*cherut*), and it is "time" (*zeman cherutenu*) for the Jews to dive right into its rich imagery, grandeur, pageantry; to "dine and recline" (*derech haseiba*) just like the affluent emancipated folk do (or as the Rambam describes them, "the aristocrats").[104] And so we have lots of drinking and an abundance of wine. Casually dipping our food is lavish, unconventional; having others pour our wine for us is table etiquette for those (nobility) who are so rich and carefree that they can do as they please. We begin in memory and hope, *hashata avdei, leshana haba bnei chorin*; yes, we are subservient *now*, but our Judaic spirit can envision dignity and liberation. Which is why we create an atmosphere of liberty and luxury, a self-imposed happy-go-lucky evening, via spirit and conduct, and indulge in freedom, the ambitious motif of the Seder.

Question 76

Where are Succot and Ethom?

The first stop on their escape route from Ramses (a city built by Jewish slave labor) and Goshen is a place called "Succot," near the Delta where the Jews lived.[105] How were the Jews able to get out of Egypt so quickly? Just look at the map: Egypt is extremely long, with very narrow east/west boundaries. Succot, a traditional line of Egyptian fortification, was both "close to" Ramses yet outside of Egyptian borders. Do we know where Succot is? Not exactly, although "a great fortress" known in Egyptian records as "Tharu/Takut" was large enough to accommodate a huge assembly of Jews and their flocks. The historian Josephus notes that Moses "knew Tharu" and organized his largest "army" ever to travel from there to Etham.[106]

---

104. Rambam, *Pesachim* 10:1.
105. Exodus 12:37.
106. *Antiquities of the Jews*, Book 2, Ch. 10.

So where's Etham? The Torah places it at "the edge of the wilderness."[107] Which wilderness? "The wilderness of the Red Sea [i.e., the mountainous mid- and southern Sinai Peninsula, known as 'the southern route,' taken by those wanting to avoid the coastline Philistines.]"[108] Etham is not a single place but an area around the mid-northern edge of the Gulf of Aqaba. How do we know? Because even after the Jews cross the sea, and walk three days to rest "at Mara," they are still in the Etham "area."[109] At Etham came the sudden instruction to pull back and camp at Pi-hahirot, another unknown location somewhere "between Migdol and the sea, before Baal-zephon"[110] (*migdal* means "tower, fortress," whilst the prefix *Pi* was a common prefix which means "house" or "temple," e.g., Pi-Ramses meant "House of Ramses," or Pi-thom meant "House of [the god] Athum," etc.).[111] The Torah's (unexplained) pullback from Etham caught the attention of Egyptian intelligence agents who reported back to Pharaoh that his ex-slaves were "lost, disorientated" and "trapped" in the wilderness, a report that whetted the Egyptian ruler's appetite for revenge, causing him to set off in an unwise pursuit.

---

107.   Exodus 13:20.
108.   Ibid., 13:18.
109.   Numbers 33:8.
110.   Exodus 13:20, 14:1; Numbers 33:7–8.
111.   Ezekiel 30:17.

Question 77

Does the number ten have special significance in Judaism?

Yes, and when it appears, it often does so in the context of Godly power and authority. Mention of the number ten in the Torah first appears in Genesis, when God creates the world with "ten utterances" (the word *vayomer*, "and He said," appearing ten times); the number next appears when God frees His folk from Egyptian bondage via ten plagues – and then we have Ten Commandments; ten trials for Abraham, ten generations from Adam to Noah, another ten from Noah to Abraham, ten *viduis* on Yom Kippur, ten martyrs murdered by Rome, and ten is the minimum number required to form a *minyan*.

The number ten is traced back to the story of Sodom where God agrees with Abraham to save the city if there are ten righteous men there, which is why ten is called "a congregation" (the Talmud[112] refers to a *minyan* of six or seven Jews, but this is not the normative law).

Jewish mystics arrange these "tens" in their chronological order and arrive at a startling conclusion: that the ten plagues were the bridge that transformed the ten declarations at Creation into the Ten Commandments at Sinai. The Maharal of Prague, the seminal figure of Jewish thought in the sixteenth century, elaborates on this difficult concept by matching the Creation declarations with each plague, as though each plague "switched off" each assertion (thus, "Let there be light" was offset by the plague of darkness; "Let us make man," the tenth dec-

---

112. *Sofrim* 10:7.

laration, was nullified by the tenth plague of the firstborn, the plague of locusts obliterated the creation of vegetation, etc.).[113] If the declarations could be rendered invalid, something more real and permanent had to take their place: this turned out to be the Ten Commandments as a micro-example of the Torah's *taryag mitzvot* (613 commands), the discovery of God's original universal purpose in Creation.

Question 78

Why doesn't God introduce Himself as the "Creator of the world" instead of the "Redeemer of Egypt?"

In the Ten Commandments, God introduces Himself as the "redeemer" of Egypt,[114] and not the Creator, to remind all that He intends to stay involved in human affairs (*hashgachah pratit*) in a purposeful and precise way (*Orach Yesharim*). This canon, that of exacting Divine providence, found its way into the Rambam's Thirteen Principles of Faith, an echo of a famous declaration by Rabbenu Asher (Rosh):[115] that the Jew must believe that "His eyes roam over the entire world, are upon all the ways of men, testing their hearts and analyzing feelings. For whoever doesn't believe in the phrase, 'Who took you out of the land of Egypt,'[116] also doesn't believe [the preceding statement], I am Hashem your God."

---

113. *Gvurot Hashem* 57.
114. Exodus 20:2.
115. *Orchot Chaim.*
116. Exodus 20:2.

Rabbenu Yona has another explanation: that no matter how difficult the mitzvot appear to be, remember: "I rescued you from slavery," thus you must trust Me. Although the things that I do may seem incomprehensible at times, I do them for *your* benefit.

Question 79

If the first *korban Pesach* occurred on erev Pesach, was there a "follow-up" *korban Pesach*-type sacrifice?

Yes, but, excluding the one that took place on the first anniversary, it took forty more years before the next one occurred in Gilgal, one of the most important sites in ancient Israel. After the momentous miraculous crossing of the Jordan River, Joshua took twelve large stones from the riverbed and set them up as a reminder.[117] God named the place *Gilgal*, Hebrew for "removing," in reference to the mass circumcision of Jews born during the previous forty years ("Today I have removed from you the shame of Egypt!").[118] With this ritual, the nation became eligible again for the next *korban Pesach*.

---

117. Joshua 4:20–24.
118. Ibid., 5:9.

Question 80

I live in America, the ultimate "land of the free." Why do I need Pesach to be reminded of freedom?

The Torah does not consider physical freedom sufficient, and recognizes the need for a spiritual freedom, one that uplifts, inspires, motivates. The *zeman cherutenu*, the season of our freedom, does exactly that!

Question 81

What is "the *minui* process"?

In a unique Torah law, each Jew had to reserve a piece of the paschal sacrifice for himself, in a process called *minui* (in plural, *minuyim*, which means the "delegated parties"). What if there were "leftovers"? Nothing was to be discarded: "If the household does not contain sufficient people to 'cover' the eating of a sheep, then he should include his neighbor."[119] The *korban Pesach*, the pre-liberation sacrifice, was so important to God that He made it into a *hekdesh shutfin*, "a party of many partners."[120] The value of being included was such that the Talmud describes the "original dedicators" selling their place in line[121] (Rashi softens this perception by describing the payment as an "exchange of donations," money for a part of the lamb), and "limiting" how

---

119.　Exodus 12:4.
120.　*Pesachim* 8:4.
121.　Ibid., 89b.

much each Jew could eat (equal shares) so that there was enough to go around.[122]

Question 82

Are Jewish women allowed to "show off" their beauty?

The Midrash relates how the "beauty" of Jewish women once saved the Jewish people from extinction. The Hebrew males in Pharoah's oppressive regime in Egypt were slaving day and night in the field, rendering conception virtually impossible. This coincided with Pharoah's genocidal decree to murder all male infants. Hebrew wives, however, were determined not to allow Egyptian oppression to disrupt family life so they donned their best clothes, made themselves sensuously attractive, and snuck out to the fields to continue marital relations with their husbands.

The Talmud describes how these Jewish women (guided by the motto *Passions are Fashions!*), would polish pieces of copper to check their appearance in the reflection. So proud was God of their sexual bravery (for the noble purpose of Jewish continuity), that He instructs a reluctant Moses to fashion their copper "mirrors" into the washing vessels that the priests used during the construction of the Tabernacle.

---

122. Ibid.

Question 83

How many chariots chased the Jews to the Red Sea?

Pharaoh had an "elite" force of six hundred chariots; Josephus, the historian, claims that the Egyptian ruler also had 50,000 horsemen and 200,000 infantry that died when the waters collapsed on them.[123]

Question 84

Why ask questions on Pesach?

We want to involve our children, not as onlookers but as participants. We believe that essentially Judaism cannot be taught – it must be caught! We encourage our children to ask questions, for no stimulus to education is more effective than the development of curiosity. Only a questioning, inquisitive mind is drawn to the adventure of study and exploration (Dr. Immanuel Jakobovits).

In the sixteenth century, the Maharal of Prague warned his followers not to get too satisfied with their view of life, for complacency is a spiritual ailment that leads to the deterioration of the mind and spirit. Its chief weapon begins internally with the asking of new questions, an acknowledgment of humility, and that something (knowledge) is lacking.

The Seder is structured to partially fill this void, in that the mode of "asking" opens Jewish minds to the depth of the

---

123.   Exodus 14:7, 9, 15:4, 5:23–30; Josephus, *Antiquities* 2:324, LCL 4: 307.

Exodus experience, described by the Chatam Sofer as the "foundation of Jewish belief." The new Jewish empire that arose from freedom was not just one of power and land, but an empire of thought; Pesach is thus a chag of the mind, a retelling of how a "new world order" (the ethics and morality of Torah) replaced the "old" world of hubris and paganism.

Question 85

Why should we, as Jews, worry about human rights in other countries?

Although there is no Hebrew or rabbinic word for "rights," affinity for human rights, and not just Jewish rights, as articulated in the Haggada, is rooted in Jewish thought and practice (today's term, *zechut*, denotes purity, virtue, innocence).

The key Torah concept is *duties*, not entitlement; and these duties were governed not by man's definition of right and wrong, but by a "plaintiff" process, a tort liability motivated by moral responsibility within penal and civil laws as dictated by God (thus, the Torah frowns upon Jews, even kings and rulers, doing "that which was right in his *own* eyes").[124] And what did God promote? Justice, justice, *above* all, to *all*, by virtue of their common humanity and ancestry – a binding *Anschauung*, not just on mankind but also on God Himself.[125]

God might have set the examples of "rights" (property rights, worker's rights, lender's rights, beneficiary rights, chil-

---

124. Judges 17:6; Deuteronomy 17:14–20.
125. *Sanhedrin* 37a; Genesis 18:24–25; Leviticus 19:15; Deuteronomy 16:20.

dren's rights, women's rights, etc.),[126] and introduced human rights, in the form of law and justice (one of the seven fundamental laws for non-Jews [*Bnei Noach*]),[127] but it was the rabbinate, concerned with human dignity (*kavod habriot*) who stretched the Torah's obligations (*lifnim mishurat hadin*) to ensure that universal human rights were implemented in a "path of respect and peace" (*mishum derech eretz vedarchei shalom*).[128]

Question 86

What exactly is the Haggada trying to tell us with its "In every generation..."?

A month after Purim we open the Passover Haggada and there it is, a sneak preview: *omdim alenu lechalotenu*, "In every generation there are those who rise against us to annihilate us" – an admonition that anti-Semitism has not been relegated *ad ata*, for all time; that just like a Jack-in-the-box, it solemnly pops up again and again, regardless of how often history hits it over the head, powered by the hidden spring of irrationality.

Throughout Jewish history, many Jews have been perplexed as to why their embrace of universal brotherhood suddenly became futile whenever anti-Semitism arose. In 1917, the eloquent Rosa Luxembourg told a Jewish friend, "I feel at home in the entire world." In less than two decades, courtesy of Adolf, there was not a single Jew left alive in her hometown (Zamocz),

---

126. Deuteronomy 23:25–26, 24:6, 12–13; Exodus 22:24–26; Leviticus 19:1–18.
127. *Sanhedrin* 56–57; Ramban, Genesis 34:13.
128. *Baba Metzia* 83a; *Gittin* 59 a–b.

confirming the Talmud's observation that "the urge to evil enters as a guest, and soon becomes the host."[129]

The privileged Jews of the Roman Empire, whose very Judaism was *religio licita*, officially State-recognized, woke up one day to discover their communal serenity drowning in the bloodbaths of Hadrian. The Jews of Shushan were totally convinced that their gentile neighbors had accepted them unconditionally. And yet their wealth, respect and acceptance in the Oriental capital of the world came to naught, literally overnight.

Similarly, when Adolf Hitler was born, the Jews of Germany were well entrenched into societal middle class. By the time the stiff-armed moustached monster died, there was not a single Jewish child left alive in Germany. In their complacency, these Jewish communities had forgotten that there exists within Creation an arbitrary and pathological irrationality regarding societal anti-Judaism; and that "*it*" (whether a gallow, pogrom, Auschwitz or homicidal bomber in a keffiya) can happen anywhere, anytime, by such satanic aberrations as a Torquemada, Antiochus, Chmelnitsky, Eichmann, Arafat – or a Haman, whose simple machination of death by lottery is a reminder that those who plan genocide don't need complicated methods or machinery to carry out their deeds. Remember: about fifteen percent (a million) of the Jews who died in the Holocaust died from nothing more complicated than being deprived of food!

---

129. *Midrash Rabba.*

Question 87

How many years were there from Creation to the Exodus?

A span of 2,448 years. The Temple was built in 832 BCE. How do we know? Add 480 years to 2,448 to arrive at 2,928, then deduct 2,928 from 3,760, the year the Common Era began.[130]

Question 88

We hear a lot about matza, but what else did the Jews leave Egypt with?

The Jews left with their (wooden) kneading bowls, clothes and sandals (God promised that these "would not wear out"),[131] Egyptian gold and silver, and used goat hair for tents. We get some more tidbits from Flavius Josephus (Joseph ben Matthias), a Jew raised in Jewish aristocracy despite the Roman occupation of Palestine who, at 29, defected to the enemy after being drafted into the Jewish war of liberation as a general (the enemy rewarded him with an apartment, a pension and Roman citizenship). Josephus adds that the Jews took vessels of brass instead of pottery (which was more "breakable") for use in "manna, metals, woven fabrics, armor decorations (taken from the drowned Egyptians), beasts of burden, and military implements."[132]

---

130. Rashi *Sanhedrin; Rambam, Shmita Yovel,* Kings I.
131. Deuteronomy 8: 4; 29: 5, 6.
132. Exodus 3: 21, 22; 11: 2,3; 12:34, 35; *Antiquities of the Jews* 3:57; LCL 4: 347.

Question 89

What has sustained the Jews over the centuries?

Jewish mystics take the Haggada verse, "And this is what has sustained our forefathers and us," and apply *gematria* (Jewish numerology) to *vehee*, the word used for "this." The homiletic result? The four letters in the Hebrew word for "this" reveal the source of Jewish national endurance. The first letter is a *vav* which is the sixth letter of the alphabet (representing the six sections of Talmud); the next letter is a *hey*, the fifth letter of the alphabet (which represents the five books of Moses); next we have a *yud*, the tenth letter (i.e., the Ten Commandments), and finally an *aleph*, the first letter of the Hebrew alphabet, which symbolizes the *Shema Yisrael's* "God is One" belief.

Question 90

Why don't we know more about Egypt?

The Jews' lack of interest in history is a result of the Torah's perception of time, that past, present and future are nonsequential. Thus, from the second Temple to the nineteenth century, there are hardly any historiographical works. Even the Rambam, perhaps influenced by Greek rationalist philosophy or Muslim philosophers who avoided history so as to avoid being seen as admiring bloodshed or glorifying futile battles, was indifferent to history ("anecdotal writings, vanities with nothing to contribute to knowledge"), as evidenced by a paragraph in his commentary on Tractate Sanhedrin: "It is a sheer waste of time; as in the case of books found among the Arabs describing historical events, the government of kings and Arab genealogy, or books of songs and similar works which neither possess wisdom nor yield profit for the body but are merely a waste of time."

During the twelfth and thirteenth centuries, Torah scholars and students throughout Christian Europe frowned on history books, which they considered, at best, "adventure novels, with light fiction and no intellectual or moral merit." That is why neither the Torah nor the Haggada are history books; they do not describe the lengthy servitude of the Jews, nor do they relate what happened to the Jews who stayed behind in Canaan, facing the severe drought that forced Jacob & Family to go to Egypt in the first place.

The purpose of the Torah is simple: to reveal God's role in history. Anybody interested in reconstructing the circumstances that preceded the Exodus has plenty of non-Jewish sources at their disposal; in fact, the totalitarian empires of ancient Egypt are some of the most written-about and examined societies in history. Well-known were its Pharaohs and their passionate lust for absolute power, culthood, self-divinity (how do you say *l'etat c'est moi* in Egyptian!), its economy, privileged upper-class *noblesse oblige* priesthood, oppressed proletariat and enslaved gratuitous masses (not just Jews). Egypt, covering an area over a million kilometers, has always been the most populous nation of northeastern Africa, and is famous for such stunning monuments as Khufu's pyramid, the Karnak temple and the Valley of the Kings. And then there was the macabre preoccupation with death, considered just a "passing agitation," a temporary interruption of life, which is why Egyptians continued to write letters to the dead, and Egyptian judges continued to arbitrate cases where one side was dead (this is why dreams, and their meanings, were so prevalent in society). The dead were buried fully clothed, with cooking utensils, weapons and personal toiletries by their side (the rocked-out tombs contained toilets for the dead), with an instruction guide ("Book of the Dead") that advised them of the etiquettes of being dead – i.e., not coming out by day.

Yet there is Jewish material that is revealing and reliable: the Midrash, written about a thousand years after the Exodus, is a body of oral recollections (unfairly called folktales; more accurately known as Jewish folk memory) which were, at the time, the only accurate method of intergenerational information (nobody wrote anything out of fear that the authorities would find it; in any event, most people, including Jews, were illiterate). It is only from the Midrash, for example, that we learn about several thousand Jews (Ephraimites) who tried to escape Egypt before the Exodus, only to be tracked down and slaughtered by the Egyptian military;[133] we discover how, despite harsh conditions, they preserved their "Jewishness" by maintaining family purity, speaking Hebrew, giving their children Hebrew names. In public, Joseph was Zaphenat-paneah, but as soon as he meets up with his family, he says, "I am Joseph!"[134]

---

133. *Targum Jonathan*, Exodus 13:17.
134. Genesis 45:3.

Question 91

During the Exodus, was Moses a lawgiver or a prophet?

More the latter than the former. We're introduced to Moses, initially the child of an anonymous "man of the house of Levi,"[135] when he encounters God at the Burning Bush ("And there never arose in Israel a prophet like Moshe, whom God knew face to face"), however by the time we take leave of Moses he has become transformed after *mattan Torah* to a lawgiver; a judge, jurist and legislator all rolled up in one, determined to appoint "Judges and magistrates in the cities."

Question 92

How did Moses and Aaron simply go in and out of Pharaoh's palace?

As members of the Tribe of Levi, they were exempt from slave labor, and were allowed access.

Question 93

Will Jews continue to recall the Exodus even in the Messianic era?

No, says Ben Zoma, convinced that the Messianic experience, the redemption of the Jews from Exile, will totally eclipse the

---

135.   Exodus 2:1.

previous redemption from Egypt.[136] Unfortunately for Ben Zoma, his Talmud colleagues disagree, claiming that it will never be eclipsed, but will fall to "second place" behind the ultimate redemption.

Question 94

Why is the Torah so specific ("because of this [the matza and maror]") when timing the start of Pesach remembrance?

Just in case some take literally the suggestion to start thinking about Pesach two weeks earlier, and prematurely think the obligation to recall the Exodus starts at the beginning of the month (Nissan). Nissan is not just the first month in the Jewish calendar but a milestone in the creation of a national folk. *Rosh Chodesh Nissan*, the day of God's first mitzva to the Jews as a people (to declare and sanctify the new month), represents one of the most significant days in Jewish history. Why? Because by giving the Jews responsibility for Time itself, the power to sanctify its passage became synonymous with the holy mission of the Jews. The Ramban sees the month of Nissan as eclipsing even Creation, embracing the mystical belief that directing History is greater than creating Creation. (This is why the Shabbat *kiddush* remembers both Creation and the Exodus, two spiritually intertwined events that mark not only the week of Creation, but God's ongoing involvement in history as Master of Mother Nature.)

---

136. *Brachot* 12b; Jeremiah 23:7–8.

But why do we need to start "thinking" of something before it happens? The Seder is symbolic of such a major life-changing, transformative experience (from serfdom to freedom) that one needs to make mental preparations beforehand; especially since we're ordered to go into a time capsule, and propel ourselves backwards to feel as though we are being personally liberated.

Question 95

Why does God need our praise? Does He have an inferiority complex?

In Judaism, it is each person's duty to thank, praise, glorify, exalt and honor another for the kindness, mercy and compassion displayed. In this case, we thank God for transforming a slave gang into a free nation, going from a state of sorrow and mourning to joy and festivity. The Jew who is unable to express this feeling of gratitude (which is the central theme of the Seder) is considered a boorish ingrate, unable to ever appreciate what he has.

Question 96

Why does Chassidut equate the freedom of Pesach with the freedom of speech?

All Chassidic masters and mystics, including the Baal Shem Tov and the Rebbe of Slonim, reach this conclusion based on a Zohar that describes Egyptian slavery as the "exile of speech."[137] Slavery is a state of silence, while redemption is reflective of a free mind and spirit. Jewish mysticism interprets the word "Egypt" literally to mean "narrowness," and the Kabbalah compares Egypt to the throat, a "narrow, constricted" passage between the heart and mind.

Redemption requires retelling; retelling requires a voice, speech, words; in conversation all is sacred. And so Rabbi Isaac Luria, sixteenth-century kabbalistic innovator, split Pesach into two words: *peh* for "mouth," *sach,* for "talk" (i.e., *Pe- Sach* means the "mouth that talks"),[138] and reminded his followers that freedom only began with the sounds of Judaic crying breaking the silence, penetrating the Heavens. "When Moses came," writes the Zohar, "voice came!" in that the arrival of a charismatic revolutionary gave voice to the people. Nachum of Chernobyl thus translates the word *Mashiach* (Hebrew for "messiah") to mean, "from dialogue" or "conversation."[139]

Question 97

Well, which one is it? Does Pesach recall the highs (of freedom) or the lows (of slavery)?

Pesach is a mirror image of Jewish history, a tension ringed with poignancy as it tries to balance the dichotomy of danger and the promise of deliverance. Jewish law and custom try to reflect this

---

137. *Netivot Shalom,* vol 27; Baal Shem Tov, *Zohar Va'era* 25b, *Bereishit* 102, *Amud HaTefilla* 99.

138. I. Luria, *Kitvei Ha'Ari, Sha'ar Hacavanot,* 79; *Peri Eitz Chaim, Sha'ar Chag Hamatzot.*

139. *Me'or Enayim, Parshat Pinchas.*

duality of the Jewish experience (which is why we break a glass under the *chuppa*), and Pesach is the epitome of this unusual Judaic trait of pride and defiance in the face of unspeakable terrors: swinging between the depths of horror (*bechol dor vedor omdim alenu lechalotenu*, "in every generation they rise up to annihilate us") and the heights of triumphs (*mishibud ligeula*, "from bondage to redemption").

Question 98

How do Jewish mystics differentiate between chametz and matza?

There is a great body of kabbalistic work that discusses the differences between chametz and matza. Chametz is considered a symbol of arrogance, while matza, being "flat," signifies the greatest of all Jewish traits, humility (searching for chametz is basically spring cleaning for the soul!); in Hebrew it's *bittul*, which means suppression of self. The Zohar, having defined arrogance and conceit as self-worship (a form of idolatry), compares those who eat chametz on Pesach to those who bow down to idols.

Rabbi Moses Luzzato reminds us that Pesach falls halfway between last Yom Kippur and next Yom Kippur, with chametz acting as a mid-way "wake-up" alarm, its "setting aside" a symbol to the Jew to also banish the accumulated disorder ("the crumbs of sins") that may have entered his life since last Yom Kippur. The charismatic sixteenth-century kabbalist Rabbi Isaac Luria told his followers that if they disciplined themselves to abstain from the tiniest piece of chametz over Pesach, they would spend the rest of the year free of sin. (The Ari even composed his own prayer while burning his chametz: "Just as I am destroying chametz from my home so shall all 'outside forces' and the spirit of impurity be removed from the earth and may God remove our evil inclination [*yetzer hara*] from within us and may all darkness and wickedness be consumed in smoke!" What else can one say, except *amen*!

Question 99

Why do we start the Seder in shame and end in praise? Was is it the Jews' fault that they were slaves? Weren't they just victims of Pharaoh's brutality and state terror?

You're right: the obligation of *sippur yetziat Mitzrayim* requires *matchil begnut u'mesayem beshevach*, "starting in shame."[140] What shame is this Mishna referring to? It's in dispute: Rav links it to the embarrassment that our ancestors were idol worshipers (*Mitchila ovdei avoda zara hayu avotenu*); Shmuel attributes the shame to being slaves in Egypt (*Avadim hayinu leParoh bemitzrayim*). It was not the slavery *per se* that was the shame, but the disgrace and dishonor of the depths of indignities to which the Jewish folk had sunk. This is why the Torah praises God for taking the Jews out of Egypt fifty times, symbolic of the fifty extra *sha'arei bina*, "Gates of understanding," given to them after they had "sunk" to the forty-ninth level of *tuma*, "impurity."

---

140. *Pesachim* 116a.

Question 100

Are there any accounts written by Egyptians that describe the Exodus?

Yes, lots! The first non-Torah account of the Exodus was written by Hecataeus of Abdera, who arrived in Alexandria, Egypt around 320 BCE.[141] He begins his account with a plague that ravaged the country, and sees it as a direct divine punishment (from *his* gods, *not* the Jewish God) for allowing "aliens" and "alien cultures" into Egypt. The "aliens" are expelled, and, under the leadership of Moses, go off to populate Palestine (he describes how Moses orders the Jews not to make any Divine images, "because God does not own a human shape [and] cannot be depicted in images.")[142]

And then we have Lysimachos whose version was written in the second century BCE; he begins with a famine that is blamed on the "unpure, impious people (*anagnon kai dyssebon*) who settled in the country." The Egyptian author describes how the king of Egypt orders that the "lepers" be drowned, and how they gather around a Moses who orders them to "destroy every temple and altar of the gods (*theon to naous kai bomous anatrepein*)," after giving them new "unlawful rules (*ta misanthropa kai paranoma ethe*)."[143] Manetho, an Egyptian priest in the first half of the third century BCE,[144] during the time of Ptolemy

---

141. Diodorus, *Bibliotheca Historica*, 40.3.
142. Stern, *Greek and Latin Authors*, Vol. I, No. II.
143. Apollonius Molon, *Apud*; Diodorus, *Bibliotheca Historica*, 34–35; Stern, *Greek and Latin Authors*, Vol. I, No. 63.
144. W.G. Waddell, *Manetho*, Loeb Classical Library, Cambridge, Mass; Harvard UP, 1940.

11, wrote a history book (*Aigyptiaka*) in which he calls Moses "a rebellious Egyptian priest who made himself the leader of a colony of lepers." Excerpts from his book (which describe a people's aversion to mixing milk and meat, socializing with the "uncircumcised ones" and abhorrence of the multiple gods) are quoted by Flavius Josephus, who tries to refute the blatant anti-Semitism, calling its hatred just more "tales and legends (*mutheuomena kai legomena*)."[145]

Chaermon, an Egyptian priest who lived in Alexandria during the first half of the first century BCE, and tutored Nero in Rome, writes how the country's rulers kicked out "Two-hundred-and-fifty thousand lepers...led by Moses and Joseph."[146] (This was a precursor for future European anti-Semitism which blamed the Great Plague on the Jews, and fueled such Jew-haters as composer Richard Wagner, who had enormous influence on Adolf Hitler, to depict the Jews in such terms as "contagion.")

In Pompeius Trogus' *Historicae Philippicae*, Moses is described as the "son of Joseph" who forms a new religion called "*sacra Aegyptia*," and is responsible for bringing "disease and epidemics" to Egypt, which forces the king to expel them from Egypt.[147] Tacitus basically confirms the Exodus tradition, the "purging" of the Jews (*genus*, "this race") from Egypt, led by Moses, because they were detested by the Egyptian gods (*ut invisum deis*). He notes how Moses has started a new "counter-religion [that] is the exact opposite of all other religions (*novos ritus contrariosque ceteris mortalibus indidit*)" – an obvious reference

145. *Contra Apionem* 2.148.
146. Chaeremon, *Aegyptiaca Historia, Apud Josephus, Contra Apionem*; P.W. van der Herst, *Chaeremon: Egyptian Priest and Philosopher*, Leiden; Brill, 1984.
147. Gager, *Moses*, 49.

to monotheism.[148] In fact, when Tacitus describes how the Jews sacrifice rams,[149] he comes close to the Torah's own description of the *korban Pesach* (paschal lamb sacrifice), and confirms the animal's place in the litany of Egyptian gods. The animal was not just tied to the stars (Onkelos, the Roman convert who became the first Jew to translate the Torah into Aramaic, calls it "an abomination of the Egyptians"), but was linked to Amun, the "highest" god of Egypt.

Question 101

Matza? Bread of food or faith?

Matza is *lechem oni* – bread of affliction, bread of austerity. The Zohar, however, calls it the food of faith. Bread of affliction or austerity we can understand, but faith? When the Jews hurriedly left the known (Egypt) for the unknown (wilderness), no one asked, "How will we survive?" Matza thus symbolizes a faith that God would care for them no matter the destination. Matza, Jewish mystics patiently explain, is "soul food"; as a bread of affliction and austerity, it nourished *emuna* ("faith") because the Jews left Egypt, not just in haste but in blind obedience, in favor of a desert, with no provisions, no food, no shelter, no cell phones, and not a clue as to their destination.

---

148. Stern, *Greek and Latin Authors*, Vol. 2, No. 281; A.M.A. Hospers-Jensen, *Tacitus over de Juden*, Groningen: J.B. Wolter, 1949.
149. *Contumeliam Ammonis.*

Question 102

When the Jews saw the drowned Egyptians, why does the Torah refer to the "dead" in the Hebrew singular?[150]

Because the number of Egyptians who died was immaterial; what was more important was that Egyptian culture on that day died a singular death.

Question 103

Why is Egypt equated with gods?

Because Egypt considered itself to be a "god" country (the Torah's goal, that *man* should strive to be "holy," would have been incomprehensible in Egypt). Egypt had an astonishing, unlimited number of gods (*netjer*), bizarre beliefs (the most "civilized" country on earth at the time was convinced that the sky was a cow goddess held up by another god) and animal fetishes (ram-gods, falcon-gods; which is why we uncover vast "pet cemeteries" of mummified cats, dogs, bulls, baboons and crocodiles whose grotesque "gatekeeper" is another animal, the jackal, master god of embalmment) – yet possessed not a single dogma nor central book of teachings. (It was not until the time of the Greeks that an effort was made to substitute limited mythopoeia, mythmaking, with some intelligent coherence). And there were competing gods: in Heliopolis and Hermopolis, the number one god was the Sun; in Elephantine, it was

---

150. Exodus 14:30.

Khnum, a ram who made all living creatures on his potter's wheel. When one Pharaoh (Akhenaten) decided to replace polytheism with the monotheism of only one cosmic god, he was, ironically, branded a heretic (unfortunately, he chose the wrong god, selecting the Sun-god Re). Many of these gods had bizarre hybrid forms (e.g., the goddess Hathor has a woman's face with cow's horns and cow's ears; the goddess Taurt has the head of a hippopotamus, the tail of a crocodile, the breasts of a woman, and the claws of a lion).

Question 104

Is there anything mystical about Shabbat and Pesach coinciding with each other?

Several Midrashim consider the merger of Shabbat and Pesach as a mystical *shidduch*, "made in Heaven," so to speak. The seven days of Creation, ending in Shabbat, is matched to the seven days between leaving Egypt and the miraculous division of the Red Sea, which corresponds to Pesach (Jewish law demands that the Shabbat *kiddush* explicitly mention the Exodus, *zecher litziat Mitzrayim*).[151] The Ashkenaz Tosafot scholars equate the thirty-nine "forbidden activities (*avot melachot*)" on Shabbat with the thirty-nine forms of slave labor forced upon the Jews in Egypt. Meanwhile the laws of Shabbat are some of the first laws (*chok umishpat*) that Moses teaches the Jews at Mara the moment the people have a respite after the splitting of the sea.

---

151.   Ibid., 13:3, 20:8.

Another Midrash introduces Shabbat as a day-of-rest request that the young Moses makes of Pharaoh upon first witnessing the burdens of his brothers.[152] Pharaoh initially agrees, but then later, when Moses reappears as a confrontational adult messenger of God, rescinds the Shabbat and increases the workload of the slave gangs by refusing to provide them with straw (the Midrash adopts the Torah verse, *Ve'al yish'u bedivrei sheker*,[153] as a play on *mishtashem*, "delight," referring to the delight, *oneg* of Shabbat).

Question 105

Apparently, seventy Jews went down to Egypt. Is this number significant?

Although the number seventy is described in this context as being "few in number," there is a great implication to seventy Jewish souls, who eventually became so prosperous as to echo God's promise, "as numerous as the stars of the sky."[154] What's its significance? There were seventy nations at the infamous tower that babbled, suggestive of the fact that the initial Jewish family that became a nation was a microcosm of humanity.

---

152. Ibid., 2:11.
153. Ibid., 12:9.
154. Deuteronomy 10:22.

Question 106

Why does the Torah use such a demeaning expression (*vayishretzu* – "and they swarmed") to describe how "great and mighty" the Jews became in Egypt?

This Hebrew phrase, derived from the root *sheretz*, is an unflattering description for creepy crawly insects or lizards. It is unbecoming and undignified. Surely God was not ashamed of the Jews because they "were fruitful, prolific, multiplied and became extremely mighty, filling the land"?[155] What made God despair?

The Jews didn't just multiply in numbers, they "grew" in assimilation, they "enhanced" their embrace of idolatry, and "swarmed" to adopt the immoral Egyptian values. "Filling the land" does not necessarily refer to statistics and demographics, but to influence and cultural digestion. And so the Haggada carefully chooses its words, borrowing a dramatic phrase ("Through your blood you shall live")[156] from a Hebrew prophet (Ezekiel) who was able to see through your "great charm, beauty of form, long hair" and notice that the Jewish emperor had no clothes ("You were naked and bare. And I passed over you and I saw you downtrodden in your blood!").

Why the reference to blood? The Haggada counters the catastrophic "swarming" to assimilation with a blunt reminder that to stay Jewish, to preserve their identity, Jews must maintain the mitzva of *brit mila*, circumcision.

---

155.   Exodus 1:7.
156.   Ezekiel 16:6–7.

Question 107

How important is the concept of memory in Judaism?

Very. When the Torah commands Jews to "remember," it uses the term *zachor* no less than 169 times. Isaiah would often quote the Torah's "Remember the days of old!"[157] – and the prophet wasn't the only thinker inspired by memory. Memory is critical. Consider Moses' final oration, which is the underlying theme of the entire Book of Deuteronomy. It is not an expression of sad resignation but is delivered in a free-flowing, poetic and passionate crescendo, beginning with an unambiguous, stirring challenge: to contemplate history (*Zachor yemot olam, binu shanot dor vador,* "Remember the days of old, consider the years of ages past..."); an ode to the concept of *experientia docet,* that there is no more reliable teacher than past experience, a reverence for previous generations, a glow in a past archival glory. This is why Moses calls upon *hashamayim va'aretz,* "the Heavens and the earth," as witnesses to his valedictorian farewell, because they are immortal and everlasting witnesses to Jewish history.

Memory of the Exodus story is so central in Judaism that it features 67 of the 613 mitzvot (including a top slot in the first of the Ten Commandments, "I am the Lord thy God who brought thee forth from the land of Egypt out of the house of bondage"). Egypt represents the old; a stagnated culture of paganism and sorcery, despotism and hubris, the "origin of all cults," tried and rejected, replaced with the truth of monotheism. When Jews

---

157.   Deuteronomy 32:7; Isaiah 46:9.

annually recall its irrelevancy, they underline a famous George Santayana observation, "Those who cannot remember the past are condemned to repeat it!" Pesach's role in Judaism can be summarized in one sentence: we are what we remember!

Most Jewish adults, regardless of their level of religiosity, carry in their hearts, and pass on to their own offspring, warm childhood memories of parents, brothers, sisters and children sitting around a Pesach table. "All pleasures," writes Ruth R. Wisse, one of the leading scholars in the field of Jewish literature, "spring from the Seders of my childhood, the excitement of which I adored."[158] Pesach does not only attract the wise and wicked sons, but also scoffers, sinners and cynics. (Heinrich Heine, the ultra-assimilated German Jew, admits that "Even Jews who have long drifted from the faith of their fathers...are stirred in their innermost parts when the old, familiar Passover sounds chance to fall upon their ears.")

Question 108

Why do we need a special festival of remembrance (Pesach) if the Torah has already ordered us to remember the Exodus daily ("all of our lives")?[159]

The duty of Pesach is *not* just to remember (which is an individual act), but to "retell" (which requires the *sharing* of Jewish history with an audience), which is what the word *Haggada* literally means. Remembering can be conducted in private, on

158.   Ruth R. Wisse, "Between Passovers," *Commentary*, December 1989.
159.   Deuteronomy 16:3.

an impersonal level, but retelling, sharing, requires involving oneself personally and sharing the memories with others.[160]

Question 109

What exactly are we giving "thanks and praise" for?

The Vilna Gaon agreed that Jews need to know exactly what they are praising, so he made a list of five pairs of "saving-adjectives": *me'avdut l'cherut* (Exodus from Egypt), *meyagon l'simcha* (parting of the Red Sea), *me'evel leyom tov* (from mourning to a festival – the *evel* being the golden calf sin, the *yom tov* being Moses' receipt of the second tablets, "*luchot*"), *me'afela l'or gadol* (literally, from the darkness [of the desert] to the great light [of *eretz Yisrael*]), *mishibud ligeula* (from slavery to redemption; the Vilna Gaon was referring to the slavery of later foreign forces during the time of the Judges to the redemption of sovereignty under Kings David and Solomon).

Question 110

If you had to reduce the Exodus to its core, what would it be?

The core of the Exodus saga, which started the chain reaction of events that led to freedom, Mount Sinai, the Torah, the conquest of the holy land, and a sovereign nation, is contained in

---

160. Rav Chaim of Brisk, *Minchat Chinuch* 21; *Brachot* 21a.

five opening words from Pharaoh: "I do not know this God!"[161] This denial-of-God attitude forced the Heavens to respond with a massive, public show of force.[162] And it was carefully choreographed for spectators, victims and future generations. If the first nine plagues seemed to be nothing but a manipulation of natural phenomena, the tenth plague put all doubts to rest. This final deathblow was absent of any "messenger," and was delivered by God Himself,[163] using the four-letter Name of God known to the earlier Patriarchs but not in the context of such unlimited clout.[164]

The death of his own firstborn shattered Pharaoh's own self-deification, and became the catalyst for his 180-degree turnaround in thought: "Who is God who has the overwhelming power to which I must bow?"[165]

---

161.   Exodus 5:2.
162.   Ramban, Exodus 5:3; *Zohar, Miketz* 198, 1; Exodus 6:7, 7:5; Rav Hertz on Exodus 4:21.
163.   *Baba Metzia* 61b; Psalms 104:4; 148:8 Rashi, Rambam, Be'er Yitzchak, Exodus 12:12.
164.   Rav Hertz commentary on Exodus 6:2, 3: Exodus 9:16.
165.   Abravanel on the Haggada.

Question 111

Why does the Torah pause to record Moses' and Aaron's genealogy before they proceed on their mission to entreat Pharaoh on behalf of the Jewish people?

By listing His messengers as descendants of Jacob,[166] and revealing their ages, God is removing all doubts that Moses and Aaron are anything but human and fallible; and that despite the soon-to-be-released powers and plagues, these two Jews are not supermen.[167]

Question 112

Why does the Torah call this festival Chag Hamatzot while the Jews call it Pesach?

From God's perspective, the paschal lamb offering, linked to the term "Pesach" via its Hebrew name, *korban Pesach*, was a one-time only affair, while the "unleavened bread" (*Hamatzot*) link applied to an entire week. From God's perspective, Israel is praised for their faith in plunging into a wilderness with no life-sustaining provisions, except matza – thus the Torah's preference for *Chag Hamatzot*. From the Jews' perspective, they

---

166. Genesis 46:8–12.
167. S.R. Hirsch on Exodus 7:11; Rav Hertz on Deuteronomy 34:6.

prefer the term "Pesach" due to their relief that their homes and families were saved (i.e., "passed over").

Question 113

Why did God lead the Jews through the desert as opposed to the more convenient, direct route through Philistine?

Rabbi Israel Meir of Radin (the Chafetz Chaim) explains why:

The advantage of the Philistine territory was that it was inhabited and there was bread to eat and clothing to wear. On the other hand, there was the danger that the Jews would learn from their ways. And so God led them through the desert, which was spiritually pure. Regarding the question where they would find bread in the desert, God said that it would be better to rely on miracles from Heaven than to seek their livelihood and a luxurious life in a land of assimilation and impurity.

But what was the most direct convenient route? Along the Mediterranean coastline, the most northern part of the Sinai Peninsula, a 150-mile path (240 kilometers) that was a well-known artery used throughout history by business travelers, kings, military, etc. When Egyptian King Thutmosis II invaded Asia it took his troops no more than ten days to get to Gaza.

To protect its Canaan border against the hostile Asiatics ("sand-crossers"), the reigning Pharaohs built a defense wall ("The Wall of Horus" – *horus* means both "ruler" and the name of a god, while "wall" was meant to be the incarnation of the latter).

The Torah refuses to use this pagan-tainted name and simply calls it *Shur*, "wall" (the same wall is mentioned in Hagar's flight back to her native land).[168] Instead, God directs the Jews to go "roundabout by way of the wilderness" (*midbar*), but we don't know the exact route. Nor is the "Sea of Reeds" (*yam suf*)[169] specific enough to locate it (Isaiah calls it, the "Way of the Sea," from its old Latin name *Via Maris*).[170]

Question 114

Why are the miracles of the tenth of Nissan associated with the Shabbat before Pesach instead of on their actual date?

The fact that the tenth of Nissan was a Shabbat is meaningful because, despite it being a traditional day of holiness and sanctity, the Jews still selected and tied up lambs in preparation for the upcoming sacrifice. This was a day of "shock 'n awe" for the enemy, the confused and disoriented Egyptian neighbors who knew that Shabbat was supposed to be a day of rest. Also, Miriam died on this date forty years later and the well that

---

168. Genesis 16:7, 20:1, 25:18, 49:22; Exodus 15:22; I Samuels 15:7, 27:8; II Samuels 22:30; Psalms 18:30.
169. Exodus 13:17–18.
170. Isaiah 9.

accompanied her and supported the Jews suddenly dried up. Thus it was inappropriate to mark the tenth of Nissan as a day of "miracles." Some even fast on this day in honor of Miriam's unique role in Jewish history.

Question 115

What was the duration of the plagues?

According to the Mishna, the plagues continued for a whole year.[171] Since the first nine plagues are basically intensified blows of Mother Nature, Rav Hertz is able to link each sequel of plagues to the natural cycle of the year. For example: the "flax and barley [i.e., wheat] being smitten" points to January; the locusts, arriving by an "east wind" and departing "westwards," is suggestive of early spring; the darkness comes around during the hot sandstorms (*hamsin*) that block the sun, and so on.

Question 116

Who amongst us is truly "free"?

Rabbi Yehuda Loew of Prague (*Maharal*) believed that a Jew should first know who he is *not*, before he can acknowledge who he is or who he can become. In the Haggada, we are told in one simple phrase, "We were slaves to Pharaoh in Egypt." How does this statement reveal to us who we are? By dividing slavery into two forms, one of "Pharaoh" and one of "Egypt," the Torah informs us of what the Jew is *not*.

---

171. *Eduyot* 2:10.

The word *Pharaoh* is linked to both *paruah*, "wildness," and *oreph*, the "back of the neck," a dual charge that this form of slavery is one that traps mankind in a stubborn, "hard-headed" culture of immorality, lawlessness, licentiousness (the reference to the back of the neck is suggestive of acts that are instinctive and stubborn because they are not thought through). This type of arrogant rule stifles the spirit and moral fiber that Jews must possess.

What about the other type of slavery? The Hebrew word for "Egypt" is *Mitzrayim*, from the root *tzar*, which means "narrow, constrained, limited." (It can also mean "calamity," as in, "Egypt was the country of calamities.") The Jew cannot survive in a narrow environment, helpless in personal and community growth and potential, an atmosphere that is antithetical to the liberating results of a Torah reality.

The Alter of Novorhadok (Rabbi Yosef Yoizel Horowitz) was once on a train where he was being made fun of by some freethinkers who ridiculed his way of dress. "You call yourselves 'free,'" he replied to their taunts, "for you have liberated yourselves from the restrictions of religious belief. But in actual fact, you are slaves. I have disciplined myself to the extent that I am prepared to do whatever my Creator asks of me. You, on the other hand, are ruled by your passions and desires. That is *real* slavery!"

Question 117

Is there any historical evidence that proves the occurrence of the ten plagues and the Jews' saga in Egypt?

There is archeological evidence that proves that the Jews were enslaved in ancient Egypt, but there was not a great deal of documentation about the Exodus itself (which is not surprising since the vanquished rarely reduced their defeats to writing). An Egyptian papyrus dated from the end of the Middle Kingdom, discovered in the nineteenth century and currently in the Leiden Museum, Holland (known as the *Ipuwer Papyrus*, after its author), claims to be a detailed eyewitness account. Ipuwer describes an Egypt rocked by mayhem, turmoil, starvation and drought, and details the escape of slaves who took the wealth of their Egyptian oppressors with them:

> Plague is throughout the land. Blood is everywhere…
> And all the Egyptians dug around the river for water
> to drink; for they could not drink of the water of
> the river… Lower Egypt weeps… The entire palace
> is without its revenues…and the fire ran along the
> ground… There was hail, and fire mingled with the
> hail, very grievous…and the hail smote every herb of
> the field, and broke every tree of the field… There
> remained no green things in the trees, or in the herbs
> of the fields, through all the land of Egypt…

But what is the most compelling evidence? The direct unbroken tradition, passed down from father to son, for 3,000 years, recalling the same experience.

Question 118

Is there really such a thing as a "second" Pesach?

Yes. *Pesach Sheni* is "a second chance,"[172] requested by "certain disappointed Jews (*anashim*)"[173] who missed the mitzva of *korban Pesach* because of their ritually impure state as a result of coming into contact with a dead body. This premier mitzva, considered a stand-alone chag (*regel bifnei atzma*),[174] is conducted a month after Pesach, and comes replete with matza and maror.

Question 119

What if the Jew fulfilled the first Pesach offering, but wanted more? Could he participate twice?

Yes. Then why don't we get a second chance if we miss the Rosh Hoshana *shofar* blowing or forget to shake the *lulav* on Succot? According to Rabbi Meir Simcha haKohen of Dvinsk, unlike the mitzva of blowing the shofar or shaking the *lulav*, the mitzva of *korban Pesach* is central to the very formation of Israel as a nation. Is there still a "second" Pesach today? No. Why not? Because you can't make a sacrifice if you don't have a Temple!

---

172. Numbers 9.
173. Ibid., 9:5–8.
174. *Mishneh Torah, Korban Pesach* 5; *Pesachim* 92b.

Question 120

OK, so Pharaoh was told to "Let my people go!" – but for what purpose?

For one reason only: "To serve Me!" The rallying cry "Let my people go" always seems to be quoted out of context, usually attributed (incorrectly) to Moses. They are in fact God's words. It's only half a sentence, and thus a distortion. The rest of it equates Pesach with freedom – but only *for a purpose*! And that is? To forge an energetic and motivated relationship with God, which can only come about when physically free. "Let my people go" is the start; "so that they may serve me" is the destination.

Question 121

Why does the Torah keep reminding us that the celebration of liberation encompasses the entire month of "Aviv" when Pesach itself is only an eight-day chag?

Aviv, the month we call Nissan, is Hebrew for spring ("for in the month of Aviv you went forth from Egypt").[175] "Abib" also means fresh ears of barley, and is so important that we even add an additional pre-Nissan month (Adar) to make sure that Pesach and spring are synonymous in the Jewish calendar.[176]

---

175. Exodus 12:15, 34:18.
176. *Tosefta Sanhedrin* 2:2.

Why? When this "transitional" month, which marks the end of the winter rains and the improvement of the weather, was first singled out by God (as "the beginning of months; the first of the months of the year for you"),[177] Moses and Aaron were told to keep it to themselves, and not tell their folk until after they explained the details of the Pesach offering. And even then, God describes Pesach as a celebration not of any one specific month, but "throughout the ages."[178]

The Jews were thus *first* conscripted into taking an active role in their own freedom, and were no longer spectators but active partners in liberation. They were now able to focus on their new beginning, a radical fresh start in both history and "Jewish" time, one kick-started not by a single week but by a month (Nissan) and a season (spring). This is why God mentions neither "Aviv" nor "spring" until *after* the Jews leave Egypt, when in retrospect, liberty and "Aviv"[179] are synonymous. Spring is now the recognized symbol of renewal, of man and Mother Nature, the arrival of hope, optimism, future sunshine – in other words, it's tantamount to the redemption from Egyptian bondage. In fact *Shir Hashirim* is more than just another love song, it is a Song of spring...

> For lo the winter is past, the rain is over and gone,
> The flowers appear on the earth,
> the time of the singing of the birds is come,
> And the voice of the turtle is heard in our land.

---

177. Exodus 12:1–3.
178. Ibid., 12:14–20.
179. Exodus 13:4, 23:15.

Question 122

Is there any special *Haftora* reading on Pesach?

The *Haftora* for *Shabbat Hagadol* (the Shabbat immediately preceding Pesach) is "borrowed" from Malachi who warns of the "great, awesome day of the Lord" (the final "Day of Judgment").[180] In the last chapter of the Prophets, God promises that before this will occur, Eliyahu will arrive on the scene, charged with inspiring the Jewish folk into doing *teshuva* ("He shall return the hearts of parents with the hearts of children, and the hearts of children with the hearts of parents, so that when I come, I do not strike the whole land with utter destruction!").

Why Eliyahu? Because unity was a goal of his that he failed to achieve during his lifetime. There was a tragic period in the history of Israel when King Achav of the Northern Kingdom married Princess Jezebel of Tzidon, a union that resulted in diminishing the holy land into a pagan land that worshiped Baal. When Eliyahu witnessed this abomination, he declared a three-year drought,[181] which, according to the twelfth-thirteenth-century Rabbi David Kimchi, had some impact upon the people.[182] With a follow-up miracle at Mount Carmel, the prophet succeeds in bringing some more of the folk back to monotheism; but ultimately he fails, asking God to take his life as he wanders, dejected and depressed, in the wilderness. What does God do? He appoints Elisha as a prophet, hoping that

---

180. Malachi 3.
181. Rashi, *Melachim I* 17:7; *Genesis Rabba* 33; *Sanhedrin* 113a.
182. *Radak, Melachim I* 18:1.

his more genteel approach will inspire a return to monotheism. Pesach's *Shabbat Hagadol Haftora* reflects Malachi's hope that the Jewish people, about to suffer centuries of exile, will one day be ready for the return of Eliyahu and his message of *achdut*.

Question 123

Did the Jews "fly flags" when they left Egypt?

Some of the first "flags" in history were carried by Jews. Upon leaving Egypt, the nation identified each of its tribes via an ensign (Menasseh's was jet-black with a figure of a Capricorn, Zevulun's was white with a ship, etc.). In order to be seen from afar, these were mounted on banners and tied down with streamers that flew in the wind (but, as usual, it was left to the enterprising Chinese to perfect the concept; in the twelfth century BC the founder of the Chou dynasty never left home without his [white] flag). Today's flag of Israel – designed by David Wolffsohn, for the first World Zionist Congress in 1897 – is adorned with a blue-and-white *magen david*, a nod to a Messianic future and the *tallit* ("Let us," wrote Wolffsohn, "take the praying shawl [*tallit*] and unfold it before the eyes of Israel and the eyes of all nations!").

Question 124

Why did Pharaoh require so much slave labor for producing bricks?

Pharaoh's obsessive building program required more than just state-imposed enslavement; it required bricks, bricks, and more bricks (the pyramids at Dahsur alone contain nearly twenty-five *million* bricks!). Great quarries of stone lay on either side of the Nile Valley; the bricks, however, came from the alluvial mud supplied by the Nile River. The Jewish slaves would mix the field stubble to form brick shapes. The brick was then left in the sun for three days before it was turned over for another three days. In other words, it took a whole week before a single brick was ready for use, unlike today, when Egyptian factories produce three thousand bricks in one eight-hour shift.

A letter scroll discovered and dated to the fifth year of Pharaoh's rule reveals the quota: forty men had to produce two thousand bricks. An inscription carved into the side of a slab dated to the era of Thutmosis III[183] shows a taskmaster mouthing the words, "The rod is in my hand, do not be idle!"

Question 125

If chametz is so bad, why is it only forbidden eight days out of the year?

Obviously there's nothing intrinsically "evil" in bread! When the Jew declares "war" against chametz – by seeking out even the

---

183.   Ca. 1490–1436 BCE.

tiniest speck of it, and then destroying it – he is acknowledging that the time has come to rid himself of arrogance, the absence of which can lead to wisdom and enough (Judaic) confidence that by the time we reach Shavuot, seven weeks later, eating chametz ("two loaves of bread, baked with leaven") becomes a mitzva![184]

Question 126

If you had to provide a short definition for matza, what would it be?

It's an impossible task: there are many definitions for the term matza. The Zohar calls it *michla de'atzvasa,* the "bread of health" (an abbreviation of *mikol tzara hatzilenu,* "save me from distress"); the tradition calls it the "bread of redemption" (a symbol of freedom, *cherut*); the Torah refers to matza as *lechem oni,* "the bread of affliction"; the rabbis of the Talmud homiletically call matza the bread of intellect, about which we answer many questions (*"she'onim alav devarim harbeh"*); the Dvar Aaron calls it the "bread of poverty" (its recipe is bare, avoiding such "rich" ingredients as oil, honey, eggs); the Jewish mystics take the letters of matza (*mem, tzaddi, heh*) as an anagram for *hatzom,* a fast day, in that it is prepared so quickly that it can immediately end a famine.

---

184. Leviticus 23:15.

Question 127

By "hardening Pharaoh's heart," didn't God deprive him of free will?

Yes, it's true: by "hardening" Pharaoh's heart, anti-Torah forces claim that God did not allow Pharaoh to repent, depriving him of his free will, paralyzing his response to the plea of *Shlach et ami*, "Let My people go." Yet prior to five of the plagues, Pharaoh was warned of the consequences and *still* refused, putting himself in a position described by Shimon: "When God warns a person on three occasions and he does not turn from his (evil) ways, God closes the door of repentance." Pharaoh, in his refusal to comply with Moses' and Aaron's request, hardened his own heart. And so the Midrash states that it was not only the Jews who were prisoners, but Pharaoh himself; prisoner to his *own* political and psychological system of utter governmental oppression.

Question 128

In Judaism, are leaders born, or made?

The latter, if we go by Moses, whose unwitting introduction to leadership occurs in a split instant, "And he [Moses] turned this way and that way, and he saw there was no man, and he smote the Egyptian and hid him."[185] Thus was a leader born (I mean *made*!). When asked how a leader becomes a leader, the

---

185. Exodus 2:12.

Baal Shem Tov claims that one can only reach high places when standing on the shoulders of others – and, of course, no Jew is born that tall!

Question 129

What were the differences in leadership between Abram and Moses?

The first Jew, in his first encounter with God, simply does as he is told ("Abram went forth [just] as God had [asked him to]"), but Moses hesitates, talks back and worries ("What shall I say to them?" "What if they don't believe me?" "What if they don't listen to me?").[186] The difference is this: Abram is searching for God, while God, seeking an agent to deliver His folk from suffering, finds Moses. What attracted the Heavens to Moses as a potential national leader? His instinctive sense of justice ("He saw an Egyptian beating a Hebrew, one of his kinsfolk… He struck down the Egyptian!").[187]

Question 130

Why does the Haggadah compare Jews to "plants, eggs, olives"?

"I made you thrive," quotes the Haggada, "like the plants of the field," a reference to the Torah's description of a people who were "fruitful, prolific, multiplied and became extremely mighty, filling

---

186. Genesis 12:1–5; Exodus 3:13, 4:1, 6:30.
187. Exodus 3:12–13, 2:17.

the land"[188] – and more! "Numerous. I made you thrive like the plants of the field, and you grew big and tall." So why compare Jews to "plants of the field"? Because the more you cut grass, the more it grows. Thus, "the more they [the Egyptians] afflicted the Jews, the more they increased and spread out!"[189]

The idea that oppression and persecution not only doesn't weaken the Jews, but actually strengthens them, in their resolve to survive, answers another question: why, when leaving Egypt, were the Tribe of Levi the smallest in numbers? Because they were the only Jews never enslaved. (This also explains why Jews are compared to an olive, whose clear oil only emerges and rises to the top when pressed.)

Question 131

What is *gomel bensching* and does it have any connection to Pesach?

This is the act of blessing and thanking God after emerging safely from a dangerous situation (*gomel* means "bestows [goodness]"). This prayer replaced the "thanks offerings" brought in Temple times. When do we say it? Usually in the presence of a *minyan*, within three days of coming out of harm. Does one have to wait until a full recovery? No. Can it be said in private? Yes, but without God's name.[190] What defines a "dangerous situation"? A serious illness or operation (including childbirth); a risky journey (e.g., air flight, especially in a world of terrorism);

---

188. Ibid., 1:7.
189. Ibid., 1:12.
190. *Shulchan Aruch, Orach Chayim* 219.

surviving an accident; release from prison. What's the source of these four categories? The Psalmist defines four types of folks that are God's "redeemed" – travelers, captives, invalids and sea voyagers.[191]

Is there any connection between *gomel bensching* and Pesach? Not directly, but the Jews who fled Egypt surely belong to the Divine classification of "the redeemed."

Question 132

Why are Succot and Pesach called the "fragrant" festivals?

The scent of chag is in the air ("How sweet it is!"); from the Seder to the seven days and nights of the succa, it's impossible to avoid the whiff of a Jewish festival. That sweet smells "gladden the soul" is why incense was used in the Temple; Mount Moriah was called the mountain of *mor* (the spice myrrh);[192] Tehillim asks that prayers be akin to sweet-smelling incense;[193] Jewish mystics believe that every good deed (mitzva) creates extra fragrance in the world (based on a Midrash that links each of God's Words at Sinai to a spice that filled the world); and during every Shabbat and chag, thanks to *havdala* spices, the Jew is given a last opportunity to savor the sweetness of the day of rest. The traditional answer to "Why is Shabbat food so delicious?" is, "Because of a spice called Shabbat"!

---

191. Psalms 107; *Brachot* 54b.
192. Rashi, Genesis 22:2.
193. Psalms 141:2.

Question 133

Night of the Heads? Sounds like a B-grade movie! What is this?

In Morocco, Seder night is known as *Layl al-rass*, "Night of the Heads," based on the custom to eat heads of sheep, which is symbolic of the paschal offering. One year the Talmud called this "The Passover of the Crushed" (or, "The Crowded Passover") after an elderly Jew was crushed to death by "the enormous crowds in the Temple court."[194]

Question 134

What is the main purpose of Pesach?

Pesach has a magnetic allurement, a fascinating appeal, a powerful attraction. It towers mightily and majestically in the Jewish calendar over all the other festivals. As one of the three festivals devoted entirely to Jewish national liberation (the other two are Chanuka and Purim), Pesach reigns supreme because it is the only one anchored in the Bible itself. As a source of Judaic inspiration, it is thus *fons et orgio* (exquisitely preeminent), a window through which the vastness of Judaism in its entirety can be glimpsed.

Unlike the multiple Shavuot and Succot injunctions of *vesamachta be'chagecha*, "rejoice on your festival," there is no similar dictate for Pesach. Why? Because it is obvious that one should be *sameach* (happy) on a chag that celebrates freedom.

194. *Pesachim* 64b.

The sole purpose of all Pesach symbols and rituals is to prod, probe and provoke Jewish children, on "whom the world exists."[195] Why? Because the Torah seeks active participants, not mute bystanders. And in order to ensure that this Seder barter of ideas be a cathartic experience with, adds the Rambam, "all the eloquence we can muster," our rabbis, knowing that stories are the lifeblood of Judaism, mandated the concept of "up-close and personal," a scripted dramatic arrangement known as the *mitzva of Maggid*, of storytelling. Parents are obliged to engage in *vehigadeta levincha*, a creative dialogue with their children. And more! "When your son asks, what is this?" the reply must be long. Why? Because "the more a person dwells on the Exodus, the more praiseworthy it is!"[196] Even the plagues are stretched to ten so that "you should tell your son and grandson"; if not for this parental obligation, the Heavens would surely have inflicted the tenth plague (*maka*) first – and be done with it.

The Torah itself, which is usually concise and parsimonious in its use of words, mentions "Exodus" thirty times, each time with an inherent passion and excitement. The Seder is thus a giant yet intimate classroom, with the Haggada serving as the subject matter, and the father as the main educator entrusted with the role of engaging his pupils in a discussion based on a question and answer format (*derech she'eila u'teshuva*), in the hope of involving everyone present. Listening is passive and stagnant; far better to inquire, probe, analyze our oldest Jewish festival. Pesach is thus fascinating and timeless, compelling and timely, a tale of some thirty-five centuries ago, 1400 years before the Common Era, when Jews were the first to rise up, in

---

195. *Shabbat* 119b.
196. *Sefer HaMitzvot* Positive Mitzva #157; Exodus 13:8.

a massive show of justice, against oppressive tyranny, slavery and discrimination, seeking the basic human rights of man, the right for liberty, the equality of the stranger and needy, the hopes and aspirations for liberty and the freedom to practice their religious liberties.

Question 135

Are there times when prayer is the wrong response?

Yes. Imagine this scene: the Jews are trapped in tumultuous terror in a place called Pi-hahirot. Behind them the thundering horse sounds of six hundred well-armed, vengeful Egyptian chariots can be heard; ahead lie the pounding, drowning waves of a Red Sea. What is their immediate reaction? Hysteric desperation! They first "cry out to God [*vayitzaku*]" in "panic and prayer," but then launch into a sarcastic assault against Moses, blaming him for their predicament, accusing their liberator of perfidy in leading them to a certain death at the swords of Egyptian horsemen ("We would rather serve the Egyptians than die in the desert!").

A stunned Moses turns to God and pleads for Divine intervention. God's response is unexpected and uncharacteristic. Stop wasting My time in "lengthy" prayers (*Ma titzak elai?* "Why do you cry out to Me?"). "Go forward," advises God, in the Torah's premiere lesson of survival; take matters into your own hands! Action thus takes precedence over contemplation. You cannot trust in God alone if you lack the courage to trust in yourself.

One Jew, Nachshon ben Aminadav, gets the message: his

spirit suddenly shifts from passive to active as he bravely steps into "the midst of the sea," causing the waters to split into "a fortress wall" (*choma*) of protection. This single act of faith and ennoblement causes an entire nation to march forward through a dry seabed, an act that symbolizes the final and full transition in the people's mindset from slavery to freedom. The moral of this small (physical) step, yet giant (spiritual) leap, is not lost on the Rambam who, in a famous halachic codification, marries the themes of prayer and action into a "positive commandment."

Question 136

What exactly was manna? Bread or cake? Did it require a blessing?

"What is it?!" cried the baffled Jews of the desert.[197] We know what manna tasted like ("dough kneaded with oil"), but have no clue as to the actual nature of this "food from Heaven." Thus no one really knows which blessing, if any, was appropriate (*mezonot? hamotzi lechem min ha'aretz* or *min hashamayim?*).

Additionally, if the manna was a "test" from God (the same word, *anasenu*, described the test of Abraham), we do not know exactly what was being tested.[198] The Midrash translates it not as a "testing," but a "raising" of the spiritual awareness of the folk.[199] Others disagree: Rashi calls it a test of restraint, Ramban as a test of devotion, whilst the Talmud defines *anasenu* in the context of unfamiliarity – i.e., a test of faith with the emergence

---

197. Exodus 11:8, 16:15.
198. *Yechaveh Da'at* 6:12; Genesis 22:1.
199. *Genesis Rabba.*

of unfamiliar food, distributed in an unfamiliar manner, in an unfamiliar place (of "snakes, serpents, scorpions"),[200] with no assurance if the morrow would bring the same!

Question 137

Sure, we were liberated from Egyptian slavery. But what type of freedom was it? The Egyptian Exile was only the first of a three-thousand-year odyssey through generational persecution, pogrom, torture and genocide, a gauntlet of terror from one nation to the next. So why are we still commemorating one particular Exodus?

Yes, the Jewish people have been cast not from exile to freedom but from exile to exile, but this only reinforces the need to keep Pesach in a central slot in our Jewish calendar. For the miracles of the Exodus are the prototype of optimism and hope, the Jews' vision of ultimate Redemption, when God will no longer "hide His face" (*hester panim*) and will permanently protect His chosen children. Remember: the unfortunate Jews of Egypt thought exile was a permanent state of being; there was no historical precedent in the Jewish psyche for redemption.

---

200. Rashi, Genesis 16:4; *Yoma* 76; Deuteronomy 8:15.

Question 138

D'tzach Adash Ve'achav – What does this mean?

The dramatic *mano a mano* Moses-Pharoah confrontation represented an unprecedented revolt for liberty, and was different from every previous insurrection. How so? All earlier rebellions had been selfishly motivated by the ruthless goals of one self-absorbed man, or one country's urge for power, plunder, prestige. It was Pharoah's arrogant outburst ("I know not the Lord!"), however, that stirred God into a series of plagues, designed to inflict all of Egyptian society, targeting water and earth, air and vegetation, animals and humans.[201]

Rashbam points out that the first nine plagues can be divided into three groups, summarized by their mnemonic initials *D'tzach Adash Ve'achav*, and that, in each group, the first two plagues are preceded by a public, then private, warning. Since the warnings had no effect on Pharoah, the third plague in each group comes suddenly and publicly, with no further warning – with the exception of the tenth (and worst) plague, which is announced twice.

Question 139

Who were the *eirev rav*?

The expression is not a complimentary one (its Hebrew root means "to mix" or "mingle"), occurring only *once* in the entire

---

201. Zecharia 9, 12; Exodus 2:15, 5:2.

Torah.[202] It refers to the Jews who did not participate in the freedom of Exodus; incredibly, even the lure of liberty was not enough to move the entire Jewish community out of Egypt. The Torah truthfully admits: only one in five were sufficiently adventurous and imbued with faith to take up the challenge of emancipation, and embark upon the journey from Ramses to Succot. Who were they? No one knows. The Torah refuses to identify them, but such is the beauty and mystery of the *am segula* (chosen folk) that only a handful, a bare minority, an insignificant statistic, dramatically changed the course of Jewish and world history.

Question 140

Does "Exodus" mean "to come" or "to go?"

The dramatic Torah portion that chronicles the departure of the Jews from Egypt is called *Bo*, as in, "Come to Pharaoh, and I will be with you!" a literary hint that the confrontation is about to become up-close and intensely personal. Joseph ben-Isaac (Bekhor Shor), twelfth-century French scholar, reads the "I" as a royal "We," signifying God's effort to lift Moses' spirits after the failure of several plagues, encouraging him to carry on ("*Come*, let's join forces and *go together!*"). What's the term for "go"? This was already established by God's *lech* ("go") directive to Abraham; thus, "Exodus" is an expression of a continuing process, one of coming *and* going.

---

202. Exodus 12:38.

Question 141

Why did Jews go back to Egypt when the Torah prohibited this?

The Jews were told not once, but *thrice*, not to go back to Egypt, land of heretical beliefs, causing the Rambam to make a startling codification: "A Jew may settle anywhere except in Egypt!"[203] The implication of returning to the "crime scene" of bondage motivated our rabbis to link Israel's survival to its avoidance of Egypt. They even blame the disappearance of the large, faithful Jewish community of Alexandria to its continued stay in this "evil and sinful" place.[204] But wait! Didn't the Rambam *himself* live in forbidden Egypt? Yes. This "history" led the sixteenth-century Radbaz to conclude that the ban only applied to "permanent" residency (the Rambam stayed there only to earn a living as a doctor), and the seventeenth-century Maharshal to argue that the ban was only operative when Jews lived in their own land as a free folk, a physicality of holiness intended to make the Diaspora less inviting.

Question 142

Who is Nachshon of Aminadav?

Nachshon son of Aminadav, chief of the tribe of Judah, embodies Pesach's most important lesson: "God will help; meantime help me, O God, until God helps!" In other words, God helps

---

203. Deuteronomy 17:16; *Hilchot Melachim* 1:1, 5:7.
204. *Succa* 51b; *Sefer Hachinuch*, Mitzva #500.

those who help themselves, confirmed by the Haggada's account of frightened Jews wedged between a raging sea and 600 Egyptian chariot troops. Naturally, they turn to Moses. Who else? But their leader stands disabled, frozen, immobile; paralyzed in prayer. God responds, but not in the way Moses expects. The Heavens admonish him for wasting precious time by praying. Miracles are suddenly withheld, but only temporarily. It takes the courage of a single daring Jew (Nachshon, who is rewarded with the Messianic Davidic dynasty) to affirm that "there is nothing greater than faith," as he steps out into the waters, thus forcing God's "great hand and outstretched arm" to make a "wall" (*choma*) and part the waters.[205] Nachshon, fifth-generation descendant of Judah, thus teaches us that individual courage results in communal Jewish liberation.[206]

Question 143

Are there any instances of biological battles in the Torah?

The fifth and sixth plagues that God hurls against Pharaoh involved a fatal attack on the skin and lungs; the former's deadly disease affecting "horses, asses, camels, oxen and sheep," killing "all the cattle of Egypt." The plague *dever* is translated as "a very grievous murrain" (the only place in the Torah where this disease occurs), *murrain* being the merger of two Latin words, *mor*(ir) plus *ine*, "a death plague" (or pestilence), which could be foot-and-mouth disease, or even anthrax, a deadly bacillus

---

205. *Exodus* 14:15; *Mivchar Hapninim*; *Sota* 37a.
206. *Pesachim*; *Psalms* 118:5.

which affects the animals' lungs and is found mainly in cattle in the ancient Mediterranean terrain. In Modern Hebrew, afflictions are named in the following way: rabies is *kalevet* from the Hebrew word *kelev* (dog); whooping cough is *sha'elet* from *she'ul* (cough); jaundice is *tsahevet* from *tsahov* (yellow), etc.

Following this principle, Philologos, the formidable lexicon giant of the *Forward*, extends this method to *gahelet*, which in Modern Hebrew means anthrax, and links it to the Greek *anthrax*, "coal" (from the Latin *carbunculus*, a "small glowing ember" whose *carbo* means "coal," but refers to an inflamed boil on the skin). So what is the connection between coal and anthrax? In the sixth plague, God orders Moses to take "handfuls of furnace ashes" (disintegrated coal) which, when released in the air, turned into a lethal skin disease, a "boil breaking forth with blains (*shechin avabu'ot*) upon man and upon beast." Ash in the Torah is *pi'ah*; coal is *peham*; and voila – we get *pahemet*, another modern Hebrew word for anthrax!

Question 144

Were there exactly ten plagues?

That depends on who's counting and who's interpreting. As J.M. Keynes put it so well, "I'd rather be vaguely right than precisely wrong!" The Hebrew word for plague (*maka*) doesn't even appear during the ten plagues; it shows up, only *once*, in the Book of Samuels, and is spoken not by a Jew but by a gentile Philistine: "He is the same God who struck the Egyptians with every kind of plague [*maka*]."

But which *maka* is he referring to? Rashi limits the word

to God's blow against the Egyptian army at the Red Sea. Why? Because the Torah does the same, using the word only in this context, identifying the splitting of the sea as the greatest of all the Exodus miracles. Since *maka* was a *goyish* word, our early rabbinic tradition used the expression *otot moftim* ("signs and marvels") for the first nine plagues, and characterized only the last one (firstborn slayings) as "a true plague (*nega*)." Wait! It gets even more confusing. Several scholars insist on including Moses' rod-into-a-serpent (*tanin*) act, ordered by God, into the category of plagues, leaving us with a total of eleven, not ten, plagues! And then, if you add "the greatest of them all (Red Sea)," you get twelve.

So how does Rabbi Judah fit "ten" plagues into his mnemonic *D'tzach-Adash-Ve'achav* device? By combining "boils" and "pestilence" into one plague.

Question 145

Which plague turned the corner with Pharoah?

At the start of the ninth plague, Pharaoh's stubborn streak shows cracks of further weakening. In fact, it is the earlier assault of hailstones (*barad*) that causes Pharaoh to blink first, blurting out an admission ("God is righteous") and a confession ("I and my nation are sinners"). The sight of the next, eighth plague (*arbeh*) was also surely horrifying: a disintegration of the country as Egypt's greenery is devoured by locusts that descend in such great numbers that "they cover the surface of the land." Don

Isaac Abravanel classifies these last three plagues to be a group with special significance: each shares the element of darkness.

Question 146

What is the Pharaoh Syndrome?

To understand the "Pharaoh mentality" you rearrange the Hebrew letters of "Pharaoh" to arrive at *arufa*, which refers to the back of the neck, the Biblical symbol of stubbornness; hence the expression *kasheh oref*, "stiff-necked," a physical description which denotes obstinacy. It is the "hardening" of his *heart*, not his hands nor brain, that hints at his evil. And so, appropriately, Jews pray to God not with all their might and body, but with all their "heart and soul." The Torah term for heart (*lev*) appears no less than eight hundred fifty times in the Torah, in recognition that the heart is *the* central discerning organ (*lev shamaya*) of emotion, intellect, character, morality. Thus, when God judges an individual, He "probes the heart"; and when He wishes to reform, He promises to "replace the heart of stone with a heart of flesh." Pharaoh's "hardened heart" Syndrome is synonymous with a predisposition to cruelty, a cognitive dissonance of those who are so cold and callous ("a heart of stone") as to be immune from feeling the pain of others. This is not just a Jewish insight. Egyptian tomb paintings show the weighing of dead hearts against feathers, the supposed hieroglyph for truth, to ensure they are empty of evil before rewarding the dead with eternal life.

Question 147

Is Pharaoh a title or a person?

A title. The term "Pharaoh" literally means "great house," and refers to the king of Egypt. In fact, two chapters in the Torah mention three Pharaohs![207] Who's on first? The Pharaoh who is around when Abraham and Sarah pass through Canaan; next comes the Pharaoh who features in the Joseph episode, and finally we have the third Pharaoh (who "did not know Joseph"), the villain of the Exodus saga.

The peak of Egyptian oppression occurred under the sixty-seven year reign of Ramses II. The Jews rejoiced at his death (prematurely it seems, for it was under the tyranny of his successor, Mernephtah, that "they cried to God,"[208] in an agonizing period of serfdom). The Pharaoh of the Exodus story was a phony Pharaoh: according to the Midrash he would study the times of the tides of the Nile, and enter the water precisely the moment that the water began to rise, so that it should appear to be rising to honor him.

Question 148

Is ignorance bliss?

This idea is alien in a religion that believes that every "why" invites a "because." Centuries of religious literature reveal an overwhelming catalogue of challenging questions and humble

---

207. Genesis 12:14–20, 13:18, 41:40, 41:45; Exodus 1:8, 1:16.
208. Exodus 2:23.

answers ("Let My people know!"). To help prepare for the festival, we are even encouraged to begin asking questions about the laws of Pesach thirty days before the festival begins. "If the other does not know how to ask," teases the Haggada, "ask for him!" Why? "Because the finest quality of Man is asking questions, since his wit is judged better by his questions than by his answers."[209] That is why the Pesach Seder immediately opens with the first of four *ma nishtana halayla hazeh mikol halelot*, "Why is this night different from all other nights?" sung in the same melody that students use when studying the Mishna, in order to kick-start the inquisitive element of childish curiosity.

Furthermore, knowledge and expertise in Torah confers on no one Jew the right to determine the meaning of Pesach; in this regard, all Jews, the wise and simple and ignorant and lost, are all equal in their quest to discover the meaning of the Exodus. "The true duty of a Jew," writes the brilliant Rav Abraham Isaac Kook, "is to expand and deepen [the tale], therefore none is such a sage that he may say I have filled my plate, that I know the essence of all the secrets of the Exodus." In fact, when Abaye saw a Pesach tray being removed, he cried out, "Wait, we haven't even eaten, why are they taking the tray from before us!" His colleague (Rabba) got angry at him ("You have exempted us from [the requirement of] reciting 'Ma Nishtana!'") for depriving the children of asking the question first ("Why do we remove [what is on] the table? So that the children will notice and ask!").[210]

---

209. Alcalay; *Pesachim* 6a; *Megilla* 29b; *Sanhedrin* 12b; *Avoda Zara* 5b; *Mivchar Hapninim*; *Mishlei Yehoshua*.
210. *Pesachim* 115b.

Question 149

What is the *cheit ha'eigel?*

When asked what was the difference between the generation that left Egypt and his generation, Rabbi Eizel Harif replied, "The wilderness generation disposed of its gold and silver to make for itself a god, while in our wilderness generation, people dispose of God in order to make gold and silver!" The Torah's most infamous incident of idolatry, the original sin of the stiff-necked Jewish people, is known as the *cheit ha'eigel* (sin of the golden calf), signifying a moment when "the Jews exchanged their glory for the image of a bull that feeds on grass!"[211]

As a catastrophic watershed in Jewish history, the sin of the golden calf and the later spy debacle were both considered the two most disastrous events that took place during the Jews' forty-year sojourn in the wilderness. Welcome to the first national tragedy of the impatient Jewish people, one that proves that not all that is gold glitters. Under the watchful eyes of Aaron and Hur, son of Miriam (who vanishes immediately after this incident), the folk dance and sing around a calf of gold, a god they could "see," having made him out of their own silver jewelry and gold ornaments.

---

211.   *Sifrei* 1; Exodus 32; Psalms 106:20.

Question 150

Do the Elders of Israel accompany Moses and Aaron on their quest to confront Pharaoh?

They try to, but after decades of subservice are unable to sustain their courage and faith. At first, they accompany Moses and Aaron to their first encounter with Pharaoh, but begin to slip away, one by one, as they approach the palace. When Moses and Aaron arrive at the gates, guarded by some 60,000 enemy guards, the two elderly Jews are totally alone, the Elders having given up and returned to their slave quarters.

Question 151

How do Moses and Aaron get past the guards?

An angel (Gabriel) magically transfers them to Pharaoh's throne room. The timing is inaudacious yet perfect: for it is the tyrant's birthday, the *only* birthday mentioned in the entire Torah. Kings from all over the Oriental world are there with presents (golden crowns) for Pharaoh's pompous birthday party, but when the two Jews walk in, they tremble in awe and fall to their knees ("Moses and Aaron resembled the ministering angels, their stature was like that of the cedars of Lebanon, the pupils of their eyes were like the spheres of the morning star, their beards were like palm branches, and the radiance of their countenances was like the splendor of the sun").[212] After the first disastrous meeting with Pharaoh, which resulted in a doubling of the slave labor ("no more straw shall be given to you, and yet you shall continue to deliver the same quota of bricks!"),[213] the Elders decide to bypass Moses and take their complaints straight to Pharaoh, unsuccessfully of course. And yet they still take out their frustration and anger not on the throne but on the sudden would-be liberator, Moses ("You have put a sword in Pharaoh's hands to slay us!").[214] The Midrash identifies two of the accusers: Dathan and Abiram, two Jews who had betrayed him years earlier to Pharaoh when he slayed the taskmaster.

Question 152

Christians claim the Last Supper was the Pesach Seder meal. Are they right?

No. The Church takes it for granted that Jesus' Last Supper was a traditional Pesach Seder, but it was not. How do we know? Because all three of the synoptic gospels (Matthew, Mark, Luke)[215] who describe the connection totally ignore Judaism's plethora of compulsory Seder elements (e.g., there is not a single reference to paschal lambs, matza, maror, *charoset, Ma Nishtana*, narration of the Exodus story, etc.). And more! The fourth gospel (John)

---

212. *Exodus Rabba.*
213. Exodus 5:11, 12–14, 17–18.
214. Ibid., 5:21.
215. *Matthew* 26:17–30; *Mark* 14:12–31; *Luke* 22:1–10.

doesn't even get the date right, placing the final supper one day *before* Pesach![216]

In any event, even if Jesus & Co. *thought* they were participating in a Seder *tisch*, the whole meal was totally invalidated by Jewish law. Why? By substituting the paschal lamb symbol with Jesus (the "lamb of God"), they made a heretical mockery of the entire custom (the first Catholic Council of Nicaea in 325 ordered their calendar be adjusted to ensure that Easter falls in spring, on the first Sunday after the first full moon following the vernal equinox. Today the Church's new catechism is to call Easter "the Christian Passover").

Question 153

Why so much emphasis on kids?

"Who exactly is going?" Pharaoh asks Moses, in response to the request to let the Jews take a three-day leave of their serfdom to pray to God. "*Our young* and our old," replies Moses, providing the inspiration for the daily Psalmist's "Lads and maidens, old men *and youths*." Moses mentions Jewish children first, demonstrating that in contrast to pagan Egyptian religions – wherein the young are of no significance – Jews place their children on a spiritual pedestal, and therefore would not contemplate not having the young (who symbolize the future) stand side by side with the old (a holy link with the past). Even Pharaoh knew this! Pharaoh allowed only the "adult men" to leave, with the intention of holding back the youth; in this way he hoped to slash

---

216. *John* 13:1–30.

the chain of tradition in which fathers teach sons ("Remember the days of old, ask your father and he will tell you").

The offer is subsequently rejected by Moses, and the ninth plague, a palpable, three-day deathlike eclipse of "total darkness" (*choshech*), is on its way. The pre-birth of Judaism thus revolves around children, a heritage, sang King David, "of God's," and how "happy is the man who has his quiver full of them." To Yitzchak Leibush Peretz, nineteenth-century Yiddish poet-novelist, children were "man's eternity"; to the Midrash's Rabbi Meir they were "the best surety, better than patriarchs and prophets!" To the yiddishists, insanity was hereditary, inherited from one's kids!

Question 154

Who was Eliyahu Hanavi?

Eliyahu ("my God is God") *HaNavi* was the invisible Prophet Elijah, a man of great mystery, a phenomenon *sui generis*, defender of God and champion of monotheism, who lived during the seventh century BCE in the northern kingdom of Israel. The multidimensional Elijah appears in the Bible out of nowhere (in various cameo roles; a quiet visitor, guardian of orphans, beggar at the door, mystery guest, miracle worker), and, after years of revolutionary leadership persistently battling religious leaders and such monarchs as King Ahab and his foreign wife, Jezebel, for their worship of pagan gods, he is miraculously "taken" to Heaven "in a whirlwind," thus ending his incognito good deeds on earth as a nomadic protector of the underprivileged and oppressed. We never hear from him again until the very last words of Micah, the very last prophet, who promises Jewish history that Elijah will return as the unifier of generations, the reconciler of parents and children, a unity of families, based on the verse "He will return the heart of parents to children, and the heart of children to their parents."[217]

This is why, since he is regarded as the protector of young children, a special chair (called *kisei shel Eliyahu*) is brought in at every circumcision for Elijah. Elijah is not mentioned once in the Torah nor in the Book of Prophets, and only appears in the Grace after Meals;[218] and yet, Jewish tradition has assigned to Elijah a larger-than-life presence, a wise Jew and dispenser of special insights whose sheer presence was the ultimate invitation to redemption and reconciliation; the Messiah's forerunner with a message that better days were a'coming for us, the unseen prophet-guardian of the people of Israel whose miraculous presence attests to the Pesach *seder tisch* as being *Leil Shimurim*, the "night of Divine watchfulness."

Question 155

I just heard the expression "Rambam Leviim." What does it mean?

This expressive phrase reflects the idealism of the Rambam, who encouraged all Jews with the spiritual battlecry, "Everyone can be a Levi!"[219] This affirmation has a Pesach basis: all Jews should

217. *Malachi* 3:24.
218. Yehuda Abida, *Koso shel Eliyahu HaNavi*, Jewish Agency, Jerusalem, 5718.
219. *Mishneh Torah, Hilchot Shmita V'Yovel.*

"separate" themselves, and escape from, the physical limitations that engulf them, just like the "tribe of Levi [God's Army] were designated and separated from the others in order to devote themselves to the service of God."

Question 156

Should I take the phrase "strong hand and outstretched arm" literally?

No; God has no corporeal form, thus the expression (b'*yad chazaka u'vizeroa netuya*) is purely anthropomorphic; however lessons can be learnt from the imagery of God rescuing His folk in this way. The first half of the expression refers to God's mercy within His power and might (the killing of the firstborn), whereas the second part (*u'vizeroa netuya*) is something that Jews try to emulate by donning *tefillin* on the "upper [outstretched] arm," on the left, closest to the heart. By donning *tefillin* in this way, we are praying that the mercy shown in the previous sentence (*yad chazaka*) continues, through and past the Red Sea miracle, to guard and guide the Jewish people.

Question 157

What does *shtei bechinot* mean?

God surfaces not once but twice at Sinai, sending Jewish mystics into a search for the episode's hidden *shtei bechinot*, "two aspects."[220] When the Divine Presence (*Shechina*) first descends

---

220. Exodus 10–19, 20–25.

on "the whole mountain in the sight of all the people," the Torah text bursts with descriptive adjectives: "trembling, fear, thunder, lightning, dense clouds, loud blasts of a horn," as well as a vivid use of words ("stoned, smitten") within emphatic expressions of awe, fear, death.

The second appearance, at the "top of the mountain," is more subdued; the fire 'n brimstone rhetoric is conspicuous only by its absence. The first dramatic emergence was staged for the entire nation of Israel, united as a people of prophets; the next, however, was reserved for the nation's elite. Individual Jews, such as Moses and Aaron, were not in need of such fiery rhetoric. They were already inspired to climb the spiritual peaks of Judaism, without any encouragement.

Question 158

Why do we respond differently to the miracles of Pesach than those of Chanuka?

Our rabbis instituted two forms of reaction to a miracle: one is *Hallel*, said when the *kehilla* of Israel is saved from an enemy; the other, the *bracha* of *She'asa Nissim*, "Blessed is God that He performed miracles for our fathers in this place," is recited when a Jew comes upon a site where such a miracle happened. What's the source for this Halacha? It comes to us courtesy of a non-Jew (Moses' Midianite-priest father-in-law, Jethro) who was so impressed at God's actions that he becomes the first person to say *Baruch Hashem*, "blessed is He," for saving the Jews from Egypt.[221]

This form of miracle-praise, *She'asah Nissim*, is said on Purim (just before reading the Megilla) and on Chanuka (just before lighting candles) – but it is *not* said on Pesach, despite the fact that it was the Exodus itself that acted as the catalyst for Jethro's admiration. Why is Pesach different? Some claim it's not: the *Sefer Haminhagim* considers *She'asa Nissim* superfluous in that it's already "covered" by the concluding *bracha* of *Maggid* (*Asher Ga'alnu*).[222] The *Kol Bo* agrees, and even claims that the *Asher ga'alnu* is a far more appropriate Pesach blessing because it is specific in its miracles (unlike the more general connotation of *She'asa Nissim*). This argument also has halachic validity, for if there is a choice of blessings, Jewish law requires us to recite the one that is the most specific and encompassing). Rav Yitzchak Mirsky notes that the *She'asa Nissim* only relates to miracles done to our fathers (*beyamim haheim bazman hazeh*), in contrast to the miracles of Pesach that are relevant throughout Jewish history to "each Jew in every generation, as though he himself had been in Egypt"[223] – which is why *Asher Ga'alnu* is apropos for Pesach because it refers to the miracles of "our fathers *and* us"![224]

---

221. *Brachot* 54a.
222. *Sefer Haminhagim* 58.
223. *Pesachim* 116b.
224. Y. Mirsky, *Haggadah Hegyonai Haggada*.

Question 159

What is the connection between Pesach and the *mezuza*?

Two Torah verses that are directly connected to the Exodus story touch upon the mitzva of *mezuza*: "And they shall take of the blood and shall place it on the two doorposts (*mezuzot*) and on the lintel," and, "the blood shall be for you for a sign on the houses where you are, and I shall see the blood and I shall pass over you, and there shall not be among you a plague to destroy."[225] The Name of God that appears on the outside of the *mezuza* (*Shaddai*) is an abbreviation for *Shomer delatot Yisrael*, "Guardian of the doors of Israel."[226]

Question 160

Why do we only extend the invitation, "all who are hungry come and eat" on Pesach, and not on other festivals, when there is surely the same obligation of hospitality?

Jews are ordered to eat matza for "seven days," and one cannot eat without money; however on Succot the Jew is only commanded to "sit in a succa" – and it costs nothing to sit![227] Once, during Rabbi Akiva Eiger's Seder, a guest accidentally spilt his

---

225. Exodus 12:7, 13.
226. Rashi, *Pesachim* 4.
227. Exodus 12:15; Leviticus 23:42.

wine and stained the new sparkling white tablecloth. Rabbi Eiger immediately spilt his own cup of wine, and then complained how the table wasn't standing straight.

Question 161

Considering the enormity of the sufferings we Jews experienced at the hands of Pharaoh, why is there no order to destroy the Egyptians, as there is to destroy the Amalekites?

One of the most beautiful aspects about Yiddishkeit is our compassion; not to carry eternal grudges; and, in fact, if an Egyptian gentile lived in the holy land for two generations he was eligible to join the Jews as a full-fledged Israelite. This remarkable empathy for a hater-of-Jews is derived from a Torah verse, "You shall not abhor an Egyptian, for you were a stranger in his land. Children born to them may be admitted into the congregation of the Lord in the third generation."[228] And so the Proverbs warn...

> If your enemy falls, do not exult;
> If he trips, let your heart not rejoice,
> Lest the Lord see it and be displeased,
> And avert His wrath from him.[229]

---

228. Deuteronomy 23:8–9.
229. Proverbs 24:17–18.

Question 162

Is it wrong for Jews to hate?

No, it is not, but gratitude is also a central component of Jewish history. As the rabbinic proverb goes ("Don't throw a stone into a well from which you once drank"),[230] we recall that it was the hospitable country of Egypt that first provided refuge (and, initially, great freedoms) to Jacob & Family who were fleeing the famine back home. The fact that Egyptian generosity degenerated into Egyptian tyranny doesn't negate the initial kindness. And more! The Torah, in an attempt to preserve Judaic humanity, discourages hatred and hostility even when justice is being carried out; which is why the Haggada urges us[231] not to gloat at the sight of Egyptian soldiers and children who had to be destroyed in order for the Exodus to go ahead. This sentiment ("God takes no delight in the downfall of the wicked") is why Jews only say a partial *Hallel* (thanksgiving) on Pesach. We skip the first half of Psalms 115–116 during the last six days of Pesach.[232]

Question 163

What does *tefillin* have to do with Pesach?

The straps on the hand, a visible sign that power does not stem from might alone (which is why it goes on the left arm, the

---

230. *Baba Kama* 92b.
231. Leviticus 23:40; Deuteronomy 16:14, 15.
232. *Tur, Orach Chayim* 490, *Beit Yosef; Megilla* 10b; *Arachin* 10a.

"weaker" side), were metaphysically linked to the straps on the head, a permanent mark that signifies that Jewish redemption came from the power of the mind and spirit.[233] The *tefillin* (similar sounding to *totafos*, the Egyptian word for Pharaoh's headdress, which was also square) was an everlasting, daily reminder that the Judaic message to mankind was embodied in it (the *Shema*).[234] The Zohar designates the hand *tefillin* as a symbol "to guard," followed by the head "to remind"[235]; this idea is derived from the order of Moses' words: first the Jews must be on guard against the fallacious argument ("My strength and the power of my hand"), which he follows with a reminder to remember that it was God, the giver of strength, who took them out of Egypt.[236] (When they fought the Midianites, the Jews were praised for not reversing the order of the *tefillin*, and for acknowledging their own limitations.)[237]

A Talmudic Midrash examines the dialogue between God and Moses, which is part of the Torah reading for *Shabbat chol hamoed Pesach*, and concludes that, "God revealed the knot of His *tefillin*."[238] Moses makes a direct yet poignant request ("Let me behold Your Presence!"),[239] to which he receives a puzzling reply. God tells him to hide in the cleft of a rock as God's Presence passes by ("Then I will take My hand away and you will see My back; but My face must not be seen.")[240] When Moses

---

233. Exodus 13:9.
234. Deuteronomy 28:10; *Menachot* 35b; Isaiah 42:6,7.
235. *Beit Yosef, Orach Chayim* 25.
236. Deuteronomy 8:11–17.
237. *Midrash Rabba, Shir Hashirim* 6:12; Psalms 20:8–10.
238. *Brachot* 7a.
239. Exodus 33:18.
240. Ibid., 33:23.

takes a sneak peek at "God's back," he sees the *tefillin* knot. The link between the two (*tefillin* and Pesach) is then strengthened by an explicit Torah verse: "And it shall be a sign upon your hand, and a symbol on your forehead that with a mighty hand the Lord freed us from Egypt."[241]

Question 164

Why was *tefillin* chosen as a symbol of freedom?

It's a paradox: tying oneself in black leather straps is also an act of servitude, but this time the spiritual bondage is to God, a nod that the Jew voluntarily accepts upon himself the "yoke of the Kingship of Heaven."[242] And so our Torah linguists note the similarity between the Hebrew for slavery (*avoda*) and service to God (*avoda*). And more! The fact that God wears *tefillin* is an encouraging sign that He has likewise bonded Himself to us. And so we dismiss the concern that slaves are exempt from saying the *Shema* (since they are serving more than one master),[243] and say the *Shema* willingly as an adjunct to *tefillin*, to proclaim our great freedom.

---

241. Ibid., 13:16.
242. *Brachot* 15a.
243. Ibid., 25a.

Question 165

What is meant by the "49 gates"?

Jewish mystics talk of 49 gates of spiritual corruption. While the Jews were in Egypt, they were at their most spiritually impure, having deteriorated to the worst of those "gates," a spiritual nadir, hovering over history's precipice of spiritual annihilation. In Hebrew, the word for spiritual impurity is *tuma*, which connotes constriction. The opposite is *tahara*, which is derived from the same Hebrew root as "light, shining." Our rabbis embrace the Exodus as both a poetic and literal journey from darkness to light, slavery to freedom, or in the language of the Torah, "And there was evening, and there was morning, one day."

What is the significance of the number 49? It is 7 times 7; the squaring of a number allows it to attain its ultimate relevant expression. Thus, 49 is the furthest reach of "seven-ness," a number of great mystical significance in Creation and Judaism. Thus it is no coincidence that it took 49 (*omer*) days to bridge the gap from the spiritual lows of Egypt (Pesach) to receive the Torah (Shavuot).

Question 166

Why is the Pesach offering grouped together with the matza and maror?

The Pesach offering, according to the Maharal of Prague, is a symbol of oneness (i.e., unity), in that a lamb or sheep is considered a "groupee" animal, always associated with a larger flock.

This concept of unity is why the offering (to the One God) must be eaten as part of a group in a single location; roasted (which shrinks, i.e., "unifies" the meat, as opposed to stewing which breaks it apart); and the bones are to be left intact. By aligning the Pesach offering with the matza and maror, Rabban Gamliel is emphasizing Judaic unity, a prerequisite to a final redemption, which Judaism parallels to the exodus from Egypt.

Question 167

Is the Hebrew word *pasa* connected to the term *pasach*?

Yes, *pasach*, "passed over," is a verb linked to *pasa*, another verb which means "to go" or "to step"; yet there is a difference. The latter emphasizes the physical passage or movement (as in the Talmud's, "There were twelve steps there and Moshe took them in one [*pas'a*] stride," or the Midrashic, "That they not take a large [*pas'a*] stride upon the altar").[244] The expression *pas'a pesi'a gasa* is a physical imagery of one who takes "large strides" (i.e., walks quickly).

On the other hand, *pasach* has a more metaphysical aspect, a reference to the place left behind, the one "passed over" (as in the Torah's "… and when He sees the blood upon the lintel, and on the two sideposts, the Lord will [*pasach al*] pass over the door, and will not suffer the destroyer to come into your houses to smite you").[245] The addition of the preposition *al*, "over" (as in *pasach al*, "passed over") is not associated with *pas'a*. The

---

244. *Sota* 13; *Genesis Rabba* 30.
245. Exodus 12.

noun *pesach*, in the context of salvation and rescue, is derived from *pasach*, as is *poseach*, a verb which describes a man who limps. Since he jumps or skips from time to time, this led to the phrase *pasach al shtei haseifim*, "to halt between two opinions," in describing one who hesitates. (The source is Biblical: after Elijah meets with the priests of Baal, he warns the Jews that the time has come to decide whose side they're on; "How long will you halt between two opinions [*Ad matai atem poschim al shtei seifim?*])[246]

---

246. 1 Kings, 18, 21.

PESACH PREPARATIONS, CUSTOMS AND LAWS

Question 168

I want to make my own matza. Where do I begin? What do I need?

The first thing you need to have is a meticulous personality and to have your wits about you, for if you dilly-dally, delay, stall or procastinate, the matza becomes worthless (chametz). Next, make sure that you have *kashered* your oven and have the "right flour" – i.e., that it has been under constant supervision from the moment of harvest to ensure it is un-moistured.

ok, here goes: Line the oven shelf with tiles, turn the oven up to the maximum temperature, and keep an eye on the clock. You have eighteen minutes to:

· mix (one part) fresh spring water with (three parts) flour

- knead a round one-to-two-inch ball, and roll out the dough as thin as you can
- punch it with a special roller tool to create tiny perforated holes (to prevent air bubbles which causes puffing)
- hang the dough over long, smooth poles, and place it on the hot tiles by turning the pole over with a quick twist of the wrist
- with a long-handled flat-metal paddle (like they use in pizza shops), gently remove the freshly-baked matzot and lay them down to cool on a table precovered with clean paper to cool.

Be careful they don't break because only whole matzot are acceptable. Time's up! Put more clean paper on the work surface, and repeat...

Question 169

What is *bedikat chametz*?

On the day before Pesach, Rabbi Levi Yitzhak of Berdichev went to the local markets, approached a non-Jewish merchant, and whispered, "Psst. Do you have any smuggled goods?"

"Sure, rabbi," the man replied, "anything you want. We got it!"

Reb Levi then went to a Jewish vendor and asked, "Do you have some of that beer you sold me last Purim?"

"Rabbi," the Jew shouted back, shocked, "of course

not! It's forbidden! It's chametz!" Rabbi Levi Yitzhak of Berdichev then looked skywards and said, "God, look down from Your holy dwelling upon Your people, Israel. See how they observe Your commandments. The Czar of Russia is a mighty king. He has countless judges and policemen; he has placed countless soldiers and tax collectors on all his borders to prevent smuggling. And yet, we find smuggled goods for sale in every street and marketplace. Yet you simply warned us, 'You shall have no leavened bread,' and already on the day before Pesach, you won't find a single scrap of chametz in a Jewish home or store!"

If Judaism has a Pesach-mania, leavened bread (chametz) is it; and if matza is flat and, homiletically speaking, a badge of lowliness (*lechem oni* means "bread of humility"), then Rabbi Zusya of Hanipol would consider chametz to be a symbol of arrogance and haughtiness, a "puffed up" bread of "hot air," similar to the bloated ego. And so the order of matza comes smack in the middle of the fifteen steps of the Seder, signifying that the centrality of forging a partnership with God requires humility. Therefore chametz, being a symbol of its absence, is forbidden on Pesach. This requires its total, absolute removal from the home, a meticulous pre-Pesach search-and-destroy procedure (*bedikat chametz*) that can be summarized as CSHAB: clean, sell, hunt, annul, burn!

The Bobover Rebbe, Shlomo Halberstam, compared the sweep of the broom to "sweeping the dust of one's soul so that it can renew itself for Pesach." Chametz is a symbol of the destruction of idolatry, derived from a Torah verse ("You shall not make yourselves molten gods")[1] that is immediately followed by the order, "You shall observe the Feast of Matzot." After King Josiah destroyed all the idols in Israel, the records note with glee, "There had never been such a Passover from the time of the judges!"[2] What is the process? The head of the house, accompanied by children, goes room-by-room seeking ten (a symbolic number that makes it easy to remember how many pieces are put out) pieces of chametz that have already been hidden. He uses a candle (for light), wooden spoon (to gather the chametz), feather (to sweep it into the spoon), and ends the "search party" by saying *bittul chametz*, a legal formula in Aramaic that declares his chametz "ownerless, like dust."

Is the mitzva in the searching or finding? The search. The next morning, no later than five hours after sunrise, the gathered chametz is burnt (*biur chametz*), with the declaration, "May all chametz in my possession, whether I have seen it or not, whether I have removed it or not, be annulled and considered as dust of the earth." This legalistic statement, penned in Aramaic and first found in the twelfth-century work of the famous Rav Isaac ben Jacob of Fez, is intended to absolve the head of the household if he accidentally overlooked some chametz. Why ten "leftovers"? This custom was initiated by the sixteenth-century kabbalistic innovator from Safed, Isaac Luria, ten being a favorite number of Jewish mystics since it symbolized the ten *sefirot*, "Divine emanations." The fact that Haman's decree for Jewry's destruction was issued on the thirteenth of Nissan, the night of searching, and that he had ten sons, all hung, is not seen as a coincidence;

---

1.   Exodus 34.
2.   II Kings 23:22.

Don Isaac Abravanel linked the thirteenth to a bar mitzva boy's obligation to remove himself from all moral weaknesses during his transitional year before turning fourteen.

Question 170

When I'm in Israel for Pesach, I see lettuce hanging out to dry. Why?

If you walk through suburbs like Bnei Brak you'll find, in the midst of the usual cacophony of chag preparations, lettuce leaves dangling delicately from clotheslines held in place with clothespins. Why? It's a *kashrut* issue: the lettuce, the Seder's symbolic bitter herb, is being "dried out" for worms. Some Chassidim are concerned that wet lettuce could cause the tiny grains of flour remaining on the matza that is used during the *korech* stage of the Seder to rise and become "leavened."

How can the incongruous, innocent-looking and-tasting lettuce stand in for maror anyway? Lettuce is the perfect symbol of the times. Its leaves are soft and mild, similar to the manner in which the slavery began. Jews were initially welcomed, and only with the death of Joseph do things deteriorate to the unnecessary pain of *avodat parech*, the backbreaking "useless" work of building the cities (Pithom and Ramses). When you get past the soft lettuce, you suddenly find hard stems with a bitter aftertaste.

Question 171

What do the terms *Afiya Yisroel* and *Bishul Yisrael* mean?

These are food labels that indicate Orthodox Jews were involved in their baking (*afiya*) or cooking (*bishul*).

Question 172

How do I kasher for Pesach?

There are five different methods of *kashering* items for Pesach, and they each depend on several factors (the type of vessel, how it became *chametzdik*, etc.). The methods are:

- *Libun gamur*, which means "full incineration" – baking or broiling utensils are heated until the metal glows
- *Libun kal* is a "lighter" form – utensils are heated until they show signs of burning
- *Hagala*, which means "purging" – immersion of utensils such as pots, forks, spoons, etc. in boiling hot water
- *Erui*, which means "pouring bubbling boiling water" – this *kashers* kitchen surfaces, sinks, metal trays, etc.
- *Milui V'erui*, which means "soaking in cold water" – the soaking of glassware in cold water over three days.

So, am I allowed to *kasher* earthenware utensils for Pesach? The fourth-century scholar Rabbi Ashi would buy new utensils every Pesach, but his colleague Rabina retorted, "You can afford it, but what of those who can't?" Nevertheless, the Torah differentiates between the metal and earthenware utensils (*kelei cheret*) that were used to cook meat from *korbanot chatat* (sin offerings). Metal utensils can be *kashered* via a process of immersion and rinsing in boiling then cold water (called *merika u'shetifa*), but since earthenware utensils are highly absorbant, they retain some of the taste of the cooked food, which borders on chametz – and thus its kashering is prohibited.[3]

Question 173

When is the latest time I can eat chametz?

A certain man left a sack full of chametz with Yohanan Koka'ah, and mice gnawed holes in the sack, so that the chametz trickled out. He came to Rebbi [Judah the Nasi] and asked him what to do, as it was almost Pesach. The first hour [of the day, beginning with sunrise] he told him, "Wait." The second hour he told him, "Wait." The third hour, he told him, "Wait." The fourth hour he told him, "Wait." The fifth hour he told him, "Go and sell it in the market" [in other words, that was the "eleventh hour," after which he would have to destroy it].

---

3.   *Pesachim* 30a; *Hilchot Ma'aseh Hakorbanot* 8:14; Menachem Genack, *Gan Shoshanim* 13.

As usual, Hillel and Shammai respectfully disagreed on the issue of when you should cease to own or eat chametz:[4] the latter said enough time had to be left between the sale and Pesach for the non-Jewish buyer to eat all the chametz. Technically, the "drop-dead" time is midday, erev Pesach. How do we know? "You shall not slaughter [or sprinkle] the blood of My [paschal] sacrifice with chametz," declares the Torah, a reference to the paschal offering that occurred after midday, erev Pesach.[5]

But the rabbis were faced with a problem: when time was calculated by sundials, or simply by looking at the sun in the sky, an overcast cloudy day caused confusion. So our Sages, to be on the safe side of the Torah, started the prohibition earlier in the day; one hour was added to the prohibition of owning, or deriving benefit from, chametz (i.e., the beginning of the sixth hour of the day); and two hours were added (i.e., four hours after sunrise) to the prohibition against eating it. Remember: "Halachic time" is totally independent from the clocks you use: it is based purely on the concept known as *Sha'ot Zemaniyot* ("proportional hours") that depend on the seasons (e.g., a halachic hour is not sixty minutes; it is a division of a day, from sunrise to sunset, into twelve equal parts. Therefore, in summer, an hour can be as long as seventy-five minutes, and as short as forty-five minutes in winter).

---

4.   *Shabbat* 18b.
5.   Exodus 34:25.

Question 174

Why do we see "kosher-for-Pesach" seals on products that don't require such certification?

The answer comes from Rabbi Yehoshua Koifman, the *kashrut* supervisor of the Chatam Sofer school in Israel, who is asked to declare as kosher such bizarre items as brooms. When he asked the manufacturer why, he responded, "because it helps sales." The rabbi's criteria is "whatever goes into the mouth" requires certification, including such non-food items as pacifiers, bottles and toothbrushes.

How can you be sure that a product is Kosher for Passover? It's simple: it must have rabbinic certification. What about fresh fruits and vegetables? No, they do not need special Pesach *kashrut* certification, but the custom in our home is not to serve unpeeled fruits and vegetables on Pesach.

Question 175

Why do we not eat matza on erev Pesach?

One reason is that we are commanded to eat "unleavened bread *in the evening.*"[6] Another reason is more pragmatic: by waiting until the Seder, we have a much greater appetite so we can fully appreciate eating matza.

---

6. Ibid.

Question 176

If I become a tenant on the fourteenth of Nissan, whose responsibility is it to check the apartment for chametz – mine or the owner's?

It depends. When were you given possession? According to Rav Nachman, if you got the keys *before* the fourteenth of Nissan, you're obligated to check the premises for chametz. If, however, on the morning of the fourteenth, the owner still has the keys, then it's his responsibility.

Question 177

I'm going on a pre–Pesach trip. Do I still have to destroy any chametz in the house?

Depends on when you're leaving. According to Rava, if you depart at least thirty days before Pesach (Rabbi Shimon ben Gamliel says two weeks) and have no intention of returning then you don't have to ("One who embarks on a sea voyage or joins a departing caravan more than thirty days before Pesach need not destroy the chametz [in his house]").[7]

Distance is also an extenuating circumstance that absolves you from *bedika* (checking) and from the responsibility for the presence of chametz in your home during Pesach (just re-

---

7.   *Pesachim* 6a, b.

member not to cut your trip short; you can't return until after chag!). Having said that, you are still responsible for searching for, and destroying, chametz, whereever you happen to be on the fourteenth.[8]

Question 178

When did Jews start "selling" chametz?

There is no source in the Talmud for the custom of selling one's chametz. The Mishna only contemplates a direct sale of chametz to a non-Jew.[9] The "sale" appears for the first time in a Tosefta that, according to the Rivta, seems to indicate it's OK but *only* "as a last resort."[10] So, is it permissible to make a sale *conditional* on a buyback basis? The *Tur* and *Shulchan Aruch* allow it.[11] Can I sell the room, or closet, in my house that contains chametz? Yes,[12] as long as "possession" is done correctly, either through a physical *Kinyan Meshicha* or the more incidental "chattel-style" method of *Kinyan Agav*.

---

8.   *Ra'avia, Beit Yosef Orach Chayim.*
9.   *Pesachim* 21a.
10.   *Tosefta, Pesachim* 2:6; *Rivta, Pesachim* 21a.
11.   *Beit Yosef, Shulchan Aruch, Orach Chayim* 448:3.
12.   *Bach, Magen Avraham.*

Question 179

What is *mayim shelanu*?

One year Rabbi Meir Margoliot, author[13] and rabbi of 240 villages in Lvov and Ostraha, was carrying a pitcher on the thirteenth of Nissan to draw *mayim shelanu* (water to be left overnight) when he met Rav Yeibi riding in a carriage, a jug on his seat for drawing water.

"Reb Meir," Rav Yeibi asked, "why are you walking? The roads are muddy!"

Replied Reb Meir, "This great mitzva comes once a year. Should I then give it to the horses?!"

Rav Yeibi then jumped out of his carriage, grabbed his jug, and continued on foot. *Mayim shelanu* is a technical, somewhat enigmatic, halachic term used in the context of baking matza; it literally means "left to rest," and refers to the requirement to use water in the morning that was drawn the previous evening. Why? No reason is given, but one theory, in the spirit of the Torah's command of supervision (*u'shmartem et hamatzot*, to keep "a vigil" over the matzot), is that it allows the water to cool down in order to slow down the leavening of the dough.

Question 180

So, what's the best way to destroy chametz?

It's a dispute. Why? Because those Sages (Rabbis Yehudah and

---

13.   *Me'ir Netivim.*

Akiva) who saw chametz as not just "unwanted" bread, but as an object of great impurity, demanded that it be burnt (in order to "obliterate" not just its form but its very substance). Others (Rabbi Yehuda), while agreeing to the "impure" label of chametz, disagreed with how deep this impurity extended, and allowed chametz to be simply crumbled and thrown to the wind or into the waters, acts that made it no longer edible or usable.

Meanwhile, Rabbi Yose Haglili, alone amongst his peers, accepted the disposition of chametz simply by selling it, even though one derived a benefit from the sale.[14] Is there a blessing on the destruction of chametz the following morning? No: it has already been "nullified" by the search the night before.

Question 181

Can I use a flashlight to search for chametz?

No. The Talmud requires "the light of a candle [and not] the light of the sun, moon or torch."[15] Why light a candle? Rabbi Aaron Berechia of Modena traces this to the verse "Man's soul is the candle of God," whilst the Sfat Emet paired the numerical value (*gematria*) of *ner daluk*, "a burning candle" with *Shechina*, "God's Spirit."[16] Or as *Pirkei Avot* puts it: the greater the effort, the greater the reward![17]

---

14. *Pesachim* 2:1, 5b, 23a; *Likutei Sichot* 16:87.
15. *Pesachim* 7b.
16. Proverbs 20:27; *Shabbat* 30b; *Ma'abar Yabbok*, 15:94b.
17. *Avot* 5:22.

Question 182

What's the point of fasting for the firstborn? I thought miracles were supposed to be joyous occasions?

The erev Pesach fast for the firstborn is a commemoration of the survival of Israel's firstborn in contrast to the death of Egypt's firstborn on the night God "passed over" their houses. To "avoid" the fast, one can attend a *seudat mitzva* (i.e., a *brit*, *pidyon haben*, completion of a *siyum* celebration, etc.). It's a paradox: this is the *only* fast in the Jewish calendar that can be "broken" with a meal!

Question 183

Why can't I "search" for my chametz during the day, when there's more light?

Jewish law requires a candle, which is meaningless and obsolete during the day. From a purely practical perspective, since the *al biur chametz* search is a family affair, it makes sense to search for the *chametz* in the evening when everybody's home.

Question 184

Can I do my laundry on erev Pesach?

No, not after midday (*chatzot*). In fact, you cannot have a haircut, shave, sew new clothing, or cut your nails – but you can iron, polish shoes, sew buttons, do minor mending, etc.[18] How about a shower or bath? Probably, but it's not so clear. Why the strictness? These acts are considered "work" (*melacha*), and during the time of the Temple, erev Pesach was considered a chag, with an obligation to bring sacrifices (*korban Pesach*).[19] Others forbid it for purely pragmatic reasons: why are you having a haircut when you should be preparing for Seder?[20]

Question 185

I'm scared of fire. Can I dispose of my chametz in some other manner?

Yes. The procedure of destroying chametz (*biur chametz*), a mitzva known as *tashbisu*, can technically be fulfilled by simply crumbling it and throwing it to the winds, or into an ocean or river. Can you simply throw it in the garbage? No, since the garbage removal may not take place until after Pesach begins. However it's better if you burn the chametz (especially if it's in the closing hours just before Pesach) for two reasons: If you're

---

18. *Mishna Berura* 8, 468:5,7; Chazon Ish, *Orchot Rabbenu* 2; *Rama Orach Chayim* 468:2.
19. *Pnei Yehoshua, Pesachim* 50a; *Mishna Berura* 468:1.
20. *Biur Halacha* 468:1.

a *mitnaged*, it's the traditional way; if you're Chassidic, burning symbolizes the power of *tuma* and the destruction of the evil inclination (*yetzer hara*).[21]

Can you appoint someone else to do it for you? Probably, but it's not ideal.[22] How and when should it be burnt? By wood (not gas or paper), and on your own property.[23] The proper time is the fifth hour of the day[24] (a halachic hour is one-twelfth of the day). How do you know when it's burnt enough? When even "a dog would not eat it" (i.e., when it has turned into charcoal).[25] By the way, don't use gasoline to expedite the process. Why not? Because then the chametz is not being burnt by fire, but is being destroyed by a different medium, a combustible material.[26] In our house, it's a custom to burn other "mitzva items" together with the chametz, for example, the spoon or feather used to gather the chametz.[27]

Question 186

What does *eruv tavshilin* mean?

This refers to the preparation of a token Shabbat food on erev chag that allows for cooking and baking on chag, or when the

---

21.   *Pesachim* 21a; *Mishna Berura* 445:5, 6, 442:33; *Orach Chayim* 118:3; *Minchat Yitzchak* 4:56; *Sha'ar Hatzion* 17; *Kaf Hachayim* 445:11.
22.   *Kinyan Torah* 5:37; *Mishna Berura* 232:8, 234:15.
23.   *Rashsash, Shabbat* 66a, *Minchat Yitzchak* 2:53.
24.   *Rama* 445:1.
25.   *Orach Chayim* 242:2; *Mishna Berura* 445:1.
26.   *Hagaddah Moadim Uzemanim*; *Siddur Pesach Kehilchato*.
27.   Arizal, *Kaf Hachayim* 432:1, 445:16; *Mishna Berura* 445:7; *Chazon Ish, Orchot Rabbenu.*

second day of chag coincides with Shabbat.[28] Is there a minimum size? Yes. At least a *kezayit* for cooked food, defined as anything you would serve as a main dish (e.g., meat, fish), and a *kebeitza* for baked food, defined as a whole *challa* or matza, to be used for Friday night, and Shabbat day's *lechem mishneh* and *seuda shelishit*.[29]

Is *eruv tavshilin* only applicable to food? No, this is a common misconception. It involves any activity (e.g., grinding, choosing, carrying, washing dishes, lighting candles) needed for Shabbat.

May one cook on chag for chag? Yes. May one cook on chag for Shabbat? Yes – the two are considered as "one day." Even the Torah refers to chag as a Shabbat!

Question 187

How serious should we be when making the bracha during *bedikat chametz* (the search for chametz)?

According to Jewish law, the verbal renunciation of chametz, known as *bittul*, must be serious and sincere. Rav Soloveitchik and Rabbi Akiva Eiger claim that this "search" is affected by one's thought (which is why the "seeker" stays quiet during the process, in order to concentrate his thoughts and deeds on the elimination of chametz). Ambivalence and a halfhearted "*bit-*

---

28. S. Wosner, *Eruv Tavshilin haAruch* 2 16:3.
29. S. Wosner, *Koveitz Mibeit Levi* 1; *Biur Halacha* 527:5; *Eishel Avraham* 527:7; *Mishna Berura* 527:11; 48.

tul" declaration are thus negative impediments to the mitzva of
bedikat chametz.

But wait. Doesn't this contradict the fundamental halachic axiom, *"devarim shebelev einam devarim,"* that what the
Jew thinks in his heart has no legal effect on what he does? A
perfect example: if a groom follows all the legal requirements of
betrothal (e.g., giving a ring that acts as *kiddushin,* saying *"Harei
at…"*), and then says, *"Whoops,* sorry, I didn't mean it," he's still
legally married. Rav Soloveitchik notes the difference: one's
intentions are relevant only when dealing with a legal process
that is directly affected either by speech or acts. Some Torah
scholars (Rashba and Rabbenu Peretz) claim that it's inappropriate to make blessings of joy or praise over a mitzva that
involves destruction. Remember: the search for chametz is not
a stand-alone act, but a halachic beginning to an ultimate aim,
the disposal of chametz (*biur chametz*). Rav Azriel Hildesheimer
elaborates: In general, the elimination of "a negative" (i.e., chametz), in contrast to the effort for something positive or self-
improvement, never warrants a *bracha* nor a *shehechiyanu.*[30] Rav
Ovadia Yosef prefers to hedge his bets: he recommends taking
a new fruit out just before doing *bedika,* saying the *bracha* (*al
biur chametz*), starting the search, and then reciting *shehechiyanu*
over the fruit (with the intent of satisfying the *bedika* simultaneously). This then requires making another (regular) *bracha* over
the fruit and eating it. Remember: the act of *bedikat chametz* is
only symbolic. A Jewish home, one day before Pesach, should
already be chametz- free!

---

30.   A. Hildesheimer, *Teshuvot,* Vol. 1, *Yoreah Deah* 198.

Question 188

Why such scrutiny on how a Jew performs the duty of disposing of chametz?

Rav Yitzchak Sender links the Halacha prohibiting even a minimal amount of chametz on Pesach (*chametz asur bemashehu*) to one's attitude towards observing the commandments. Rav Sender's position stems from a Mishna ("The world is judged four times each year: on Pesach for grain; on Shavuot for fruit of trees; on Rosh Hashana all human beings pass before God as sheep before a shepherd; and on Succot for water [rain]),"[31] in that the Jew is judged on Pesach as to how he relates to "grain." Since Jewish mystics view chametz as a symbol of the *yetzer hara* (the evil inclination), one's approach to chametz is revealing.

Question 189

Can I ask someone else to search my house for chametz?

The basic obligation rests on the owner of the house (including his office and car), but you can appoint an agent to perform the search for you. The punctiliousness of house cleaning is best articulated in a famous legend regarding a famous rebbetzin who had a pet cat. After Purim she covered her cat's paws with booties so that it would not drag chametz into the house. Her learned pious husband, the rabbi, reminded her that even the ultimate code of Jewish law (the *Shulchan Aruch*) didn't require

---

31.   *Rosh Hashana* 17a.

such stringencies, to which she replied, "You and your *Shulchan Aruch*. If I would follow its rules alone this house would long ago have been *treif!*"

Question 190

Do I have to kasher electrical appliances?

Yes. The kashering of oven racks, which have absorbed actual chametz through fire, requires a *libbun chamur* (heating until sparks fly).[32] This is difficult, so some Jews keep separate racks for Pesach.[33] The oven itself is different. Why? Because no cooking is done on the walls of the oven itself. So why *kasher* an oven? Because the steam from chametz reaches its walls and chametz crumbs frequently fall on oven floors during cooking. The ideal method is through *hagala*, boiling water, however since this is virtually impossible, the boiling process is replaced by *libbun kal*, which requires heating the utensil until it is so hot that straw burns on its outside.[34] In summary: first clean the oven, removing every crumb of chametz, leave it unused for 24 hours before kashering, then turn the heat up to its highest setting for an hour or two, and replace the racks with new ones (the other choice is simply not to use the oven at all over Pesach).

---

32. *Shulchan Aruch, Orach Chayim* 451:4.
33. *Mishna Berura* 451:32.
34. *Rama Orach Chayim* 451:4; *Mishna Berura* 451:30.

Question 191

Is Pesach fattening?

Are you kidding! Is the Pope Catholic?! Despite its entree into the Jewish kitchen as a bread of "affliction," matza has replaced flour as an ingredient in creating exquisite, mouthwatering Pesach dishes. Just think of matza pies, matza balls (*kneidlach*), matza *brei* (or *gefrishte* matza), etc.

It's truly astounding. Every year, as we approach Pesach, we encounter even more adventurous recipes, and a greater selection of wine than all the other Jewish festivals combined! With one heavy Seder meal eaten late at night and early into the morning, and many high-fat leftover dishes lining the fridge shelves, pharmacies in Israel report a fifty-percent increase in the sales of digestive stomach medication after Pesach. So how many calories are there in a typical Seder meal? Three thousand! How many in a single matza? One hundred forty, the equivalent of two pieces of bread. And how about wine and grape juice? One standard glass of sweet red wine or grape juice contains 170 calories. The final word on the matter goes to Shalom Aleichem: "A wise word is no substitute for a piece of herring!"

Question 192

Why do I always see salt on a Jew's dining room table?

Not a single sacrifice in the Temple was offered without salt.[35]

---

35. Leviticus 2:13; Numbers 18:19.

Today "pass-the-salt" acts as a reminder of those times when salt was considered a near-holy substance that helped purify offerings to God. "All dishes require salt!" declares the Talmud; the Palestinian sage Johanan was convinced that "the world can get along without pepper, but not without salt!"[36] On the Seder table, *karpas* (parsley or any green vegetable) is dipped in saltwater to represent the tears that the Jews shed.

However, it is not only the Jews who hold salt in such high esteem. Greeks embraced salt as a symbol of justice and kept it on their tables; Arabs, recognizing it as a preservative, still hand salt to strangers as an act of goodwill; the superstitious consider spilling salt a bad omen (countered only by throwing some over the left shoulder); even the word *salary* comes from salt, a remnant from the days when the Roman Empire paid their soldiers' and slaves' salaries in lumps of salt.

Question 193

Something fishy is going on here! Is fish a central part of Jewish culture?

What do the *kvetching* Jews complain about when they leave their enslaved existence in Egypt? The lack of carp, pike and fish mullet (incredibly, exactly the *same* fish – the genus *Mugilidae cephalus* – that we use today for gefilte fish), which they had an abundance of back in Egypt,[37] conveniently forgetting the oppressive desserts (whips, lashes, slavery) that came with it. The Chassidic *tzaddik* Abraham Joshua Heschel of Apta attributed

---

36. *Beitza* 14a; *Horayot* 3:5.
37. Numbers 11:5, 6.

the Jews' hankering for fish to God's manna that had every possible taste – except fish![38] Thus it became a mitzva to transform
their symbol of grievance into a symbol of gratitude by eating
fish every Shabbat and chag.

The Mishna and Talmud provide an extraordinary amount
of information about fish, from its production to its marketing
to its consumption. Was Rabbi Yose ben Halafta just a Torah
Sage? No: he was also a serious fish connoisseur ("The taste of
fish from Acco cannot be compared to fish from neighboring
Sidon or Aspamia!").[39] The rabbis of the Mishna discuss the
marketability of imported "Egyptian fish" during the time of
the Rambam; Jerusalem had a special fish gate (*Shaar hadagim*)
for importers;[40] and Nehemiah would rebuke the Tyrians for
selling fish to the Jews on Shabbat.[41] When asked what makes
Shabbat "a delight" (an *oneg Shabbat*), Rav Yehudah replies in
the name of Rav, "large fish," to which Rav Papa adds, and "a
pie of fish-hash!"[42]

On Friday nights, when the "poorest of the poor" go to the
communal kitchen, the Rambam, echoing the Talmud, demands
that they be served…yep, fish (with vegetables).[43] Rava, the
famous rosh yeshiva of Mehosa, helped his wife prepare for
Shabbat by "salting the turbot (fish)."[44]

What about the kabbalists? They had a field day with fish.
The sixteenth-century kabbalistic innovator Isaac Luria (Ari)

---

38. Apta Rav, *Sefer Torat Emet*, section *Eikev*.
39. Rashi, Genesis 1:10.
40. Nechemia 3:3; II Chronicles 33:14.
41. Nechemia 13:16.
42. *Shabbat* 118b.
43. *Laws of Charity* 7, 8; *Tosefta, Peah*.
44. *Shabbat* 119a.

believed that fish were retransformed human souls from a previous generation, and urged his followers to eat fish (*thrice!*) on Shabbat to create a "proliferation of mystical sparks."[45] Because fish were "the first created living beings," Rabbi Simcha Bunem of Przysucha linked them to the "the root of life," and thus deemed them appropriate for the holy Shabbat.

In reality, the popularity of gefilte fish is simple: being boneless and skinless, it complies with Halacha (i.e., one doesn't have to "separate" the edible from the inedible).[46] In Eastern Europe, the "poor" Jews were identified by which part of the fish they ate (the herring tail), Pesach seder plates were adorned with fishes, symbols of *mazal*, and parents named their children *Fishl* as a shield against the *yetzer hara*.

The last word goes to Moritz Gottlieb Saphir, a Hungarian-born Jew who was later baptized as a Lutheran. Saphir, born to a Yiddish-speaking Orthodox family, and an attendee of several yeshivas in Pressburg and Prague, devotes several pages of his (*goyishe*) biography to...yep, "Jewish fish"!

Question 194

Is matza considered *mazaldik*?

In some Jewish communities, matza was used as a good-luck amulet, e.g., Italian-Jewish women would bite into matza during childbirth, some hung it at home while others carried crumbs in their wallet or purse. Having said that, I wouldn't recommend you try to make matza necklaces!

---

45. *Sefer Hemdat Hayamim*, the "Book of Delight of the Days."
46. *Shemirat Shabbat Kehilkhata*, Jerusalem, Feldheim, 1965.

Question 195

Which meal is the "Meal of the Gra?"

Did you know? Pesach not only begins with a feast, it also *ends* with one, a light merry meal in the afternoon of the last day. Lithuanian Jews (*Litvaks*) call this "the Meal of the Gra," an acronym for the formidable eighteenth-century Gaon Rabbi Eliyahu of Vilna (who considered it a mitzva to honor the "departure" of matza). Chabad Chassidim call this meal a *seudat Mashiach*, the "Messiah's Feast" (to demonstrate faith in his imminent arrival); Yiddishists call it the "final supper" (*begleiten dem yomtov*), which means, "escorting out the festival."

Question 196

I want to experiment with recipes this year. Which Pesach food is conducive to a large variety of recipes?

The *charoset*. Its recipe of fruits (try raisins, pomegranates, apricots, oranges), nuts (try chopped pistachio nuts or walnuts), and spices (try cinnamon), makes it the most varied of all Pesach foods because it is reflective of the customs of different Jewish communities. The best *charoset*? Mix date honey (*haleq*) with figs, apples, nuts, cinnamon – and add wine! Why these fruits in particular? The lyrics of *Song of Songs* compares these five (figs, nuts, dates, pomegranates, apples) to the Jews,[47] and we throw in three more for symbolic reasons: almonds (in Hebrew

---

47.   Song of Songs 2:13, 6:7, 11, 7:9, 8:5.

shaked, "anxious," as in God was anxious to speed up His folk's rescue from bondage), wine (to soften the mixture and add "red," symbolic of the plague that turned the Nile into blood and the blood of Jewish infants killed by Pharaoh), and ginger-cinnamon (when ground together, they resemble the fibrous straw used to make bricks).

If you don't like horseradish and you're looking for a substitute for a sour herb try escarole or endive, which Sephardic Jews use as *chazeret*, a bitter vegetable. Rabbi Chaim of Sanz was very stringent in bitter herbs, and would eat large quantities of sharp horseradish. When he became sick, his doctors ordered him to cut out bitter herbs. The next Seder night, Reb Chaim followed his custom and had a large plate of bitter herbs placed in front of him. He stared at it for a while, then picked up a handful of horseradish, made a blessing ("Blessed are you God, who has sanctified us with His commandments and commanded us: 'You shall *safeguard yourselves*'") – and then placed the herb back on the plate.

Question 197

Am I right in saying that all Jewish festivals revolve around food?

Yep, you're right – although the quintessential Jewish food, bagels and lox, is *not* linked to any festival! All Jewish festivals involve a specific delicacy and a cornucopia of symbolic foods that borders on a halachically mandated Culinary Gastronomic Judaism. (In fact, three out of the first five commandments that Israel receives as a nation relate directly, or indirectly, to eating!)

Food seems to be very prominent in our home. Is this a "Jewish" thing? Yes. Interestingly enough, God's sole positive and negative commands to the First Couple of Eden involved what to eat ("from all the trees"), and what not to eat ("from the Tree of Knowledge").[48] Thus food, discipline and survival are synonymous from the get-go, which is why our rabbis consider the act of eating to be a powerful act of sanctification. By washing hands, making the appropriate blessings, "breaking" *challa* and sprinkling salt, we make each meal a mini-reenactment of the priest's Temple procedures.

Rashi explains God's vocabulary ("Set these laws before them")[49] in terms of digestion, "Like a table set with food ready to eat!" Try to imagine a Rosh Hashana without apples and honey cake; a Purim void of *hamantaschen*; a Shavuot without blintzes and cheesecake; a Succot without stuffed cabbage and *kreplach*; a Chanuka minus doughnuts and potato *latkes* – and what is a Shabbat without *challa*, *gefilte* fish, *cholent* and *kugel*? The Jewish calendar may be a roller coaster of feasting and fasting but, in the end, they balance themselves out.

Consider this: Rosh Hashana (feast), Tzom Gedalia (fast), Yom Kippur (more fasting); Succot (feast); Hoshana Rabba, Simchat Torah and Chanuka (more feasting); tenth of Tevet (fast); Tu b'Shevat (feast); Taanit Esther (fast); Purim, Pesach and Shavuot (feast, and more feasting); seventeenth of Tammuz (fast); Tisha b'Av (very strict fast); month of Elul (end of feast-fast cycle, time to enrol in Center for Eating Disorders before the High Holidays arrive again).

---

48.   Genesis 2:16, 17.
49.   Exodus 21:1.

Question 198

Does *lechem* always mean "bread"?

No. In colloquial Hebrew, *lechem* means bread; but not so in Biblical Hebrew where the word comes from *ki lachmenu hem*, "for they are our *lechem*."[50] Yes, it can mean bread (*lechem panim* and *lechem matzot* mean "showbread" and "unleavened bread"), but it can also refer to *lechem ishi*, particular items of food, or just food generally, *lo al halechem levado* (i.e., "not on food alone").[51] And then we have the "*lechem* [of burning]," which is the lard of a burnt peace offering, and *lechem min hashamayim*, "manna from Heaven."[52] So, like most Hebrew words, it all depends on the context.

Question 199

What is *yoshon*?

During Temple times, Jews resisted eating from their new crops (*chadash*) until a special offering (*omer*) was brought on the second day of Pesach. The grain from the previous year was called *yoshon* ("old"), and Jews who wish to be stringent will refrain from eating any food products on Pesach that might be "new" (i.e., *chadash*). Since there are no more *omer* sacrifices, the status of grain depends on when it is planted. How do you know

---

50.   Numbers 14:19.
51.   Exodus 25:30, 29:2; Leviticus 3:10; Deuteronomy 8:3.
52.   Exodus 16:4.

what's *yoshon* and what's not? Look at the labels (e.g., *kemach yoshon*, "old flour" or "*Made with yoshon flour*," etc.).

Question 200

Is there a difference between the *korban Pesach* and the other sacrifices?

Yes. Unlike the regular sacrifice at the Temple, which was counted as only *one* of the 613 mitzvot, the *korban Pesach* constituted *two* separate mitzvot — the sacrificing of the animal, and the eating, a *ma'aseh achila*, a halachic act in and of itself.[53] There was an order to eat more meat at the *korban Pesach* (at least a *kezayit*),[54] while the order for the standard for the ordinary sacrifice was much less (one *cohen* describes how he got the equivalent of a bean, a *lechem hapanim*).[55] With the ordinary sacrifice, the order is simply that meat be eaten (by *anyone*), whereas every Jew had to personally participate in the *korban Pesach* meal. And while the ordinary sacrificial meal is not restricted to one time zone (day or night), the *korban Pesach* is (it can only be eaten at night).[56]

The consequences of *not* eating the *korban Pesach* highlight the difference between the sacrifices: the punishment cited in the Torah for abstaining from the *korban Pesach* is *karet* (excision).[57]

---

53.   *Rambam, Sefer Hamitzvot*, 55, 56; *Semag* 223, 225; *Chinuch* 5, 6;
       Yere'im 90, 405.
54.   Beit Halevi 1:2.
55.   *Pesachim* 3b.
56.   *Yere'im, Mitzva* 405; Mordechai Breuer, *Pirkei Mo'adot*, vol. 1.
57.   *Rashi, Zevachim* 100b.

Question 201

Are locusts *kosher l'Pesach*?

They used to be nutritious, delicious, pareve – *and* kosher ("Of these you may eat any kind of locust, katydid, cricket or grass-hopper");[58] but not anymore. How is that possible? Because the rabbis doubt that today's locusts are the same as those from ancient times. The Ashkenazim were the first to drop locusts from their diets; Yemen and North African Jewish communities continued to enjoy the locust until seventeenth-century Moroc-can Rabbi Haim Ben Attar decided its kosher status was too suspect and banned the insect.

Question 202

What! I can't eat *kitniyot* on Pesach?

The term literally means "bits," from the Hebrew root for "small," but is often mistranslated as "beans" or "legumes." *Kitniyot* are tiny, fleshless seed-grains that can be ground into flour, or be-come derivatives in other products (e.g., chick peas, corn, dried beans, peas, icing sugar, rice, sesame seeds, soya products, sun-flower seeds; it's even possible to make bread out of the flour of legume). The prohibition began during the Middle Ages when Ashkenaz rabbis, such as the thirteenth-century French Rabbi Moshe of Kouchi (Semak),[59] declared the ban on *kitniyot* a *gezeira*, "a preventative decree," on the basis that *kitniyot* was so

---

58.   Leviticus 11:22.
59.   *Sefer Amudei Golah* 222.

similar in texture to chametz that one could easily be misled into sin – i.e., if one could eat "corn bread" on Pesach, then surely wheat or rye bread was OK as well! Is mere possession (not consumption) of *kitniyot* OK? Yes.

Question 203

What is *Huevos Haminados*?

This is an introductory Sephard dish; Ladino for "brown eggs" (Greek Jews call it *Selanlik yamurta*, "Salonika eggs" or *Yahudi yamurta*, "Jewish eggs"). *Huevos* means "eggs" in Spanish while *haminados* is derived from the Hebrew *hamin* ("oven"), a reference to the low-temperature one-day cooking of eggs. And the *ados* suffix? This is a typical Spanish ending for words. Is this only a Pesach delicacy? No. It is a Sephard custom to serve *Huevos Haminados* at life-cycle Jewish events and even for Shabbat lunch.

Question 204

What's a *beignet*?

It's a Moroccan Jewish custom to eat white truffles, French-style doughnuts (*beignets*) during Pesach. This delicacy is made with matza meal, and is often accompanied with honey, almonds, cinnamon, sponge (*Bisquitte pané d'Espagne*), nut, crescent (*Torta de muez*, *Mustachudos*), or syrup-drenched cakes (*Tishpishti*) – not to be confused with *bimuelos*, a Ladino term for fritters, another favorite Sephardic Pesach food.

Question 205

Why do some Jews avoid squash, eggplant, fish, tomatoes and peppers on Pesach?

Avoiding squash and eggplant is a Chabad custom that has more to do with continuing tradition than *kashrut*. Different Chassidic sects have different customs: for example, Chabad Chassidim eat matza out of cling-wrap in order to avoid any contact with liquid; Vishnitz Chassidim avoid fish on Pesach (despite it being a Chassidic custom to eat fish on Shabbat and chag) because the fish may still have chametz in its belly; in other homes, tomatoes and peppers are avoided because they cannot be peeled free of any leaven as a result of contact during the harvest; some Karliner Chassidim will not use tap water over Pesach because they don't trust the national water carriers to be kosher for Pesach.

Question 206

What does *gebrochts* mean?

The world of Pesach *kashrut* can become very confusing. Some Jews avoid cakes baked with matza, others are careful not to eat *matza brei* (fried matza soaked in milk and eggs), while others yet request "no *gebrochts*" (*gebrochts* is yiddish for "broken"), which refers to cooking or baking with matza, or matza meal mixed with liquid. What's the concern? That matza, although properly baked, may contain unkneaded bits of raw flour that, upon moistening, can become chametz.

Question 207

Do I really have to buy a gift for whoever finds the *afikomen*?

No. There are neither ransom notes nor any halachic repercussions if you don't redeem an *afikomen* with a Lego set; but the family holds you "guilty" for the "crime" of falsely and cruelly raising a child's expectations. Traditionally, the delaying of the *afikomen*, with the incentive of receiving a gift, helps keep children up late at night, and this is a critical component of keeping their attention during the *Maggid*, "telling" of the Pesach saga – and *that* is a mitzva!

Is the *afikomen* the last thing to be consumed at the Seder? Jewish law forbids eating after the *afikomen*, but not light drinking (water, tea); and, don't forget, you still must gulp down the last two cups of wine. Why finish the night with matza? Several scholars consider the *afikomen* as a commemoration of the *korban Pesach* (the mitzva of matza being fulfilled at the start of the Seder), which was only eaten at the end of the meal. However, a lesson can be learnt from eating the *afikomen* at the end: matza as dessert gives us a chance to stop, pause and reflect on the night of probing.

Question 208

Why do some men wear a *kittel* (white garment) at the Seder?

Reasons abound: wearing a *kittel* emphasizes the sanctity of the Seder by recalling the white robes worn by the priests in the Temple. It is a reminder, being a burial shroud, that excessive joy should be avoided during the Seder. As a symbol of purity, the whiteness commemorates the positive transformation of an impure folk who were exposed to the idolatries of Egypt. In the old days, only the ritually pure Jew could lead a Seder and so a Midrash links the word *chur*, "white," to *chorin*, "freedom," and states, "white garments are those which are worn by free men."

Question 209

Are there any differences between a Sephardic and Ashkenazic Pesach?

Yes. The Haggada text itself is basically the same, but in a Sephard Seder, there are a greater variety of songs after the meal. Ashkenaz Jews say a *borei pri hagofen* blessing over each cup, while Sephardim say a *bracha* only over the first (*kiddush*) and third (after *bensching*) cups. The reasoning behind this major discrepancy is that Ashkenazim believe each cup is a separate mitzva, as does Rav Yosef Caro, Sephard compiler of the *Shulchan Aruch* and the monumental *Bes Yosef* (a commentary on the Tur's *Arba'a Turim*), and yet bypasses such previous Sephard-Torah giants as the Rambam, Rif (Isaac Alfasi) and Rosh

(Asher ben Jehiel) and still codifies it on the basis of Rav Asher and Rav Alfas, in that "there's no diversion of attention," since it's permitted to drink between the first and third cups.[60]

The Seder plate is also different in a Sephard Seder: there are six symbolic foods, arranged according to the custom of Rabbi Isaac Ben Solomon Luria (Arizal) plus a symbolic seventh (saltwater, vinegar, lemon juice or lime juice) in a small side cup or bowl; Ashkenazim have five, based on the view of Rabbi Moses Isserlis (Ramah), plus the second maror, *charoset*. Askenazim divide their three matzot into three separate compartments away from the Seder plate, in contrast to the Sephard custom of putting everything together (which is why a Sephard Seder plate is usually larger than an Askhenaz one).

In the Netherlands, Spanish-Portuguese Jews have nine symbolic foods, which are placed in groups of three on three separate Seder plates. Ashkenazim attach no kabbalistic meanings to these food symbols, whereas Sephardim do, carefully placing each symbol, corresponding to one *sefirah* ("holy emanation"), in a pattern designed to resemble the kabbalistic tree of life. In kabbalistic tradition, there are ten *sefirot*, "attributes of God," that sustain the world. These ten are the three matzot, six symbolic foods, and one Seder plate. Ashkenaz Jews break the middle matza in no particular manner while Syrian Jews add a mystical aspect by breaking the matza into the shape of a *daled* (which is the Hebrew numeric value of four) and a *vav* (whose numeric value is six), in order to symbolize the ten *sefirot* of the Kabbalah. Jews from Morocco, Algeria, Tunisia and Libya break the matza to form a *heh*, with a Hebrew numeric value of five.

Sephardic Jews eat rice and *kitniyot* during Pesach but

60.   *Beit Yosef, Orach Chayim* 474.

check them out (thrice) prior to chag just to be certain no kernels of chametz (any one of the five grains of barley, oats, rye, spelt and wheat)[61] found their way into them. To prevent any accidental mixing of the flours (*kitniyot* with *chametz*), strict Sephardi Jews use fresh legumes. The Seder plate in Ashkenaz homes is a stationary object; Moroccan Jews hold it up, pass it over the heads of those participating whilst announcing that they have finally left Egypt and are now free (some touch the head of each person slightly, a reminder of the burdens their ancestors once carried upon their heads as slaves). Ashkenazim refrain from lamb courses since the destruction of the Temple and the discontinuation of the sacrifice of the paschal lamb; some Sephardim allow lamb meat as Pesach's featured dish.

Generally, Ashkenazi Jewish women do not recline; some Sephardic women choose to do so. Usually the youngest child at an Ashkenaz Seder asks the *Ma Nishtana*; all participating at a Sephard Seder say the Four Questions in unison. The order of the questions is also slightly different: Sephardim ask, "Why dip twice? Why eat matza? Why eat maror? Why recline?", while Ashkenazim ask, "Why eat matza? Why eat maror? Why dip twice? Why recline?" Ashkenazi Jews don't do anything physical to reenact the Exodus; Sephardi Jews do. After *Yachatz* (breaking of the middle matza), or *Halachma Anya* ("This is the bread of affliction"), the head of the Seder leaves the room, returns with a walking stick and a wrapped *afikomen* on his shoulder, about which the children ask: "Where are you coming from?" He will then begin the mitzva of *Maggid* and tell the tale of the Exodus. (There are several different versions of this: Turkish or Greek Jews add another question, "Where are you going?"

---

61.   *Pesachim* 35.

to which the head of the Seder replies, "To Jerusalem!"). Most Sephardim (but not Greek-Turkish Jews) do not open the door for Elijah; most Ashkenazim do (just before Hallel). Also, only in Ashkenazi custom is the *afikomen* hidden and searched for at the end of the meal by the children (to keep them awake), who get a present as a "ransom." And, only in Sephard custom do some Jews spread the *charoset* at the end of the meal in five places (symbolizing God's protective *khamsah* Hand of five fingers), such as the front door, near the *mezuza*, etc. Ashkenaz Jews simply sing *Dayenu*; Sephard Jews sing it whilst clutching bunches of celery, chives, leeks or scallions and lightly beating each other on the back to symbolize the stinging whip of Egyptian taskmasters. Persian Jews take it in turns to lightly "beat" each other, playing the role of Egyptian taskmasters, as they wish each other either a *Sentak Khadhra*, or *Sant-il-Khadra*, blessings for a "green, fruitful year" and "a year of good fortune."

Question 210

I love peanuts. Can I eat them on Pesach?

It depends. On what? On your family custom. The concern is whether peanuts are *kitniyot* (Rav Moshe Feinstein says they are not). However, several Jewish communities in pre-war Europe did not eat peanuts over Pesach, so if they're your ancestors, you shouldn't either. What about peanut butter? I don't know. Even if peanuts are OK, you need to know more about the other commercial ingredients (hydrogenated vegetable oil, dextrose, etc.).

Question 211

What is *shibbolet shual*?

It's Hebrew for oats. When asked if perhaps today's "oats" are different that they be prohibited (in the context of *chadash*, "new wheat"), Rav Moshe Feinstein declared that the accepted custom in Israel is unchangeable *even* if a "thousand proofs" were presented against it! Rav Elyashiv agreed that for all intents and halachic purposes, *shibbolet shual* were still oats!

Question 212

What is a *pidyon haben*, and does it have anything to do with Pesach?

It is a symbolic ceremony that takes place on the thirty-first day after a birth (unless that day happens to fall on Shabbat or chag) that "redeems a firstborn son" ("Sanctify to Me every firstborn that initiates the womb among the Israelites")[62] by way of a payment of an overdue debt. What was the debt? God's miraculous redemption of the firstborn of the Jews after killing "every firstborn in Egypt." The *pidyon haben* thus helped preserve the memory of liberation; and more, the firstborn was required to fast every year on erev Pesach (*taanit bechorim*) in commemoration of "his" deliverance from child genocide.

What if it's the mother's first child in a second marriage? If she has a "firstborn" from a previous marriage, no further redemption is necessary (even if this is the father's first child).

---

62. Exodus 13:2.

Why doesn't the father's firstborn count? Because it's impossible to determine his firstborn. Does a caesarian-born child get redeemed? No. It must be the child that "opens the mother's womb." What if there are twins – is there a double redemption? No. The first is the firstborn, the second is not. Do you say a *shehechiyanu* on a *pidyon haben*? Yes (instead of at the *brit* when it's inappropriate to say it while the baby's in pain).

What does a *pidyon haben* involve? The father gives a *cohen*-priest (of his choosing) a "fee" to redeem the boy (i.e., buy him back!). How much? No less than five *sela'im*, which is about a hundred grams of silver, or assets worth that much (the silver *sela* was common, worth about half of the *shekel ha-kodesh*, "sacred shekel").[63] Why five? Rashi traces the amount to the twenty pieces of silver that were equivalent to the five silver *shekalim* that were paid to acquire Rachel's firstborn son (Joseph). According to Reb Yitzchak Bunim, this set the minimum cash criteria for the value of a servant of God. What is the *cohen* to do with the cash? In the olden days, he donated it to charity (I don't know what he does today!). Why a *cohen*? Because *cohanim* are the descendents of the tribe of Levi, the priestly class who were legally entitled to keep the firstborn for service to God (in stark contrast to the then practice of heathens, who sacrificed their firstborn to the gods).

What if the father's a *cohen* or Levite, or the mother's a daughter of a *cohen* (*bat cohen*)? Then no ceremony is required. The question is obvious: why does *pidyon haben* only apply to a firstborn boy, and not a firstborn girl? Because only the male

---

63. Numbers 18:16.

firstborns were threatened by Pharaoh's decree of child genocide, and so only they were "redeemed" (saved) from danger.[64]

Question 213

Is *kreplach* associated with Pesach?

If I had my way, it would be compulsory eating for all the *chagim*! However, *kreplach* is associated not with Pesach but Shavuot, in addition to the custom of eating dairy (*milchig*) foods, (cheesecake, blintzes, etc.). Jewish mystics associate the custom of eating the three-cornered *kreplach* with the number "three" ("And kreplach makes a threesome...") in that a nation of three (Cohanim, Levites, Israelites) were the descendants of three ancestors; and at Sinai they prepared for three days before receiving a Torah which consists of three parts (Tanach: Pentateuch, Prophets, Holy Writings). And who gave them the Torah? Moses, a *third*-born child (after Aaron and Miriam), in the month of Sivan...yep, the *third* month of the year!

Question 214

Is it true? The Jews invented not just the sandwich but also pizza?

By placing the paschal lamb and bitter herb onto matza (*korech*), Hillel invented open sandwiches; later, Roman Jews created the world's first (cold) pizza when they put cheese and olive oil on matza.

---

64. Exodus 13:1, 12–13; *Maaseh Roke'ach, Bechorot; Chidah, Zeroa Yemin* 6a.

Question 215

When I was a child, the matzot were round. Today, they are square. Why is that?

What's better? Round or square? It's not a question of which is better, but whether it's *kosher l'Pesach*, in which case the shape is irrelevant. Having said that, round matza was the original, traditional shape[65] and for those of you who treasure tradition, use round matza, even if it's machine-made!

But why was matza round to begin with? The Hebrew root of the Torah's description for unleavened bread, *uggot matzot*,[66] is *ug*, which means "round," or "drawn in a circle." Jewish mystics see a round shape as denoting eternity, with God and Israel existing without limit. So when did the matza turn square? In the mid-nineteenth century, when matza-baking machines were invented in Europe, and it was easier and more cost-efficient to mass-produce the square shape. It is difficult, if near-impossible, to knead, flatten and bake a square matza by hand with a rolling pin, especially with an eye on the clock to make sure the traditional process is done quickly so the dough doesn't rise (this is a special mitzva, to "guard the [round] matzot"[67] against rising).

---

65. Rashi, *Moed Katan* 4b.
66. Exodus 12:39.
67. Ibid., 12:17.

Question 216

What is Shabeh Sal?

Unlike Ashkenazi Jews, Sephardim traditionally celebrate the end of Pesach with partying. In Morocco the celebration was called Mimouna; in Iran, Persian Jews had *Shabeh Sal*, replete with sweets and tea drinking (dates, no sugar) in the home of the eldest member of the family. The next day, Persian Jews would picnic in grassy shaded areas, an ancient *minhag* known as *Roozeh Sal*. In Turkey, at the end of Pesach, heads of the household throw coins and candy (symbolic of the wealth the Jews took with them when they left Egypt), and grass (symbolic of the Red Sea reeds) for the children to collect.

Question 217

Why do we wish each other a chag sameach?

The custom derives from a Torah command, *Vesamachta bechagecha*, "you shall rejoice on your festival,[68] an order that is simple in theory but much harder in reality (the Vilna Gaon called it the most difficult mitzva in the Torah). The word *chag* comes from *chug*, "a circle," in that Jews must always be happy with their lot, especially on chag, regardless of what the wheel (circle) of life brings.

---

68. Deuteronomy 16:14.

Question 218

What is Mimouna?

Mimouna, derived from the Arabic *mammon*, "wealth, prosperity, good fortune," is a vigorous Sephardic party held at the end of Pesach, a celebration of family, freedom, friendship. Jews wish each other *tarbah* ("success"), toast each other with a honey-based drink (*mahya*), give special blessings (*Alallah mimouna, ambarka mas'uda*), and serve many symbolic delicacies (e.g., the pareve *Zabane*, a caramel-resembling mixture of sugar, nuts and whipped egg whites; the *Mufleita*, a thin, round pancake-like butter and honey food rolled up hot French crépe-style).

What is the origin of Mimouna? No one knows for sure: some link it to the anniversary of Rambam's father (Maimon) who died in Fez, Morocco, on the final day of Pesach. Others link the term *mimouna* to *emuna*, "faith," in that the final redemption will come in the month of Nissan.

Question 219

What is *kemitza*?

Immediately after the first day of Pesach, the *Beit Din Gedola* (the Sanhedrin House of Judgment) would go out into a pre-Pesach prepared field and watch three sickle-wielding men cut three "measures" of barley (*se'ahs*) which were then brought to the Temple where only one-tenth (an *"omer"*) was needed for the offering. It was then "waved" in a ceremony (*kemitza*), and burnt with the remainder going to the priest.[69]

Question 220

What happened to the practice of the paschal lamb?

The paschal sacrifice ceased after the destruction of the Temple, however, during the first century of the Common Era, Theudas, the most prominent Jew of Rome, tried to reintroduce the custom of sacrificing a lamb which led to a rabbinic rebuke from Palestine who *paskened* that this practice was permitted only in the Temple of Jerusalem.[70]

Question 221

Is today's matza the same as the one used in antiquity?

The humble matza's longevity is remarkable; mass-produced, sold on supermarket shelves thousands of years later, its simple perforated recipe – wheat, water, salt – has endured the millennia. Given the Jews' fickle gastronomic palate, it's a ritual phenomenon. The matza of old was much larger than it is today, it consisted of a different type of grain, it was more irregular and had rougher edges, and was more of a disc "cake" shape.

---

69. *Menachot* 64; Leviticus 23:9.
70. *Brachot* 19a.

Question 222

What do I do if I'm in Israel for Pesach? What does an Israeli do in Melbourne for Pesach?

The general rule of thumb is to maintain the custom you have at home (the Rambam disagrees), and the consensus is that the two-day chag is a *minhag*[71] (based on a Talmudic verse, "Give heed to the customs of your ancestors which have come down to you, for it might happen that an unfriendly government will issue a decree [against Jewish learning] and it will cause confusion [in the calculation of the Jewish calendar]").[72] Thus an Israeli only keeps one day of Pesach in *chutz la'aretz*, and vice versa, a Diaspora Jewish tourist must continue keeping two days in Israel. The chief rabbi of Israel, Rav Herzog, told tourists to keep two days in Israel just in case keeping one day became so "convenient" that they forgot to keep two days when they returned home.

Not all agree: the Chacham Tzvi, Rav Tzvi Hirsh Ashkenazi, supported by Reb Shmuel Salant, chief rabbi of Jerusalem, was adamant that *all* Jews, local and foreigners, keep only one day of Pesach in Israel, based on the supremacy of putting on *tefillin*, a *positive* Torah command, and the prohibition of *bal tosif*, "adding to the Torah." But even Rav Tzvi's own son (Rav Jacob Emden) respectfully disagreed and urged Jews visiting the holy land to keep two days of *chag* (if he had his way, Rav Emden, who saw no difference between Israel and other countries since

---

71.   Yosef Caro, *responsa, Avkat Rochel.*
72.   *Beitza* 4b.

Israel was ruled by gentile foreigners, would have had *all* Israeli Jews keep two days to comply with the previous order, "Give heed to the customs of your ancestors!").[73]

It gets even more complicated! In the days of the Talmud, Rava, Rav Ashi and Abaye differentiated between different parts of *chutz la'aretz*. Because Babylonia boasted the two most formidable *yeshivot* in the world, they gave visiting Babylonian Jews "a pass," equating the holiness of Babylon with *eretz Yisrael* (however, Jews coming from North Africa or Egypt were treated as "foreigners" and had to keep two days of Pesach).[74] But this causes a problem: there is another ruling that Jews must follow the *minhag* of the Jewish community they find themselves in, in order to avoid disputes and disunity. In his major works (*Beit Yosef, Shulchan Aruch*), Yosef Karo spends a great deal of time discussing what an Israeli should do in, say, Johannesburg or New York, but is totally mute on what a Jew from Los Angeles or Johannesburg should do when in Jerusalem for Pesach. Others (the Rama, Rav Moshe Isserles, the Ashkenazi voice in the *Shulchan Aruch*) are also mute on this subject, aware of the obvious contradictions involved.

Question 223

Is the *Shir Hama'alot* of Pesach's *Birkat Hamazon* different than the one said the rest of the year?

No. The night may be "different," but some things just never

---

73.   *Responsa, She'elot Yavetz.*
74.   *Ma'aseh haGeonim; Pesachim* 51a.

change! This short song (also known as Psalms 126) is one in a series of fifteen psalms – symbolic of the fifteen steps in the holy Temple – that all start alike, with the words *Shir Hama'alot* ("Song of ascents"), all penned by King David. This popular happy ditty (which touches on the restoration of Zion) has joy dripping from its *niggun* and lyrics (*Az yemalei sechok pinu*, "then our mouths filled with laughter and cheers were on our tongue") and was sung by Levites on the steps of the *Beit Hamikdash*, and by pilgrims making *aliya* to Jerusalem to celebrate the *shalosh regalim* (three pilgrimage festivals).

Since *Shir Hama'alot* was not written specifically for a meal, its words make no direct reference to God and the food He has provided; instead, a song of generic appreciation is sung for everything God has given us.

Question 224

Why do we say *Ya'aleh Veyavo* on Pesach?

This special prayer, inserted into the *Birkat Hamazon* and the *Shmoneh Esrei*, is said on *Rosh Chodesh*, the High Holidays, and the three pilgrimage festivals. Rabbi Samson Raphael Hirsch equates its first eight words ("May our remembrance rise before God and be favorably received") with eight different expressions of prayer. One passage in *Ya'aleh Veyavo* ("Remember your promise of mercy and redemption") is directly linked to Pesach. The rest is a plea for God to be gracious and kind – and grant us life and peace.

Question 225

What's the difference between *se'or* and chametz?

Se'or is old leavened dough which, over time, has reached a high level of fermentation or yeast. By itself, it is inedible; however, when mixed with flour and water, it helps the dough rise and becomes chametz. Nineteenth-century Russian Rabbi Naftali Tzvi Berlin of Volozhin (Netziv) saw *se'or* as the mystical manipulation of God's natural state, which is why it was banned from the Temple altar.[75] The Netziv was convinced that only natural elements (flour, water) were supposed to make dough rise, and that technological ingenuity (e.g., sourdough making bread rise, a major breakthrough in food technology) interfered with this natural order. The Zohar recoiled from anything that would assist dough in rising, defining these "unnatural" elements as sheer *yetzer hara* ("evil inclination"), causing the mystic Rabbi Alexandri to add to his daily prayers, "Master of the Universe, You know full well that it is our desire to act according to Your will; but what prevents us from doing so? The yeast in the dough!"[76]

Question 226

Is it OK to eat out on Pesach?

The practice in many Jewish communities is not to eat outside

---

75.   *Ha'amek Davar*; Commentary, Exodus 13:3.
76.   *Brachot* 17a.

the home on Pesach, not because of *kashrut* reasons but because of various customs and different standards. Ashkenazi Jews avoid rice, beans and anything that can be defined as *kitniyot*; some Jews eat only hand-baked matzot; others avoid matza soaked in a liquid (*shruya* in Hebrew, *gebrochts* in Yiddish), etc.

Question 227

Why do we omit saying *Tachanun* during the entire month of Nissan?

The solemn *Tachanun*, usually said after the daily *Shmoneh Esrei*, is inappropriate for times of joy. But why is the *entire* month "joyous"? For the first twelve days there was a daily festive dedication in the Tabernacle, brought by a different chief of each of the twelve Hebrew tribes (starting with Judah, ending with Naftali).[77] Then, Pesach started a few days later, and the day after Pesach was a festive *Isru Chag*; thus the entire month was basically full of delight.

Question 228

Should a person in prison search for chametz?

In 1978 an emaciated Yosef Mendelovich, a Jewish hero if ever there was one, sat in a dark, dank cell in the Soviet Union's Christopol Prison, charged with being "too Jewish." When April

---

77. Numbers 7:12.

twelfth arrived, Yosef, despite his conditions, knew it was the fourteenth of Nissan, erev Pesach, and immediately rose to the "Jewish" occasion. He needed a candle to search for chametz, which he crafted from a bit of string, a drop of oil, and a sliver of wax that he had been hoarding just for this moment. He used mustard, which the infirmary had provided for his backaches, for bitter herbs (maror), an old onion bulb kept in water as greenery (*karpas*), and soaked raisins for wine (*kiddush*). Behind those lifeless walls, he then recited the Haggada by heart. Today, Yosef Mendelovich walks the streets of Israel a free man. Thus the search for chametz is a symbolic obligation for the Jew, no matter where he is.

Question 229

Can I use raisin wine on Pesach?

Wine from raisins is acceptable for those who cannot stomach regular wine (or grape juice), although one is allowed to (slightly) "dilute" the wine with water. Some rabbis even allow the four cups to contain "the beverage of the country,"[78] which, theoretically, could mean tea (or even coffee), although this would be odd. When asked if a person could drink soda water instead of wine, Rabbi Moshe Feinstein answered no, because this drink merely fulfilled one's thirst, but is not a mitzva![79]

---

78.   *Mishna Berura* 472, 37.
79.   *Igrot Moshe, Orach Chayim* Vol 2.

Question 230

Is there any order to the festivals within the Jewish calendar, or are the dates of the holidays purely random?

It's orderly with many moving parts, but there are dependable "constants" in the Jewish calendar. An example? No Jewish (non-leap) year begins earlier than September 16th, nor ends later than October 5th. And a Jewish year that begins on Adar 1st (if twenty-nine days) and ends on Cheshvan 29th is *always* 265 days, and *always* contains the Torah's specific six festivals (Pesach, Shavuot, Rosh Hashana, Yom Kippur, Succot, Shemini Atzeret). On what day is Rosh Hashana most likely to fall? Thursday (a frequency of 31.9%). And what is the least likely day? Tuesday (11.5%). An oddity: although tradition has it that Pesach occurred on a Thursday, it's more likely to fall on a Tuesday! Pesach is formulated so that its first day can never fall on a Monday, Wednesday or Friday – and its second day *always* falls on the same weekday as Shavuot. A coincidence? No. It's the result of *at-bash*, a mnemonic rabbinic device. How does this work? You match the first and last seven letters of the Hebrew alphabet (i.e., *alef* = *tav, bet* = *shin*, etc.) in order to determine the first days of festivals. Try this! Take the letters *alef* to *zayin*, which represent the seven days of Pesach, and link them with *tav* to *ayin*, the last seven Hebrew letters taken in reverse order, to indicate the day of the week. Here's the pattern: *alef* (for the first day of Pesach) equals *tav* (for Tisha b'Av), thus their days are the same. Similar with *beit* (for Pesach's second day) which is linked to *shin* (for Shavuot), *gimmel* (third day) to *reish* (for Rosh Hashana), *daled* (fourth day) to *kof* (for *kriat haTorah*, i.e., Simchat Torah), *heh* (fifth day) to *tzaddi* (for *tzom*, "fast," i.e., Yom Kippur), and *vav* (sixth day) to *peh* (for Purim). For centuries, this general concept applied only to the first six days of Pesach, until 1947 and the rise of the Third Jewish Commonwealth, which allowed modern mystics to finally match a calendrical partner: *zayin* (the seventh day) to *ayin* (for *atzma'ut*, as in Yom Ha'atzmaut).

Question 231

Why are we still required to eat matza if there is neither a Temple nor Pesach offerings?

It is true; the Torah's *korban Pesach* requirement is coupled with the order that it be eaten *"with* matzot and maror." However, our rabbis concluded that sacrificial absences, in the post-Temple period, affect only maror and not matza since *only* the word *matza* is repeated ("In the evening you shall eat matza [i.e., no mention of maror]").[80] Thus, eating *"matza shemura"* is the *only* post-Biblical obligatory Pesach mitzva remaining that relates to eating (all the others, *Pesach korban*, sacrifices, *teruma*, *ma'aser sheni*, are impossible to fulfill today).[81]

---

80.   *Pesachim* 28b, 120a; *Tosafot, Kiddushin.*
81.   *Chatam Sofer*, Responsa, *Chosen Mishpat* 196.

Question 232

I'm confused. When eating matza, do I say the *Hamotzi* blessing or *al achilat matza*?

Both. First put a piece of the broken matza between two whole pieces, say *Hamotzi* on the whole piece, break it, then say the *al achilat matza* over the broken piece and then take at least an olive-sized bite (*kezayit*) of both![82]

Question 233

Can a blind man say the Haggada?

The mitzva of *sippur yetziat Mitzrayim* requires, according to Rav Acha bar Yaakov, being able to see in order to point to certain symbolic foods (Pesach, matza, maror).[83] However, the Talmud relates that both blind rabbis Yosef and Sheshet conducted their own Sedarim. When asked why, they replied that the "mitzva of matza is only rabbinic in nature." Is this the accepted position? No. Both Rabban Gamliel and the Rambam[84] make these foods an integral part of *sippur yetziat Mitzrayim*.

---

82. Rosh, *Hilchot Pesachim*; Responsa of the *Rosh*, 14.
83. *Tosafot Megilla* 19a.
84. *Hichametz Umatza* 7:6.

Question 234

Why the confusion over the size of a *kebeitza*?

Different calculations are reached depending on whether an average-sized egg is measured with its shell on (*kav*) or peeled. Some (*Mishna Berura*) measure the egg with its shell;[85] others (the Vilna Gaon, Chazon Ish) disagree.[86] The Rambam researched the matter thoroughly on the basis that the Torah's measurement of a *revi'it* equals a *beitza*, and announced that one *revi'it* was the same as twenty-six Arab silver coins (*drams*) of wine and twenty-seven drams of water. The conclusion? One *revi'it* equals a *beitza* and a half, and a *kebeitza* equals eighteen, which is two-thirds of twenty-seven drams.[87] But how big is a dram? The Rambam doesn't say, but Rav Chaim Na'eh (*Shiurei Torah*) figured out that it was 3.2 grams, which made the volume of a *kebeitza* 57.6 cubic centimeters. Did this put an end to the dispute? No. Why not? A dram in the Turkish time of Chaim Na'eh was different than the dram of the days of the Rambam (when it was smaller, around 2.83 grams, which made a *beitza* around fifty cubic centimeters).[88]

Obviously, if the size of a dram can change, so can the size of an egg. Thus, the Noda BiYehuda, in a startling Ashkenaz decision, announced that all food measurements must now be doubled, on the basis that modern-day eggs and fruits

---

85.   *Mishna Berura* 486:1.
86.   *Kuntras Hashiurim, Orach Chayim* 39:17.
87.   Ramban, Commentary to the Mishna, *Eduyot* 1:2, *Keilim* 2:2.
88.   *Midot Veshiurei Torah* 13:7, 30:6.

are smaller than in the times of the Talmud (this doubled the size of a *kebeitza* from fifty to a hundred cubic cm). Was this position unanimously accepted? No. Some disagreed (*Mishna Berura, Biur Halacha*, although they decided to follow the Noda BiYehuda in such mitzvot of Torah origin as matza and Shabbat *kiddush*),[89] whilst many halachic "heavies" agreed with him (Vilna Gaon, Akiva Eger, Chatam Sofer).[90] Remember: the Torah's measurement of length is connected to the size of body parts (*amma, tefach, agudal, etzba*), while volume measurements are determined by the volume of foods (*se'ah, beitza, gerogeret, zayit*, etc.). The discrepancy in measurements is also a result of various scholars over the years using a combination of food and body parts.[91]

The Chazon Ish, in his pamphlet *Kuntras Hashiurin*, rules that if a contradiction exists between the generational standards, one must accept the larger measurement, and confirmed that the moment the Noda BiYehuda's position was accepted by the masses, it became law. Are a *kezayit* and a *kebeitza* the same thing? No. The latter is larger (the size of an egg), while the former is much smaller (the size of an olive).[92] Is this the accepted position? Actually, no: there are ambiguities in defining their sizes. In response to a question from Rav Nachman ("What's the law if one throws an olive-sized piece of *teruma* into an impure house?"), Rava's response ("If in regard to Shabbat, [a minimum of] the size of a date is required") implies that a *kezayit* is

---

89. *Mishna Berura* 486:1; *Biur Halacha* 271:13.
90. *Noda BiYehuda*, commentary *Tzelach, Pesachim* 116; Vilna Gaon, *Ma'aseh Rav* 105; Rabbi Akiva Eger, *Shut Hachadashot* 39; *Chatam Sofer*, Responsa, *Orach Chayim* 127, 181.
91. *Tashbetz* 3:33; *Pesachim* 109a–109b.
92. *Yoma* 80a; *Keritut* 14a.

actually smaller than a date, which is about one-third of an egg. Another Talmud defines "two average meals" as the equivalent of eighteen dates (*gerogerot*), around five and one-third *kebeitzim*.[93] The Rambam claims a *kezayit* is around one-third of a *kebeitza*;[94] Rashba says that a *kezayit* is less than one-quarter of a *kebeitza*;[95] others (Rabbenu Tam, Ra'avya, Maharil) maintain that a *kebeitza* is twice the size of a *kezayit*.

The problem has increased over the centuries, since the sizes of eggs and olives are no longer what they used to be. This is why the Mechaber, Rav Yosef Karo, author of the Shulchan Aruch, not wanting to come out totally against the Rambam's conclusion, answers the question, "What's the measurement of a *kezayit*?" with the dissenting opinion, "Some say that it equals half a *beitza*."[96] Meanwhile the *Mishna Berura* differentiates between a Torah obligation (strictly, demanding that one eat half a *kebeitza*) and a rabbinic one (leniently, content with a third of a *beitza*).[97]

Question 235

I need to take medicine daily. What do I do over Pesach? Is it considered chametz?

Chametz is defined by its "edibility." You have to ask yourself the

---

93. *Shabbat* 91a; *Eruvin* 82b.
94. *Hilchot Eruvin* 1:9; *Magen Avraham* 486:1, *Peri Chadash*.
95. *Mishmeret Habayit* 96a.
96. *Shulchan Arukh* 486; Rav Chaim Na'eh, *Shiurin Shel Torah*.
97. *Mishna Berura* 486:1, 190:10, 456:2.

question – would a dog eat it?[98] Thus cosmetics,[99] ointments or medication (*even* if they contain an active chametz ingredient) can be stored over Pesach, because no dog would find them suitable for consumption, i.e., they are *nifseda tzurat hachametz*, "have lost their (chametz) form."[100] Although an item which is not fit for consumption, and has lost its chametz "form," may be stored and used on Pesach, it still may not be eaten. By eating it, its status is elevated from "inedible" to "edible."[101] This reclassification is referred to by the *poskim* as *achshavei*, literally an "elevation," or an upgrading of this item's halachic status.

Does *achshavei* apply to medication?[102] No. The person taking them because of pain or an illness (a *choleh*) obviously doesn't consider them "edible" food items (unless they are flavored or coated in a way to make them taste better), and thus it's permissible[103] – but *only* if chametz-free medications are unavailable.[104] What's the status of a product that starts off being "inedible," but can be altered (via cooking or adding other ingredients, etc.) so that it becomes "tasty" enough to eat? It's prohibited. Even if it stays in its "inedible" condition? Yes. What about perfume? Fragrances don't count! Remember: something is only chametz if it enters your mouth.

---

98. *Biur Halacha* 442:9; Chazon Ish, *Orach Chayim* 116:8.

99. *Sefer Hilchot Pesach.*

100. *Shulchan Aruch haRav* 24; *Igrot Moshe Orach Chayim* 3:62.

101. *Orach Chayim* 442:1, 4; *Mishna Berura* 20, 43.

102. *Chazon Ish* 116:8; *Igrot Moshe, Orach Chayim* 2:92; S.Z. Auerbach, *Shemirat Shabbat Kehilchata* 40:74.

103. *Sha'ar Hatziyun* 466:6; *Shemirat Shabbot Kehilchata* 40:76; *Sefer Hilchot Pesach.*

104. *Yechaveh Da'at* 2:60; *Tzitz Eliezer* 10:25–20; *Kinyan Torah* 4:44; *Nishmat Avraham, Orach Chayim* 466:1.

Question 236

Who named Nissan the month of Pesach?

In 539 BCE, the Jews, led by Ezra and Nechemia, returned to Jerusalem from exile after the Persian conquest of Babylonia, took God's order (to make "the first month of the year")[105] and named it *Nissan*. Ezra and Nechemia did not stop at Nissan and "borrowed" names from the Babylonian months and named all Hebrew months after them. Nissan thus became the first month of the Jewish year (either March or April in the Gregorian calendar), while the other Jewish New Year (Tishrei) remained the seventh month. Why the different New Years? Different events in Jewish history lead to different celebrations in the Jewish calendar (e.g., the tax year is not the same as the calendar year, etc.). The Torah confirms that the Jewish cycle is marked by two calendars: civil[106] (beginning with Tishrei, in either September or October in the Gregorian calendar), marking the month of Creation,[107] and religious (starting in Nissan, the Torah's "head month").[108]

---

105. Exodus 12:2.
106. From Genesis 1:1 to Exodus 12:1.
107. Genesis 1:1.
108. Exodus 12:2.

Question 237

Do we measure matza based on weight or volume?

Ashkenazim (e.g., Rav Yosef Shalom Elyashiv), based on the *Noda BiYehuda* and the Rambam,[109] still calculate by volume,[110] while Sephardic Torah scholars (*Kaf Hachayim*, Rav Ovadia Yosef)[111] measure matza by weight. There are problems, however, with measuring by volume since you end up including "emptiness" (i.e., hollow spaces in the matza), which is impossible to measure, and empty air-pockets are not included for halachic purposes.[112]

So what's the measurement of a *kezayit* for the Pesach matza? There's no one simple answer. You can go from strict (the Chazon Ish's three-quarters of a matza), to lenient (Rav Chaim Na'eh's half or even a third of a matza). And more! It depends which matza is being used at what time during the Seder! No, not all matzot are considered halachically "equal." The first *kezayit* of matza on the first night fulfills the Torah obligation, so it would be best to follow the Chazon Ish's position at this time; the second *kezayit* of matza, eaten together with the first (as an added stringency), has a lower level of obligation and you can be lenient here.[113]

When you get to *korech*, which is designed to recall the *korban Pesach*, you should go for the compromise view (half

---

109. *Hilchot Chametz Umatza* 5:12.
110. *Keilim* 17:6; *Mishna Berura* 486:3.
111. *Yechaveh Da'at* 1:16; *Kaf Hachayim* 168:46.
112. *Uktzin* 2:8; *Mishna Berura* 486:5.
113. Rav Nissim Karelitz, *Siddur Pesach Kehilchato*, Ch. 8.

a matza), unless you have trouble digesting matza, in which case eat a third.[114] When you get to the *afikomen*, it's best to eat three-fourths or two-thirds of a matza – unless, like me, your stomach can no longer digest matza (known as *achila gassa*, "excessive eating"), in which case you can eat a half or a third of a matza.[115]

Question 238

I'm going away this Pesach to a hotel. Do I still have to search for chametz in the hotel room?

Yes. According to Jewish law, you are a "renter" with (probably) a non-Jewish landlord, and a renter is still obligated to search for *chametz* (by performing *bedikat chametz*) wherever he is. With candlelight and a blessing? Yes, unless you arrive at the hotel on erev Pesach, when it is too late. In such a case, you "search" but don't make a blessing.[116]

Question 239

Why does every Jewish festival begin at night?

Rav Samson Raphael Hirsch compared "the waxing and waning of the Moon to Israel's renewal, for even in its darkest

---

114. *Mishna Berura* 486:1.
115. *Shulchan Aruch* 477:1; *Mishna Berura* 486:1.
116. Rabbi Moshe Mordechai Karp, *Chag Bechag*.

wanderings, Israel, like the Moon itself, is never lost." The nineteenth-century Chassidic Sage Yehuda Leib Alter (Sfat Emet), commenting on a Mishna that collates the transformation from Egyptian suffering to joyful freedom as going "from darkness to great light [dawn],"[117] concluded that, "Israel orders its calendar by the Moon, for it is used to living in the night of history."

Jewish festivals begin at night in order for the Jew to emerge in the dawn, the morning light, with an affirmation of survival. This belief that those who cling to Torah, heritage, lore and law have the power not only to persevere through darkness, but also to transform that darkness into light, stood in sharp contrast to the Egyptian mentality which considered darkness to be superior to light (which is why they deified blind field mice).

Marcus Ambivius, a Roman official during the Second Temple, is quoted by Rabbi Shlomo ibn Verga[118] as saying that "no door is locked that [Pesach] night in Jerusalem...a symbol of Jewish confidence in Divine protection."

Question 240

What does *u'sefartem* mean?

Even before we sink our teeth into the pleasures of Pesach, we are directed, twice, in a brief and enigmatic Torah command ("Seven weeks shall you count...and you shall keep the Feast of Weeks")[119] to start "counting" (in a language which is understood) in anticipation of the next festival (Shavuot). This "count-up" is

---

117. *Pesachim* 10:5.
118. *Shevet Judah.*
119. Leviticus 23:15–16; Deuteronomy 16:9–10.

sanctified with a nightly blessing said immediately after the evening prayer (*maariv*), starting from the second night of Pesach (or first night if in Israel), and continuing for seven weeks. This period is known as *sefirat ha'omer*, "counting the *omer*," a reference to the *omer hatenufah*, "a new meal offering," which each Jew was obligated to bring to the Temple in Jerusalem. The term is derived from *u'sefartem lachem*, "you shall count for yourselves."

The Riziner Rebbe saw a double layer of meaning behind the term *u'sefartem* – a duty to count and a link to *sappir*, a sapphire stone. The lesson? As you count each day, you should make that day count (and shine like a jewel!).

Question 241

Do I have to sell my shares on erev Pesach in a public food company that deals in chametz?

The status of a Jew as a shareholder in a public company that possesses, or benefits from, chametz over Pesach (*Issur hana'ah*) is complicated. Some scholars are strict about the issue – e.g., Rav David Karlin, Rav Weiss, Rav Sternbuch[120] – but many display leniency, including Rava, Chatam Sofer, Rav Yitzchak Izaak Ettinga, Rav Hildesheimer, Rav David Zvi Hoffmann, and the Swiss Rav Shaul Weingort.[121] It depends if a stockholder is seen as a "silent partner (*noten iska*)," or simply a passive creditor (waiting for a return on his investment), and what constitutes

---

120. *She'elat David; Minchat Yitzchak* III:I; *Mo'adim Uzemanim* III:269.
121. *Yevamot* 46a; Chatam Sofer *Orach Chayim* 63; *Mishna Berura* 448:17; *Mahari HaLevi* II:124; *Melamed LeHo'il, Orach Chayim* 91.

"ownership" (Jewish law equates responsibility for chametz with ownership).[122] It is complicated to rely on a halachic precedent since corporate securities laws – in terms of the relationship between investors and companies – in nineteenth-century Germany or Poland were very different than they are now in twenty-first-century America and Israel.

Question 242

Is the ban on chametz only applicable throughout Pesach?

This is true for today, but not in Temple times. When describing the laws of the flour-oil meal offering (*mincha*), the Torah deems flour to be acceptable in the shape of matzot and pancakes, but staples this warning (*twice*): "No meal offering shall be with leaven (chametz)...it shall be eaten as unleavened cake (matzot)."[123] When leaven was allowed into the Temple, it had nothing to do with sacrifice: unleavened wafers (like matza) and unleavened loaves (like pita or bread) were permitted during the thanksgiving offering (*shelamim*) of Shavuot, which is linked to Pesach by the *omer*.

Why was leaven disqualified at the altar of God? According to the Rambam, offering chametz would be a similar act to local pagan practices ("idolaters would sacrifice only leavened bread"),[124] which is why the Zohar harshly compares those who "eat chametz on Pesach [to] praying to an idol!"[125]

---

122. *Shulchan Aruch, Orach Chayim* 440:1.
123. Leviticus 2:11; *Tzav* 6:9–10.
124. Rambam, *Guide to the Perplexed* 3:46.
125. *Zohar* 2:182.

Question 243

Does the general *kashrut* principle of *batel bashishim* apply on Pesach?

No. This concept, whereby a small amount of meat is "nullified" within a large amount of milk, is inapplicable to Pesach where there is no such thing as an "insignificant" amount of chametz.

Question 244

Why do my wife and daughter have to say the Haggada's *Hallel* if they are exempt the rest of the year?

Why is this *Hallel* different from all other *Hallels*? The once-a-year obligation to retell the saga of Pesach overrides the exemption that women have from saying the Hallel, which ordinarily is a time-sensitive mitzva. Jewish women, who were also saved from Egypt and witnessed the same miracles as the men, are obligated, within the halachic framework of *Af hein hayu be'oto haness*, in the mitzva of the four cups of wine, of which *Hallel* is an integral part.[126]

---

126. *Succa* 38a.

Question 245

We are ordered to celebrate, permanently, "the day" of our Exodus. Which day is that?

It depends. The "day" differs from Torah portion to Torah portion: sometimes the "festival of Pesach" is the date upon which it occurs (14th or 15th Nissan); in others it is according to the season (i.e., in the "month of spring").[127] It gets more complicated: although it is "the day" we're commemorating ("This day shall be for you as a remembrance…for all your generations…celebrate it as an eternal statute…"),[128] the Jews left Egypt "at night" (with the obligatory paschal lamb sacrifice offered only "in the evening, at sunset, the time of your departure from Egypt").[129]

Perhaps the "date" is not as important as the exact "time" of departure? The Torah's use of dual dating also appears elsewhere (e.g., "*Today* you are going out, in the *month* of spring," in the context of the command to sanctify the firstborn).[130] How long is Pesach? In one place, it's seven days (based on the time frame of forbidden chametz during the length of the *korban Pesach*); in another location we're told that the sea split on the seventh day after the Exodus, and thus Pesach is a seven-day chag, starting from the death of the firstborn up until the miracle at the sea. Thus, the Torah provides two different explanations for

---

127. Deuteronomy 16:1.
128. Exodus 12:14–20.
129. Deuteronomy 16:6.
130. Exodus 13:1–10.

the length of this chag. Why? The moment the Jews were given control over Time, there became dates of "worldly time" and "Godly time" (sometimes coinciding, sometimes not).

The dual dating system of Pesach must therefore be seen through the prism of the eyes of the Jews (who chose the month of Nissan) and through the vision of God (who chose "the month of spring," since God retained control over the seasons of the year, fixed since Creation).

Question 246

Is everybody obligated to drink all four cups of wine?

It's in dispute. If drinking the four cups of wine is a *mitzva shebegufo*, a deed "fulfilled by a physical act," then one person cannot do it on behalf of anyone else. Rabbi Yitzchak Zev Halevi Soloveitchik (Griz) rules that every Jew must drink all four cups. Tosafot disagrees, and claims the mitzva lies in the recitation over the cup itself, akin to *kiddush*, and therefore one person can fulfill it on behalf of others.[131] Tosafot thus views the phrase "four cups" as a misnomer, claiming that it refers to breaking the Seder into four different *kiddush*-recitations, known as *amirat hahaggada al hakos*, with each delineated by one of the four. (If wine is not the focus of the mitzva, then, according to this theory, if wine is absent, one can substitute matza for the four cups, which is permissible for Shabbat *kiddush*).[132]

---

131. *Hilchot Chametz Umatza*, 7:9; *Pesachim* 99b; *Tosafot Sukka* 38a; *Orach Chayim*, 371.
132. *Shulchan Aruch, Orach Chayim* 272:9.

Rabbi Zvi Pesach Frank comes to the same conclusion as Tosafot, but for a different reason. Reb Zvi compares the *mitzvat arba kosot* to *ner Chanuka,* and defines them both as mitzvot of *pirsumei nisa* – i.e., incumbent upon the household and therefore can be fulfilled by one Jew in front of all the others.[133] What does the Rambam say? *"Each* person must drink *four* cups on this night."[134] The Rambam, according to Rabbi Joseph B. Soloveitchik (the Rav),[135] was influenced by the sheer number of *halachot (seder asiyat mitzvot elu)* that center around drinking, ranging from the precise intervals to the exactness of pouring *(mezigat hakos).*[136]

Question 247

Why don't we make the *Shehechiyanu* prayer of praise on the seventh (last) day of Pesach?

The *Shehechiyanu* is reserved for "new" festivals, and this day is not an independent chag but an extension of Pesach's first days, in contrast to Shemini Atzeret, which follows Succot as a standalone, independent Jewish festival.

---

133. *Mikraei Kodesh, Pesach.*
134. *Hilchot Chametz Umatza,* 7:7, 10; *Hilchot Shabbat* 29:7.
135. Rabbi Yitzchak Lichtenstein, *Siach haGrid,* 1995.
136. *Hilchot Chametz Umatza,* 8:1–2; *Pesachim* 114a, 116a; Ramban, *Pesachim* 117b.

Question 248

What's the earliest time in the day I can make *kiddush*?

You cannot start your Seder before the time of *tzeit hakochavim*, although, on the first night only, many Jews daven *maariv* earlier and start the Seder earlier (if someone is not feeling well, you can begin about 45 minutes after *shkiya*).

Question 249

What happens if erev Pesach falls on Shabbat?

I think that's great! Why? Because you'll be able to rest up for the Seder![137] But it does pose some inconveniences; some minor (which *Haftora* to read, skipping *seuda shelishit zemirot* so this after-*mincha* meal does not create problems with time),[138] some major. One can eat neither chametz nor matza (from "the tenth hour on")[139] on erev Pesach (Rav Moshe Feinstein was against eating matza on Shabbat starting from Friday night),[140] and yet the Shabbat sanctity, wherein three meals and "two loaves of bread" (*lechem mishneh*) are mandatory, must be preserved.

Here are some solutions. Use *challa* on Friday night, go to an early *minyan* on Shabbat morning and then use the *challa*

---

137.   Radvaz 780; *Chok L'Yisrael; Be'er Hetev* 290, *Sefer Chassidim* 266.
138.   *Eliyahu Rabba* 444.
139.   *Orach Chayim* 471:1; *Mishna Berura, Orach Chayim* 443:7, 8.
140.   *Iggerot Moshe, Orach Chayim* I, 155.

again.[141] For the third meal, use egg matza. The Vilna Gaon would split the morning meal into two meals; the Radvaz said it was better to simply skip *seuda shlishit* altogether; the Rama and Rav Moshe Feinstein, rejecting *matza ashira*, "egg matza," as an option, preferred a meal with no bread, but only fish, meat and fruit.[142]

What about destroying the leftover chametz from the Shabbat meals? Can this be done on Shabbat? No. Here are some solutions. Give the food to a non-Jew, or have a non-Jew throw it out (there is a dispute as to whether chametz can be "sold" to a non Jew on Shabbat: the Chayei Adam allows it, but the Graz and Pri Megadim do not).[143]

What about the dishes? Aren't they *chametzdik*? Yes, so use paper or plastic plates on Shabbat. Alternatively, use your regular dishes and clean and put them away in an "unusual manner," known as *shinui*).[144] When should the Seder plate and table be set? Not on Shabbat. Do it before Shabbat (if you forget, you can do it on *motzei Shabbat* with a *shinui*).[145] What about the "fast of the firstborn," usually conducted on erev Pesach? You can't fast on either erev Shabbat or Shabbat, so some Torah authorities (Rav Ovadia Yosef, Rabbi Moshe Feinstein) suggest fasting on

---

141. *Orach Chayim* 444:1.
142. *Orach Chayim* 444:1; M. Feinstein, *Orach Chayim* 155:1; *Shearim Metzuyanim Behalacha*, 115:7; *Nimukei Yosef*; *Radvaz* 489; *Aruch Hashulchan* 44:6; *Erev Pesach Shechal BeShabbat*.
143. *Shearim Metzuyanim Behalacha* 115:4.
144. *Erev Pesach Shechal BeShabbat*; *Mishna Berura, Orach Chayim* 444:15; *Shearim Metzuyanim Behalacha, kuntres acharon* 115:2; *Sdei Chemed* 7.
145. *Orach Chayim* 667; *Magen Avraham* 473:8; *Chok l'Yisrael*.

Thursday,[146] while some advise skipping it altogether (because it's only a *minhag*, custom).[147]

Do we sing *Shalom Aleichem* before the Seder? There is no set law. Some Jews skip it altogether in order to get to the Seder's *kiddush* as quickly as possible; others say it so that Shabbat doesn't become overshadowed by Pesach, and then there's a compromise: say it but don't repeat each verse thrice, just once.[148]

Question 250

Can you start the Seder before Shabbat starts (or ends)?

No. Pesach, like Shabbat, begins at sundown, and you can't start before. Starting early on the second day, if it was Shabbat, introduces another problem: the mingling of the Shabbat *seuda shlishit* meal with the Seder, an inappropriate "merger." However, you can start later – but best of all is to stay up as late as you can, for "whoever tells about it at length is praiseworthy!"[149]

---

146. *Chazon Avadia; Iggerot Moshe, Orach Chayim* 4, 69:4; *Terumat Hadeshen* 126; *Maharil* 106; *Chavot Yair.*
147. *Agur, Chazon Ovadia; Orach Chayim* 470; *Mikraei Kodesh* 2:23.
148. *Mateh Efraim* 583:1.
149. *Hagaddah.*

Question 251

Is there any problem with preparing the Pesach symbols (salt, *charoset*, etc.) on Shabbat?

Making *charoset* on Shabbat is forbidden (it's a form of "grinding and kneading," *techina* and *lisha*). With regards to the shankbone, it obviously cannot be roasted on Shabbat, but you can use any cooked meat as a symbolic reminder of the Pesach sacrifice. The problem with "salting" is that, together with "tanning (*me'abed*)," it's one of the thirty-nine prohibited works for Shabbat,[150] although the rabbis of the Mishna do allow the preparation of (a small amount of) saltwater for dipping. Having said that, they still prefer that it be prepared before Shabbat, and even before chag if Pesach doesn't fall on Shabbat.[151]

Question 252

What's the punishment for eating chametz on Pesach?

Don't even ask! It's harsh! Premature death (*karet* – i.e., "before

---

150. *Shabbat* 73a, 75b; *Shemirat Shabbat Kehilchata* 15:37; *Mishna Berura, Orach Chayim* 327:4.
151. *Shabbat* 108a; *Shulchan Aruch Orach Chayim* 321:2; *Hagahot Maimoniot Hilchot Chametz Umatza* 8:3; *Kitzur Shulchan Aruch* 118:4.

the age of sixty"). The Ramban defines the punishment as the denial of any chance of an afterlife![152]

Question 253

Can I write on *chol hamoed*?

Yes, especially if you're writing out a check to buy this book! Actually, certain forms of writing (e.g., homework or calligraphy, which require skill) are prohibited, except for special circumstances (e.g., if there's an immediate need to write out a will or write someone out of a will!).[153] If refraining from writing will cause you financial loss then writing is not forbidden, but the way in which you write should be different (e.g., on a slant). In general, writing should be restricted to works that enhance, or are associated with, Pesach. How about typing on a computer? Rav Moshe Feinstein, America's most prominent halachic expert, calls this a *ma'aseh hedyot*, an activity "which doesn't require expertise," and is thus permissible as long as the content is *yomtovdik*.

Question 254

How do we know we have to start eating matza in the evening?

From God's dictate to Moses that, "You shall eat unleavened bread [matza] from the fourteenth day of the month in the

---

152. *Hilchot Teshuva* 8:1.
153. *Shulchan Orach, Orach Chayim* 545; *Mishna Berura* 4,5, 35.

evening until the twenty-first day of the month in the evening."[154]
Remember: the Jewish day begins and ends at sundown, thus
the mitzva to eat matza begins "in the evening" [i.e., "after
sundown"].

Question 255

Why do we keep eight days of Pesach in the Diaspora?

The Jewish calendar is based on lunar months, which are approximately one day shorter than solar months (which is why a
Jewish month can be either twenty-nine or thirty days). In the
days of the *Sanhedrin* (the Jewish Supreme Court), the first day
of the new month (*Rosh Chodesh*) was based on the testimony
of reliable witnesses who report that they saw the crescent new
moon. But by the time this news reached the Jews outside of
Israel, it was too late to know exactly which day was the fifteenth
of the month (in Nissan, that meant Pesach).

Keeping two days of chag was considered a safe option,
and although we have a precise calendar nowadays, we still
adhere to that custom in the Diaspora. Jewish mystics offer
another reason: Jews outside of Israel need two days of chag in
order to experience the holiness of one day of chag in the holy
land. The eighth day of Pesach is likened to a day of *atzeret*, of
"lingering," akin to the eighth day of Succot, known as Shemini
Atzeret, also literally, "the eighth day of lingering."[155] After the
Jews celebrate a long festival, explains a Midrash, God says to

---

154. Exodus 12:18.
155. *Succa* 47b–48a.

them, "It's difficult for us to part; tarry awhile longer. Stay, just one more day!"

Question 256

If we don't shake the *lulav* on Succot, blow the *shofar* on Rosh Hashana, and listen to the Megilla reading on Purim if these festivals fall on a Shabbat,[156] why don't we likewise refrain from eating matza if Pesach falls on a Shabbat?

Rabba's reason for canceling these other mitzvot is part of building "fences around the Torah," in order to prevent the inadvertent carrying (*hotza'a*) on Shabbat ("taking it [*lulav, megilla, shofar*] in his hand to an expert [i.e, carrying] to learn how to use it").[157] However the same reasoning doesn't apply to matza since no one will reasonably run to a rabbi on Shabbat-Pesach with matza in his hand to ask questions about eating or blessings; and even if they do, it's doubtful, says Rabbi Naftali Zvi Yehuda Berlin (Netziv), that Jews would leave their house at night (remember: the mitzvot of *lulav, megilla* and *shofar* take place during the day!).[158]

---

156. *Rosh Hashana* 29b; *Sukka* 42b; *Megilla* 4b.
157. *Sukka* 42b; *Chazon Ovadia* 1, Vol. 2, Section 31.
158. *Ha'amek She'eila*, Vayakhel, She'ilta DePurim, 21.

Question 257

Since we're in the mood to ask questions, why then are we allowed to have a *brit* on Shabbat if there's a chance the *mohel* might carry his tools?

Because, explains the Ritva, the very act of *brit mila* is already a Shabbat "transgression," but since it is such an important act in and of itself, the Torah demands that a *brit* take place on "the eighth day," even if it coincides with Shabbat.[159]

Question 258

Why can't we say the *Viyhi Noam* prayer on *motzei Shabbat Hagadol*?

The general principle is this: we only say *Viyhi Noam* on *motzei Shabbat* if there are six working days (*yemei hama'aseh*, non-holy, *chol* days); since *Shabbat Hagadol* results in a "shorter" work week because of Pesach, we omit it. This logic is based on the repetition of the words, "The works of our hands (*ma'aseh yadenu*)."[160] Not all agree: those who claim that this is only a rabbinic prohibition allow it to be said.[161]

---

159. *Sukka* 42a; *Minchat Chinuch*, Mitzva 9.
160. Tur, *Orach Chayim* 295; Rema, *Orach Chayim* 195; Tosafot, *Pesachim* 50a; *Tzitz Eliezer* 13:36.
161. *Pri Megadim*, *Orach Chayim* 295; *Pri Chadash*, *Orach Chayim* 268:1; Mishna Berura.*Orach Chayim* 295:3.

Question 259

Why is *She'asa Nissim* not said on Pesach?

The expression *She'asa Nissim*, "Who has performed miracles," seems very apropos for Pesach, but it is only said on Chanuka and Purim. Why? Because it was instituted only for Jewish festivals established by rabbinic, not Torah, law – and, in fact, the Haggada already expresses the same sentiment: "We are dutybound to give thanks to the One Who has performed miracles for our forefathers and for us!"

Question 260

I have a home in Israel but am living in *chutz la'aretz*. When I go "home" to Israel, do I keep one or two days Pesach?

It's complicated. According to the Talmud's Rabban Simeon ben Gamliel, your ownership of real estate in the holy land, and its accompanying obligation to pay taxes[162] (or even if you just rent for twelve months), gives you the halachic status of a resident, no matter where you are.[163] But Rabbi Jacob Samuel Hagiz, quoting the Radbaz, disagrees: this rabbi claims your home is where your wife is![164]

---

162. *Baba Batra* 7b, 8a.
163. *Gittin* 44b; *Baba Batra* 7b.
164. *Responsa, Halachot Ketanot.*

Question 261

Why is machine-made matza kosher?

Jerusalem Rabbi Menachem Ohrbach was against machine-made matza but when he saw a Jew burning them with his chametz, in order to make a statement, he called him "a pious fool," adding, "You have the right to act more stringently for yourself, but not for others! Were you among those who left Egypt, and did you [personally] see which matzot our fathers baked, or which matza Moses ate?!"

For matza to be "kosher," it requires, like other mitzvot, *intent* – for a specific purpose. Intent cannot be delegated to another person (which is why matza made by a non-Jew is not kosher), and since a machine has no mind of its own, its automation has no "intent," other than what its operator tells it to do. In fact, Judaism encourages Jews to create "mitzva-objects," any tool that will help or improve the quality of performing mitzvot.

Question 262

Why do we omit *Magen Avot* on Friday night if it coincides with Pesach?

This particular plea was originally included in the davening in order to extend the services to accommodate latecomers. Why should the *kehilla* do this? In those days, it was dangerous for a Jew to walk home alone in the dark after prayers. However, since Pesach is considered *Leil Shimurim*, a "night of Divine protection," it was unnecessary to stretch the services. But from a pragmatic view, Jews never came late to Pesach's *mincha-maariv* prayers anyway. Why? Jewish law demands that we stop work around midday, the afternoon being considered a quasi-holiday since the Pesach lamb was sacrificed then.

Question 263

How many mitzvot are there associated with Pesach?

Twenty-four: the Rambam breaks them down into three positive and five negative mitzvot linked to Pesach itself, plus four positive and twelve negative commands relating to the *korban Pesach*.

Question 264

How soon after Pesach can I eat chametz?

Any chametz in the possession of a Jew during Pesach (*chametz she'avar alav haPesach*) cannot be used by another Jew after Pesach, therefore, you have to allow enough time to pass after Pesach before buying any food products so as not to inadvertently eat this (still) forbidden chametz. Is this a Torah or rabbinic law? It's in dispute: Rabbi Yehuda claims the former (minus the punishment of *karet*, "being cut off" from the community), Rabbi Shimon, the latter (for which the punishment would be just a fine). One of the reasons, quoted by the Rambam and Rav Yosef Caro, that all chametz had to be destroyed before

Pesach was to deprive those Jews who tried to store it for post-Pesach profits.

Question 265

Do Jews start their calendar from Pesach?

No. The Judaic measure of calendar time (Year One) begins at the Creation of the world, a Time of "waste and void."[165] But how do we know the year of Creation? By adding up the ages of those mentioned in the Torah going back to the "beginning." God's cosmic clock started to tick on a Sunday (the 24th of Elul) with a command, "Let there be light!" and completed its first weekly cycle the following Saturday. This starting point (August 22, 3760 BCE in the future Gregorian calendar) was 3760 years and three months before the commencement of the Christian Era, designated as AM I (*Anno Mundi*, "year of the world").

This allocation of a "date" to a year is a practice nowhere to be found in the Torah. Why not? The Jews preferred to place the succession of years in relation to some outstanding historic event, as in "so many years *after*" the deliverance from Egypt, the formative event of its existence as a people (the years spent in Egypt were between 1522 BCE and 1312 BCE); or the Flood, the formative event of universalism, or by the accession of rulers to the monarch (as "in the year x of the reign of King y"), or from the Seleucid era, beginning 312 BCE, used by the Jews after the Babylonian Exile up to the twelfth century. The destruction of

---

165. Genesis 1:1.

the Temple in 70 CE was such a cataclysmic event that it replaced (temporarily) the use of the Exodus as an inaugural date.

Question 266

Can I eat egg matza if erev Pesach falls on a Shabbat?

Not according to Rav J.B. Soloveitchik. It contains various fruit juices that can turn it into chametz.

Question 267

What is *matza ashira*, "rich" matza?

On the first night of Pesach, one cannot fulfill the mitzva of *achilat matza* on any matza that had wine, oil, milk or date-honey added to it during the kneading process (*she'at lisha*), based on the Torah's command that it be *lechem oni*, "the poor man's bread." These ingredients make it into a *matza ashira*, "rich" matza.[166] How about fruit juice? That was OK with the Rambam, who makes no distinction between the first night (matzat mitzva) and other times,[167] but not with the Ramban and Rif.[168]

---

166. Deuteronomy 16:3; *Pesachim* 36a.
167. Rambam, *Chametz Umatza* 5:9.
168. Ibid., 6:5; Ramban, *Milchamot Hashem*; *Rif* 10b.

Question 268

What is *shimur*?

The word means "guarding," and requires the pre-washing of the grain used for baking matza (*letita*), a positive command of precaution which Rava derives from the verse U'*Shemartem et hamatzot*, "And you shall guard the matzot."[169] The purpose? To ensure that chametz is kept out. "Guarding" is necessary only if there is a "real" risk of imminent fermentation (*chimutz*). When does this obligation begin? It's a dispute: Rava and Ramban time it from reaping (*she'at ketzira*) – despite the possibility that grain can ferment even when it's in the ground[170] – whilst others, viewing *shimur* to be more of a symbolic act, time it from when the matza is placed in the oven to bake (*she'at afiya*). The resultant matza is known as *matza meshummeret*, a term which grants this particular matza a special status (more commonly known as *shemura matza*).

What if there's no *shimur* at all? What happens to the matza? Can it be used for *achilat matza* on the first night of Pesach? It's in dispute: it depends on whether this "watchman" obligation falls on the person (*gavra*), or just on the matza itself (*cheftza*). Is the obligation of *shimur* counted as one of the 613 *mitzvot*? Torah linguists note that in the verse, "You shall guard the matzot [from becoming leavened]," "matzot" is spelt the same as "*mitzvot*," suggesting that the Jew also "guard his *mitzvot* from becoming leavened" (i.e., don't delay in performing God's deeds: do them immediately before "they leaven" – or in

---

169. Exodus 12:17; *Pesachim* 40a.
170. *Pesachim* 33a.

modern-day popular slang, "Don't put off until tomorrow what you can do today!"

Question 269

What's the minimal fulfillment of the mitzva of *vehigadeta*, "And you shall tell your children on that day"?

In pure halachic terms, if you simply recall the going-out-of-Egypt, and explain several Pesach symbols, you've done your duty! But the reason there are all those "add-ons" over the centuries is because of the desire to enhance the mitzva. In fact, these "additions" were so well received, and flow so perfectly, that it's hard to tell where the "original" Haggada ends and the "new" begins (e.g., neither *Dayenu* nor *Chad Gadya* appear in the Haggadot of the Rambam,[171] nor of Egyptian-born Rav Saadia Gaon, rosh yeshiva of Pumbedita and Sura,[172] but no publisher would dare leave them out today!).

Question 270

What does *chol hamoed* mean?

The term refers to "the intermediate days" of Pesach; *chol* means "weekday, secular" (from which comes the modern Hebrew adjective *chiloni*, "secular") and *moed* means "meeting" (it also means "holy time/festival"). Taken together, *chol hamoed* infers that

---

171.   1135–1204.
172.   882 CE–942 CE.

we are "meeting" God at a time more spiritually intimate than a regular "weekday/workday," but not with the same intensity as the chag itself (i.e., a sort of "weekday festival," the "secular" part of Pesach and Succot).

Question 271

Is it OK to impress images into the matza?

Because it could be baked quickly, matza was used to serve unexpected visitors, as in the case of Abraham serving "cakes" to his three sudden guests at Mamre, as well as Lot serving the angels ("unleavened bread') in Sodom and Saul eating matza at the woman's house in En-Dor. With more time on her hands, the woman of the house would impress images (doves, fishes, flowers, etc., according to Rabbi Isaac ibn Gayyat)[173] into the matza for decorative purposes. Was this allowed? Yes, and the rabbis of the Talmud (responding to a question from Rabbi Boethus ben Zonin) prohibited it on Pesach *not* because of the design imagery, but because it delayed the baking (and any delay created an opportunity to let in chametz).

Rabbi Elazar bar Zadok recalls the matza he and his father ate at Rabban Gamliel's house that had perforated figures on them. Did the Rambam allow this? Yes, but only from professional matza makers, not by the ordinary woman of the house who lacked the professional molds.[174] Several illustrated Hag-

---

173.   *Maggid Mishna* on *Chametz uMatza* 5:15.
174.   *Pesachim* 37a, Rashi; Rambam, *Chametz uMatza* 5:15; *Orach Chayyim* 460:4.

gadot show matzot with various designs (remember: in the Middle Ages, matza was an inch thick); one shows a design of chains, symbolizing the bondage.[175]

Question 272

What do *Yanesh Beyanesh* and *Lach Belach* mean?

The former refers to foods that do not blend together (e.g., *kosher l'Pesach* matza with non-*kosher l'Pesach matza*), in contrast to the latter which defines foods that do blend together (e.g., chametz and Pesach flour). All mixtures are prohibited on Pesach, even if the ratio is as high as 100-to-one![176] Why? Two reasons: the penalty is harsh (premature death, *karet*), and because Pesach only lasts a week or eight days there is not as much room for leniency (*lo bedilay minay*).

Question 273

Is it true that all products bought on Pesach must have a *kosher l'Pesach* seal on them?

No: this is a common misconception. On Pesach you can buy without a seal such products as club soda, seltzer, fresh concentrated frozen juices, fresh vegetables, plastic tablecloths, aluminum foil, paper plates, plastic spoons and forks. Based

---

175. *Bet Hillel, Yoreh Deah* 96.
176. Rashi, *Pesachim* 29b.

on the rabbinic principle of *batel bashishim,* some items can be purchased without a seal on condition they are bought *before chag* (such as granulated sugar, non-iodized table salt, instant coffee, tea or tea bags, cocoa, milk). Why? Because the ratio of chametz to non-chametz is assumed to be less than a 1:60 ratio, and becomes *batel,* nullified, when the *bracha al biur chametz* is made. Items not in one's possession from before Pesach, however, are not covered by the *bracha* and cannot be made *batel* once Pesach has begun.

Question 274

What's wrong with eating *kneidlach* on Pesach?

Nothing. Then why do some Jews avoid it? These Jews have imposed upon themselves a *chumra* (stringency) because *kneidlach* are made by kneading matza meal with liquid. Does this combination produce chametz? No. In fact, many Chassidim, wishing to show there's nothing wrong with *kneidlach,* make a point of eating them on the eighth day of Pesach.

Question 275

Last year I received a package during Pesach that contained chametz. Should I have returned it to the sender?

If you know what's inside it, don't open it; in other words, just leave it "ownerless" (*hefker*) until after chag.[177] If you didn't know its contents until after you opened it, then don't touch the chametz.[178] If the package arrives during *chol hamoed*, you have to get rid of the chametz ASAP. And more: it's possible that the packaging insulation itself is chametz (polystyrene is OK, but biodegradable "peanuts," made from edible corn or wheat starch, are not).[179]

Question 276

If I can't drink pure wine, can I dilute it with water?

It's complicated: according to the Rashbam, Rash's grandson, if you drink diluted wine, you have observed the mitzva of wine (*yayin*), but not of freedom (*cherut*).[180] How is that possible? This falls within the rabbinic concept known as *mitzva min hamuvchar*, a mitzva "improperly fulfilled." The Rambam agrees, defining *derech cherut* as the art of drinking undiluted wine in a way which symbolizes one's undiluted freedom (based on the Talmudic wording, "*Arba kosot* were established *miderabanan derech cherut*").[181]

---

177.   *Orach Chayim* 446:1; *L'horos Nossan* 5:30.
178.   *Orach Chayim* 446:10.
179.   *Mishna Berura* 15, 41–42; Chazon Ish *Orach Chayim* 116:8.
180.   *Pesachim* 108b.
181.   Ibid., 117b.

Question 277

How much wine do I need to drink on Seder night in order to have fulfilled the commandment?

The obligation is to drink the majority of wine in each of the four cups, so the question really is: how small can the wine cup be? At least the equivalent of a *revi'it* (which is about 80 millimeters), because of a concept known as *kiddush bemakom seuda*, wherein we make a "meal" out of wine. Why? Because the average time between making *kiddush* and eating is around thirty minutes, a near-impossibility when telling the Pesach story, thus *kiddush* is in lieu of the meal.

Question 278

Can I eat matza before the Seder?

Not on the afternoon before the Seder. In fact, the very first order in the Mishna ("*lo yochal ad she…*") focuses on eating and drinking with a reminder not to eat matza between *mincha* and nightfall. Why not? First, there is a general prohibition against eating before any chag (or Shabbat), in order to preserve the appetite for the festive meal (*simchat haregel*),[182] and second, to ensure you don't get so distracted as to not participate in the afternoon activity of the *korban Pesach*.

---

182.   *Tosefta* 10:4, *Brachot* 5:1; *Pesachim* 107b.

Question 279

What's the latest time I can eat matza on erev Pesach?

There are three opinions. The Rosh times it to when eating chametz is forbidden ("from six hours on");[183] the Rambam says the entire day (twenty-four hours);[184] and Reb Moshe Feinstein rules during the day only (i.e., daylight hours).[185] Some stop eating matza from the start of Nissan, others from Purim.[186]

Question 280

What should I do with all my chametz?

You can't eat it, own it or derive benefit from it! Therefore you have four choices (there's the number four again!): either consume, destroy, sell (through your local rabbi), or give it as a gift to a non-Jew before Pesach.

---

183.   *Baal Hamaor, Pesachim* 83; *Nimukei Yosef, Rosh, Pesachim* 3:7.
184.   *Ramban, Magen Avraham, Hilchot Chametz Umatza* 6.
185.   *Iggerot Moshe, Orach Chayim* 1, 155.
186.   *Mishna Berura, Orach Chayim* 470:11.

Question 281

Can I feed my puppy non-kosher food over Pesach?

Yes,[187] with two exceptions. Not if the food consists of a mixture of milk and meat (it's forbidden to gain any benefits from such a mixture), and not if it contains chametz (you shouldn't derive benefit from chametz).

Question 282

Isn't the dual demand to make a *Hamotzi* over matzot which need to be broken and to also start the meal with "double bread" (*lechem mishneh*) a contradiction in terms?

Yes. The mitzva of eating matza requires breaking the matza, the Torah's expression *lechem oni* being an indication of poverty,[188] whereas the order of *lechem mishneh* requires saying *Hamotzi* over two *complete, unbroken pieces* of matza. So what should we do? Rashi and Tosafot suggest we say *Hamotzi* over two complete matzot and use the (third, broken) matza as a separate, stand-alone matza for the purpose of fulfilling the mitzva of eating matza, which contradicts the Talmud's explicit order that "a broken piece is placed among the complete ones to begin

---

187. Exodus 22:30.
188. *Pesachim* 115b.

the meal."[189] The Rambam and Rif disagree with Rashi, and accept whatever one holds as one unit (i.e., hold both whole and broken *matzot* together, say both blessings, and then eat either matza). Others (Rav Menachem of Juny, Baal Hamaor) say both blessings over the broken matza. Some (Ra'avan, Rabbenu Chananel) say *Hamotzi* over the broken matza, *al achilat matza* over the whole one, and then start eating; and yet others (Ri) make *Hamotzi* over the complete matza, and *al achilat matza* over the broken one.

Question 283

Can I drink more than four cups of wine?

No, with the exception of water. Why not? Because you cannot "add" to the requirement. Another reason is that you may become drunk and therefore incapable of participating in, or leading, the Seder.

Question 284

If each cup of wine constitutes a separate mitzva, why don't we say a bracha over each cup?

Rabbi Samson Raphael Hirsch explains that each cup leads to the same place, final redemption, which is why we say only one

---

189. *Berachot* 39b.

concluding blessing (*al hagafen*) over the last cup of wine. According to Jewish law, since we drink all four cups at the same table, during the one meal, one *bracha* "covers" them all.

Question 285

When's the earliest and latest Pesach can fall in America?

No sooner than March 27 – no later than April 27.

Question 286

Is it obligatory to eat matza on the last six days of Pesach?

The verse *Af sheshet yamim reshut* indicates that the eating of matza takes on a voluntary nature (i.e., there is neither a *chiyuv*, "obligation," nor a *kiyum*, "fulfillment of a mitzvah," during these days). However, in practical terms, it is impossible to have a full-fledged *seuda* (obligatory on *Shabbat chol hamoed* and on the seventh day of chag) without matza.

This position is not universally accepted. Both the Baal Hamaor and Ibn Ezra state that the mitzva of matza extends to the entire chag period, which is why the Vilna Gaon (Gra) ate matza with particular zeal during these last days.[190]

---

190. Vilna Gaon, *Ma'aseh Rav; Tosafot* 119b; *Ba'al HaMa'or, HaRa'avad* 3; Ramban *Hilchot Chametz Umatza* 8:14.

Question 287

Is there a *bracha* for chametz?

In 1944, the Jews in Bergen-Belsen obviously had no matza for Pesach and a debate raged as to whether it would be better to fast than to eat chametz. The conclusion was that it was imperative to stay alive (*pikuach nefesh*), but the rabbis urged that the following "blessing" be said before eating chametz...

"Our Father in Heaven, behold it is evident and known to Thee that it is our desire to do Thy will and to celebrate the festival of Pesach by eating matza and by observing the prohibition of chametz. But our heart is pained that the enslavement prevents us and we are in danger of our lives. Behold, we are prepared to fulfill Thy commandment: 'And ye shall live by them and not die by them...' Therefore, our prayer to Thee is that Thou mayest keep us alive and preserve and redeem us speedily so that we may observe Thy statutes and do Thy will and serve Thee with a perfect heart. Amen!"

Question 288

Do I still need to search for chametz if I'm lying in a hospital bed?

Yes. You can search your bed, dresser and closet, however, no *bracha* is recited since you do not own the hospital.[191]

---

191.   *Yad Le Yoledet* 22, 1.

Question 289

Can I use dairy products for Pesach?

In our home, many years ago, we didn't use milk or milk products for Pesach. However, times have changed. The facts are these: there is no question of chametz being present in dairy products since milk purchased before Pesach is intrinsically not chametz. Even if some of the liquid became chametz, it is "neutralized" (*batel*) because the general Jewish law of *bitul* applies pre-Pesach.

What about milk produced on Pesach? The issue is that the animal producers of milk (cows) probably ate grain feed that has reached the state of chametz. The other issue is that Jewish cattle owners cannot feed their animals chametz during Pesach, a transgression of deriving benefit or profits [*hana'a*] from chametz).[192] There is no consensus on this issue: for example, the great halachist Rav Yonasan Eyebeshutz saw nothing wrong with drinking the milk of an animal that ate chametz on the basis that this "*hana'a*" was derived *shelo kederech hana'a*, "not in the normal way."[193]

Question 290

What is the Torah source for not possessing chametz over Pesach?

There are two Torah verses in Exodus: "Chametz shall not

---

192.   *Shulchan Aruch, Orach Chayim* 4487.
193.   Rabbi Y. Eyebeshutz, *Kreisi u'Plaisi* on *Yorah Deah* 60.

be seen to you and leaven shall not be seen to you in all your boundaries" and "Seven days there shall be no leaven found in your home."[194] We learn from these two verses that simply the act of possessing, not even eating chametz, transgresses the two negative commandments of *bal yira* and *bal yimotza*, "one shall not see and one shall not find." Some scholars[195] claim that abandoning chametz is the same as nullifying it; others (Ramban) put this into a separate category. Thus, from a lenient point of view, even if it remains in the house, chametz may be "abandoned," because this act shows the owner's intent of no longer wanting it.[196] However, the general consensus is that *all* methods of chametz "destruction," including nullification, are required even if any one method is sufficient. The main concern about "nullifying," according to Ran, is that it totally relies upon one's feelings and each Jew experiences different feelings at different times.

Question 291

What does the term "folded matza" mean?

If a piece of matza folds during baking, with one part attached to the other, it is not allowed to be eaten. Why? Because it has not baked properly. In reality, most rabbis are lenient on this matter because it is only a *chumra*, a stringency.

---

194. Exodus 12–19.
195. *Ran Pesachim* 2a, *Tosafot* 4.
196. *Noda BiYehuda* Vol. 1, *Orach Chayim* 19, *Kehillat Yaakov Pesachim Siman* 2.

Question 292

What is the foundation for the laws of Pesach?

A concern for others. The great Hillel once observed that if we are only concerned with our own well-being, then we have little human worth. And so the first paragraph on the laws of Pesach in the *Shulchan Aruch* discuss *maot chittim*, which means literally, "money for wheat," and *kimcha depischa*, an obligation to ensure that the poor and needy have enough food and means to celebrate chag properly (a reminder less than a month after Purim's similar obligatory charity demand for *matanot le'evyonim*).

Question 293

Is kashering the same as immersion?

Yes and no. For example: *treif* food vessels bought from a non-Jew must be both koshered and immersed in a *mikvah*. A vessel owned by a Jew that somehow absorbed non-kosher food requires kashering but not immersion; and new vessels acquired from non-Jews necessitate immersion but not kashering. What's the basis for these distinctions? The genesis of "koshering," a process that renders a utensil kosher (i.e., fit for use), is in the Torah.[197] After receiving utensils as booty in a war against the Midianites, Elazar, the High Priest, instructs the Jews on how to treat them ("Anything that was used with fire should be passed through fire to be purified, but [then] needs to be immersed

---

197. Numbers 31:21–24.

in a *mikva,* and anything not used with fire should be passed through water").

The basic rule of thumb in kashering is a concept known as *kevol'o kach polto,* in that "things can be removed in the same way they got absorbed"[198] (e.g., if non-kosher soup was boiled in a pot, kashering it would involve boiling; likewise, if non-kosher meat was roasted on a spit in fire, removal of the non-kosher meat absorbed by the spit requires fire).

---

198. *Pesachim* 30a.

Question 294

What does *klotz kashers* mean?

"Tis better thrice to ask your way," Guiterman's poetry advises, "than even once to go astray!" The art of questioning lies at the heart of the Jewish religion, applying even to *klotz kashers*, which is Yiddish for the most ridiculous queries of them all! Man's finest quality? In the words of Ibn Gabriol, "To inquire, probe, query."[1] Moshe Ibn Ezra agrees: "Who is ashamed to ask diminishes in wisdom." Or in the wit of our yiddishists: Each wherefore has a therefore! There is a long line of scholars and students who are in search of reasons for the Divine commandments (*ta'amei hamitzvot*). And if they fail to find a rationale for a given commandment, does this exempt them from the specific mitzva? No.

"The components of the Torah remain the law," writes Rav

---

1. *Mivhcar Hapeninim.*

Samson Raphael Hirsch, "even if we have not discovered the cause and connection of a single one!"

Question 295

What should the "needy" extract from the Seder's invitation, "Come and join the Passover celebration?"

Physical hunger is the impetus for the Haggada call, "All who are hungry, come and eat." The fact is that beyond the human physical need to eat and be satisfied, Jews "need" to be reinforced in their belief system, and this "need" is best manifested during Pesach. We may "need" food to eat and clothes to be warm, but human beings likewise "need" spiritual sustenance in the form of personal freedom and liberty. The hungry come to satisfy their stomachs; the needy come to satisfy their soul – and, adds the Rambam, "the health of the soul can only be achieved after the health of the body is achieved!" (This concept echoes Philo's philosophy: "The body is the soul's house. Shouldn't we first take care of our house so it doesn't fall into ruin?")

Question 296

Why are the Haggada's answers to the four sons different from those given in the Torah?

We go easy on the *Tam* (the simple son) and the *She'eino Yodea*

Lishol (the son who does not know how to ask) by repeating the Torah's answers in the Haggada, but when it comes to the *Chacham* (wise son) and *Rasha* (wicked son), more care is needed in replying. And so the Haggada uses the expression *af*, "even," as in, You should *"even"* say to him, to add to the Torah. Another reason is that the Torah's response to the wicked son included a reference to the *korban Pesach* which no longer existed when the Haggadah was written after the destruction of the Temple. (That's why, with the exception of the section of Rabban Gamliel, the Haggada generally minimizes this ritual which was more relevant then.)

Incidentally, the four questions are not even the same as those in the Torah, which includes one on the *korban Pesach*.[2]

Question 297

When I go through the Haggada, I see no logical "order" at all. So why do we call it a Seder (meaning "order")?

The word *Seder* comes from the Hebrew verb *lesader*, "to arrange," and its Aramaic root cognate (*samech, daled, resh*) forms the basis of religiosity – e.g., *Siddur*, the daily prayer book; *Sidra*, the weekly Torah portion; *Sedarim*, the six sections of the Mishna; *Seder mo'ed*, the "order of the Festivals," etc. – and is also the source for modern Hebrew expressions of order – e.g., *sadran*

---

2. Rambam, *Hilchot Chametz Umatza*; *Pesachim* 116.

for "usher," *seder hayom*, the day's "agenda," and the popular colloquial *hakol beseder*, "everything's gonna be alright!"

I can understand how the Seder's very eclectic recipe – throw in some sections of the Mishna with some Tanach passages, then stir in some halachic Midrashim, add some narrative and serve with prayers and songs – can make one ask, *Ma haseder shebaseder?* "Where's the order in the order?" However, there *is* consistency and a coherent structure in the Haggada's overall educational aim of the evening, *vehigadeta*, "And you shall tell." Although juxtaposed and oftentimes running parallel with each other, the Haggada is divided into four central pedagogic ingredients – not surprising, since the number *four* is predominant on this night! The four are:

1) Questions (e.g., *Ma Nishtana*, the four sons)
2) Vivid stories (e.g., *Avadim Hayinu, MiTechila, Arami Oved Avi*)
3) An obligation to say *lefichach*, "Thanks" (e.g., *Baruch HaMakom, Baruch Shomer*).
4) Praise (e.g., *Dayenu, Hallel*).

The Malbim, a preeminent Russian Torah scholar of the nineteenth century, breaks the Haggada into six sections by splitting the only verse in the Torah (*Vehigadata levincha bayom hahu lemor, ba'avur zeh asa Hashem li betzeiti miMitzrayim*) that requires parents to tell their children about the Exodus without waiting to be asked into six parts: *vehigadata levincha; bayom hahu; lemor; ba'avur zeh; asa Hashem li; betzeiti miMitzrayim*. Traditionally, the *seder* of the Seder consists of fifteen sections of spiritual awakening (*hitorerut*), starting with *Kadesh* (*kiddush* on the first cup of wine) and ending with *Nirtza* (singing "Next

Year in Jerusalem!"). It begins with *begnut* and ends in *beshevach*, from denigration ("our forefathers were idol worshipers") to praise ("now God brought us to Sinai to serve him").

Why is the Haggada structured in such a way? Because of human nature: you can only fully appreciate what you have when you consider what you have lost (from spiritual-physical slavery to spiritual-physical freedom).

Question 298

I know how to tell the story of how we got out of Egypt, but shouldn't I also say something about how we got there in the first place?

Absolutely – and it can take less than a minute! Try this: the foundation of Pesach, the anniversary of our Declaration of National Independence, began with seven people. From one couple (Abraham and Sarah), their son and daughter-in-law (Isaac and Rebecca), and their son and daughters-in-law (Jacob, Rachel and Leah), we made the leap from individuals to a family, and then a people. Due to a severe local famine, Jacob, his wives and family (now numbering seventy), were forced to leave Israel (*yerida*) and migrate to Egypt. There, over centuries, they dramatically grew in size (to three million) and prospered so successfully as to be perceived as a threat to their hosts. Admiration turned to contempt; freedom to oppression. Oppression caught the attention of God...and now you are ready to recount the tale of the Exodus!

Question 299

Who is "the Aramean" to whom the Haggada refers?

If you read the phrase literally, *Arami oved avi*[3] means, "my father was a wandering Aramean," which would refer to either Abraham or Jacob, both wandering Jews. However, our rabbis see it differently and translate *oved* as "destroy" (i.e., *Arami eebaid avi*, "an Aramean tried to destroy my father!"). Why? The Midrash points an accusatory finger at Lavan, Jacob's uncle (his mother's brother), and identifies him, and not Pharaoh, as the central evil character of Pesach. His desire to kill Jews was sneaky and deceptive ("trickery"), and thus he was to be feared much more than an overt Pharaoh who never hid his anti-Jewish intentions.

In order to make it clear to all how appalling Lavan was, the rabbis of the Mishna (who want to sever all possible family connections with the Arameans) makes it obligatory that the Seder participants discuss the *"Arami oved avi"* passage in depth and in detail.

Question 300

In the Haggada, is God portrayed as being masculine or feminine?

Neither. The Torah and Haggada speak of God as "Him" even as other texts confer both masculine and feminine attributes

---

3.   Deuteronomy 26:5–8; *Pesachim* 10:4.

of love. Tehillim compares His compassion to that of "a father" for his children, whilst Isaiah compares His comfort to that of "a mother" for her child.[4] The Kabbalah frequently switches genders, emphasizing both male-female aspects, although Jewish mystics seem to tilt, allegorically, towards His feminine attributes.

Question 301

What does hare hunting have to do with the Haggada?

I assume you are referring to the *kiddush* page in the famous medieval Haggada with its scenes of hare hunting. If Pesach begins on *motzei Shabbat*, we say both *kiddush* and *havdala*, but in which order? The Talmud[5] gives the sequence as *yayin, kiddush, ner, havdala, zeman*; in short, *Yak-n'-haz*, which resembled the German expression, *Jagt den Hasen*, "hunt the hare." And so creative Jewish artisans illustrated the *kiddush* in Haggadot and *machzorim* with hunting scenes.

Question 302

Must I read the Haggada in Hebrew?

Since the obligation is to understand the story of the Exodus, you should conduct a Seder in the language understood by the participants. (Sedarim are still conducted in Ladino, Yiddish, etc.).

---

4. Psalms 103:13; Isaiah 66:13.
5. *Pesachim* 102b.

Question 303

How important was Aramaic to the Jews?

It was very important! Even today, a Jewish child's first Israeli words (*abba, imma*) are Aramaic! This three-millennia-old Proto-Semitic tongue was the *lingua franca* of the masses of Palestine Jews, and was the second most important language in the Assyrian Empire, maintaining its prominent position during the Babylonian and Persian Empires until it was supplanted by the rise of Islam and Arabic.

The Midrash refers to Aramaic as "Sursi" (in Greek it is called "Surisit," the language of Syria), whilst our rabbis (Shmuel ben Nahman) warned the Jew not to hold Sursi "lightly in your eyes." The Haggada bypasses God's own language (Hebrew) and begins its storytelling workshop in Aramaic (*Halachma Anya*, "this is the bread of affliction"). And the Hebrew texts are packed with Aramaic parallels in vocabulary, grammar and phonetic systems. Often, one need only replace the Hebrew *shin* with a *taf* to get its Aramaic equivalent (e.g., "ox" is *shor* in Hebrew, *tor* in Aramaic; "eight" is *shmoneh* in Hebrew, *tamnei* in Aramaic, etc.).

What are the first Aramaic words in the Torah? *Yegar sahaduta*,[6] uttered during Jacob's negotiations with his Aramaic father-in-law (Lavan). More than three chapters of Ezra, and five chapters of Daniel, are all written in Aramaic. For many generations, Aramaic was referred to as "Chaldean," a term no

---

6.   Genesis 31:47.

longer in use[7] (the Qumran discovery unearthed the earliest known Aramaic translations from the second generation BCE). The Jews of Babylon even replaced their national Hebraic script (called *ktav d'etz*, the "wooden script") with Aramaic letters, still in use today. Today's Yemenite Jews still have a *meturgaman* (translator) who recites the Targum in Aramaic after the Hebrew Torah reading.

Question 304

What does *karpas* mean?

Etymologically, *karpas* is a very difficult word to translate. Why? Because it has two meanings. It's either a vegetable (celery, parsley) or a piece of cotton or fine linen (the word *pasim* comes from *ketonet pasim*, Joseph's multicolored garment, an expression of *karpas* and *techelet*, green/light blue wool or linen). The symbol of *karpas*, which is a totally separate independent element of the Seder (a type of "external prop") was specifically placed before the mitzva of "telling" (*sippur yetziat Mitzrayim*) in order to give the head of the household the chance to start with a preamble as to how the Jews got into Egypt in the first place. It was Jacob's gift to his son Joseph of this multicolored garment that led to sibling jealousy, and a chain of events that saw Joseph sold off into Egypt. Some ancient Jewish communities would dip (*metabbel*) a torn piece of cloth, indicative of Joseph's *ketonet pasim*, into a red-colored *karpas* (suggestive of the fake blood Joseph's brothers spilled on the garment and showed to their grief-stricken father).

---

7.   *Midrash Genesis Rabba*, 84, 14; *Megilla* 4; *Mishna* 4.

The Talmud[8] describes this strange act (*kedei sheyishalu hatinokot*) as a stimulant, a catalyst to get children's curious juices bubbling so they will ask questions. Jewish mystics, fascinated by the idea that every Hebrew word or letter are linguistic repositories for holy concepts, breaks the word *karpas* into its four letters (*kaf, reish, peh, samech*) to arrive at four words which they claim guide a Jew's capacity for giving. The first letter (*kaf*) symbolizes the palm of the hand, the next letter (*reish*) suggests a poor person; when merged, we visualize an open benevolent hand extended out to help the needy. And what if you yourself are poor? The next letter (*peh*) means, "mouth," and the final letter (*samech*) means "to support." In other words, if you can't help with money, help with empathy; words of kindness, compassion, friendship and concern also help to encourage and uplift the impoverished spirit.

Question 305

The *Hallel* we say on Pesach doesn't seem to be the same as the rest-of-the-year *Hallel*. Why is that?

Two reasons: first, we say it at night (an exception to a Mishna that tells us we can only say it by day),[9] and second, we take a meal-break in the middle.

Hallel on Pesach is different, and it's different for a reason. How do we know? Because when the Talmud[10] defines the times

---

8.   *Pesachim* 114a.
9.   *Megilla* 20b.
10. *Arachin* 10a, b.

when *Hallel*, or half-*Hallel*, must be said (the key components are a chag and the presence of a miracle),[11] it simply ignores the *Hallel* of Pesach night, an absence that conspicuously and automatically places it in a different category. The Talmud even ignores a previous Mishna[12] which made it clear that *Hallel was* said at the *korban Pesach*!

The Ramban disagrees, and sees no difference between the nighttime Pesach *Hallel* and the laws of *Hallel* in general, which require a *bracha*. But there is no general consensus. The Ritva, Re'ah,[13] Rabbenu Tam,[14] the Tosafot, Rav Chaim Brisker,[15] and the Shulchan Aruch[16] agree with the Ramban; but Rabbi Yehuda, Ri Migash, Rav Yitzchak Zev Soloveitchik (the Griz) and Rav Hai Gaon disagree. The Griz maintains that *Hallel* is different on Pesach because it is interrupted by a meal; Rav Hai Gaon believes that *Hallel* in its Pesach context is seen as a spontaneous, non-obligatory outburst of *shira*, "song."[17]

Question 306

Why don't we say full *Hallel* on Pesach?

The Talmud gives a reason: unlike Succot, where each day is considered a separate chag, each daily Pesach sacrifice is identi-

11. *Pesachim* 116b, 117b,
12. Ibid., 95a.
13. *Succa* 21.
14. *Berachot* 14a.
15. Brisker Rav, quoted in *Shiurim Lezecher Abba Mori*.
16. *Orach Chayim* 487.
17. *Tosafot* 6; Hai Gaon, *Teshuvot Hageonim, Sha'arei Teshuva* 102; Griz, *Hilchot Chanuka* 3:6; Ri Migash, *Teshuva* 44.

cal.[18] But the more popular answer comes to us courtesy of a famous Midrash in which God responds to Shmuel ben Abba, *Ma'asei yadai tove'im bayam, ve'atem omrim shira?* "My handiwork is drowning in the sea, and you would recite song?"[19] God's sad and disillusioned words are echoed by the moral standards of a Mishna in *Pirkei Avot* and Proverbs (*Benefol oivecha al tismach*, "Do not gloat at the fall of your enemy").[20]

Question 307

Why is the Seder the only Torah mitzva that must be performed specifically at night?

Because it all happened at midnight! Don Isaac Abravanel, the Spanish Torah statesman, was struck by how thin a line there was between slavery and freedom; all it took was a "stroke of midnight." Remember: the only plague, the last one that God actually performs...is at night! Jewish history is replete with nighttime dramas: Abraham achieved victory only after he divided his company "that night"; God judged the king of Gerar "at night," and He frightened Lavan "in the midst of the night." Israel wrestled with an angel, prevailing "at night," and the armies of Sisera were miraculously swept away "by the night stars." When were the Assyrian armies besieging Jerusalem stricken? Yep, "at night," and Bel was overthrown in the "dark of the night." Daniel had God's mysteries revealed to him "at night." The King

---

18. *Arakhin* 10a–b; Rabbi Yehiel Mikhel Epstein, *Aruch haShulchan*.
19. *Pesichta deRav Kahana*; Midrash *Harninu*.
20. Proverbs 24:17.

of Babylon (Belshazzar) was slain "at night" (after becoming drunk from the holy vessels). And Purim-time? Remember how Haman penned his edicts of hate "at night," and Judaic victory came about through the night sleeplessness of Achashverus?

So when Isaiah calls out to the Heavens, "Watchman what of the night?"[21] Rashi describes "nighttime" as the "domain of the destroying agencies." The Zohar agrees: nighttime is a "barren dust that rules over Israel, who are prostrate to it."[22] And so our rabbis composed *Hashkivenu*, a prayer that God protect Jews from the terrors of nightfall, a plea based on pure precedence: all thirteen events, as compiled by the Beit Halevi and listed in the lyrics of *Vayehi bachatzi halayla*, take place on Pesach eve, *at night!* This convinced Jewish mystics that the final redemption, an event which will be "as clear as day" (*u'keor boker yizrach shemesh*), would appear during the darkness, when all hope seems lost; at a time of heightened fear, insecurity, deep anxiety. Why? So that the Jew could awake to the light and confidence of a new world order, and know no more of the dark, inauspicious, "it-came-to-pass-at-midnight" dread.

Question 308

Is the *aggada* of the Haggada just legend or should it be taken more seriously?

Dismiss it at your own risk, for *aggada*, "narration," derived from the Aramaic root, *ngd* ("to flow"), is indispensable to Judaism. Its imaginative narrative, homiletic material, free-floating

---

21. Exodus 21, 11.
22. Rashi, Exodus 12:22; *Baba Kama* 60b; Psalms 90:14.

metaphors and heavily annotated parables flow with such spirit and dazzle that it is a Judaic teaching tool *par excellence*. As an end product of Midrash, *aggada* is a (non-halachic)[23] vehicle of aspiration through which each individual Jew can "understand," rather than be forced to accept, Halacha.

Those who were its masters (such Palestinian *Amoraim* as Rabbis Yonathan, Abba bar Kahana, Tanchuma), known as *Rabba De'aggadata*, "Rabbis of the Aggada," were determined to utilize this method to ensure ethics were part of their teacher-student Torah curriculum (known as *shimush hachamim*, "serving the learned").[24] Traditional Judaism doesn't hesitate to use *aggada* as a character-building tool to lead Jews to predetermined moral truths and spiritual conclusions, hoping, along the way, to inject the trio of faith-wisdom-ethics as the Torah's sole *Weltanschauung*[25] – "wisdom" defined not as being wise in thought and knowledge but wisdom in good actions (i.e., doing the "right thing"). In fact, without it, we wouldn't have such central Torah concepts as reward and punishment in the afterlife, the nature of prophecy, and the coming of the Messiah.

And yet, it is true! *Aggada* contains exaggerations and contradictions, which led to an early argument as to whether it should even be reduced to writing ("Anyone recording it has no share in the world to come," announced Yehoshua ben Levi, third-century CE *Amora*, adding, "and whoever uses a written copy for teaching it is liable to excommunication!").[26] But his colleagues (Rabbi Yochanan, Resh Lakish) won the argument,

---

23. *Peah* II:6.
24. *Ma'aserot* I:2.
25. Psalms 119:86.
26. *Gittin* 60a; *Shabbat* 16:1; *Ma'aserot* III:4; *Chagiga* 14a.

convinced that it wasn't worth depriving future generations of the opportunity to learn "the message." The result? *Aggada* occupies about thirty percent of the Talmud.

The final word goes to the Rambam: "*Aggada* cannot always be taken literally; rather, it must be interpreted with the understanding that a higher truth is being alluded to...Thus, it does not matter that the medium used for its expression is inexplicable. What is important is the philosophical or ethical truth that underlies the story."

Question 309

Isn't the Seder night plea, "Pour out Your wrath upon the nations," a little bit harsh?

No. This is not a prayer *per se* but simply a collection of four verses[27] from the twelfth century, written during a time of unspeakable medieval persecutions. But why is it in the Haggada? Because the worst pogroms always occurred around Pesach-Easter time. The bitterness, cruelty and brutality left in its wake helpless Jews who turned to God to arise and confront the evil before them, those who had "devoured Jacob and laid waste his dwelling place." Remember: Jews could not strike back, so they "prayed back" – seeking not vengeance but intercession – briefly interrupting the joy of a Seder, and prior to resuming the thanksgiving of *Hallel*, to remind all of the darker side of Jewish history.

---

27.   Psalms 79:6–7, 69:25; *Eicha* 3:66.

This jolting interruption makes its first appearance in a Haggada in around 1100, in the Ashkenaz *Machzor Vitri*, a massive collection of prayers and commentary that was compiled by the Torah students of Rashi after the traumatic First Crusade[28] (the first time in Jewish history when entire communities killed themselves and their children in order to escape forced conversion). In fact, today's description is a shorter, *edited* version of the more extensive denouncement of tormentors in the *Machzor Vitri*. Later rabbis reduced the expressions of vengeance to "four," a number heavily associated with Pesach.

Jewish history cast its shadow, forcing certain decimated Jewish communities to "retell" the story of Haggada not in unadulterated reclining joy but in sadness, tears and angst, as strikingly articulated by the pathos of this medieval French Hebrew poet...

> In the Egyptian Passover,
> my captives went free.
> In the Passover for the ages,
> harsh rulers swallowed us.
> Turn toward me and see!
> In the Egyptian Passover,
> You redeemed Your people mightily.
> In the Passover for the ages,
> I was silenced by Your wrath.
> Turn toward me and see!
> In the Egyptian Passover,
> You smote every one of their firstborn.
> In the Passover for the ages,

28. 1096.

my own offspring conspired to undo me.
Turn toward me and see!
In the Egyptian Passover,
each household sacrificed a lamb.
In the Passover for the ages,
desert wolves devoured it.
Turn toward me and see![29]

Question 310

Exactly what "crime" did the fourth son commit to get such a bad rap, and be labelled a rasha ("wicked one")?

The answer lies in how this son phrases his question: "What does this service mean to you?" The wicked son takes himself out of the equation by stressing, "to you." This displays a selfish segregation from society, denying a fundamental principle of Hillel. *Al tifrosh min hatzibbur*, "Do not separate yourself from the community."[30] The son is thus "wicked" in his attitude, language, tone of voice; his is an *exclusionary* statement, one of division, making him an enemy of Judaic unity, a *kofer be'ikar*, a "denier of the foundations of Judaism."

The question is obvious: sure, loyalty and solidarity are great virtues, but why does the Torah go so far as to call him a *rasha*? There is no specific prohibition against disunity. The Vilna Gaon attempts to answer this question by examining the wise son's question: "What are the laws which God has com-

---

29.   Daniel Goldschmidt, *Haggada*.
30.   *Avot* 2:5.

manded you?" In this question, the wise son clearly acknowledges the presence of God, while the wicked son completely removes God from the equation. Excluding God in this way is what makes this boy "wicked."

But wait: doesn't the "wise" son also use the same directive, "What are the testimonies which God has given *you*?" Yes, but he includes "God" in his search for answers, making his phraseology a sincere quest for knowledge.

Question 311

Why is the Seder conducted at home and not in the shul?

Our rabbis wisely made the premier Pesach activity, the Seder *tisch*, "a family affair," one held at home, at night, rather than in the synagogue. This festival thus became one of sharing and kinship, brilliantly bonding Jews not only internally (to their own families) but externally as well to the larger family of their scattered people. This Judaic camaraderie made it inconceivable that one would stay home alone for a Seder or leave one's own family to attend another's Seder, even though both acts are halachically permissible. (Rabbi Eliezer even rebuked his own pupil, Rabbi Illai, for leaving his family to spend time with him, his teacher.)[31] It is this emphasis on togetherness, of belonging, the most intimate of all human experiences, that has contributed to Pesach's longevity and explains why ninety-two percent of unaffiliated American Jews still attend a Seder every year, despite the otherwise blatant apathy to all things Jewish.

31. *Succa* 27b.

Question 312

Why do we "double dip"? Isn't once enough?

The most obvious answer? To arouse the curiosity of children. Hopefully the unusual sight of dipping bitter herbs into sweet *charoset* and (relatively sweet) parsley into saltwater will motivate questions and answers, the primary goal of Pesach. An esoteric reason? When the enslaved Jews, based on an order from God, dipped hyssop into the paschal lamb's blood, they did so as a symbol of redemption. Jewish mystics embrace the admixture of sweet and bitter as creating just the right mood (and dual motif) for the *Seder tisch*, the sourness of slavery and the sweetness of redemption.

When we dip *karpas* into saltwater, and then again, matza and maror into *charoset*, we also have an opportunity to reflect that perhaps, through the tears and bitterness, there is a ray of hope and optimism, that the experience of Jewish history is made up of a bittersweet recipe. The second dip? This allows us to pause and not just dwell on the (sad) taste of experience, but also flavor the sweetness of the future.

Question 313

Every mitzva has a blessing, right?

Wrong. An example? There is no blessing for saying the Haggada, a premier mitzva. Why? This is a mitzva of memory ("remember the day when you came forth from Egypt") that has neither a limit nor a quantifiable measure, extending to *"all the days* of your life."[32] Therefore it's just like endless prayer, which, incidentally, also doesn't require a blessing!

There are those who believe that we *do* say a *bracha* on the Haggada with the opening *kiddush* (which contains references to going out from Egypt). For the most intriguing reason we turn to the Chatam Sofer who compares the Haggada to the laws of conversion, whereby one doesn't say a blessing until *after mikva* immersion, and reminds us that the Pesach story begins with a blunt reminder: "In the beginning our forefathers were idol worshipers...." Thus, we aren't *officially* "Jewish" until the *end* of the story, when the Haggada has us saying the final blessing, "Blessed are You...who has redeemed Israel." Meanwhile, the Sfat Emet considers a person exempt from saying blessings on all "rational" mitzvot (e.g., *tzedaka, bikkur cholim*), and being freed from slavery is as rational as rational can get!

However, although there is no explicit *bracha* on recit-ing the Haggada, there is a quasi-blessing (*Baruch haMakom, Baruch Hu; Baruch shenatan Torah le'amo Yisrael, Baruch Hu*) at the beginning of the "four sons" that emphasizes its special mode of Torah study (*Talmud Torah*) – note how the word *baruch* appears four times! It resembles the morning *birkat haTorah* blessing that is said before studying Torah, and just before getting an *aliya*. What's the difference between these two blessing? The Haggadah replaces God's Name (*Shem uMalchut* (i.e., *Melech ha'Olam*) with "*HaMakom.*"

---

32.   Deuteronomy 16:3.

Question 314

Why doesn't the Haggada mention the name of Moses?

Moses is left out of the Haggada (except for one isolated reference) because the rabbis knew, from (Christian) experience, the dangers of idealizing one man. This is why, Rabbi Samson Raphael Hirsch explains, the Torah describes in great detail the birth of Moses, "to teach us that Moses, the man of God and the greatest of all prophets, also was born as all others, and not in any supernatural fashion." Likewise when Moses dies, we are told that "Moses died, as does all flesh and blood!"

Moses is also absent from the Hagadda in order to stress that what happened was only due to Divine intervention (God brought us out – not by the hand of an angel, not by the hand of a seraph, not by the hand of a messenger!"). This is the reason for Moses' early stutter, notes Rabbenu Nissim, in order that all recognize that his influence came not from great oratory or demagoguery, but from the Divine Presence who spoke "through him" despite his all-too-human speech impediment. In general, the Torah and rabbinic literature shy away from the notion of celebrating Jewish heroes. In fact, declare the Sages, if it hadn't been Moses, someone else would have come along. The Haggada directs all its attention on God as the Liberator, and not His agents ("I and *not* an angel, I and *not* a seraph, I and *not* a messenger, I alone").

In the portion of *Tetzaveh*, the Torah seems to go out of its way to omit Moses, referring to (maybe) him as "you" ("And *you* [whoever *'you'* is meant to be] command the Children of

Israel...")[33] Is this gratitude for everything Moses did for God and the Jews? No. And since it is Moses himself writing, under God's direction, the actual Torah words, why not protest against this deliberate omission of his name? It's true: he's no egotist ("Moses was the humblest of men").[34] Jewish history doesn't depend on brave supermen or any individual champion to bring about redemption. Why? Because God left it up to you and me, to the power of mind, spirit and conscience of the individual, the Jew who conducts a Seder here, shakes a *lulav* there, and educates Jewish children in Torah and mitzvot. Now, there's a Jewish hero!

Question 315

What's the source of having *charoset* at the table? Doesn't it seem like a waste? We never eat from it, and only use it for dipping purposes! Why not just eat the maror straight?

Yes, at first glance, *charoset* seems to play a secondary role, just something to dip bitter herbs in. Its inclusion on the Seder table is derived from a two-line Mishna and follow-up explanation,[35] but, other than its educational value for the children present ("Why are we dipping?"), it still remains a bit of a mystery. Tosafot and Rashi saw it as a health precaution (obviously the *charoset* in their times was more "potent" than it is today),

---

33.   Exodus 27:20.
34.   Numbers 12:5.
35.   *Pesachim* 10:3, 116a.

neutralizing, either by smell or by dipping, the *kapa* poisonous bug in the maror.

The reason for *charoset?* It provides a balance, it "sweetens" the bitterness, adds hope to despair, and reiterates the Judaic longing for life. And so traditional recipes all seem to "marry" the sweet (apples, wine) with the bitter (vinegar, chestnuts).

So, is *charoset* a mitzva? Yes, say Rabbis Eliezer ben Tzadok, Yochanan (it's a reminder of *zecher latit*, "mortar") and Levi (it's a reminder of the *tapuach*. What's a *tapuach?* I don't know; maybe, based on Rashi's explanation, it's the apple from the *Shir Hashirim?*).[36] Ben Tzadok recalls how the Jerusalem storekeepers would yell out, "Come and buy your spices for the mitzva [of *charoset*.]" Rabbi Moshe Shternbuch claims the mitzva is just to have it on the table. Do we say a *bracha* over *charoset?* Yes, says the Rambam.[37] Is there a minimum requirement? Yes, eat a *kezayit* worth. Is there a traditional recipe? Yes. "It must be thick, like mortar," notes Abaye, "and tart, like apples!" Greek Jews crushed dates and nuts until they had a mortar-like thickness, and then added pears to match the color of brick.

Question 316

I'm ready to start conducting my own Seder. Any tips?

Yes, just follow the order (*seder*) in the Haggada. There are fifteen steps. Who decided on this number? We're not sure, but it dates to the eleventh century and could be Rashi, or one of

---

36. Song of Songs 8:5; *Sota* 11b.
37. Rambam, commentary on the Mishna.

the many Tosafot scholars who flourished in northern France and the Rhineland in the early Middle Ages. The "fifteen" start with *kiddush* and end with songs of praise, *Hallel*, and *Nirtza*'s concluding declaration, "This year we were in foreign lands and were slaves, but hopefully next year we will be in Jerusalem for the building of the Third Temple and experiencing the ultimate redemption of the Jewish people and of all humankind."

Question 317

Why is the wicked son included in the Haggada if there is a rabbinic adage that one must not teach Torah to a wicked person?

This rabbinic belief, that one must not teach Torah to a *rasha* (wicked person), out of fear that the knowledge would be used against Jews, only applies to the *apikores*, and, in any event, is supplanted by the auspicious mitzva of *Maggid*. But what did the wicked son do that was so evil? He separated himself from his community. But, says the Rebbe of Ropczycer, the wise one misunderstands. "Removing yourself from your people is not a unilateral decision. We say to this wayward son, 'You might think you're no longer part of the family, but our tradition includes you in our Seder anyway. We have a seat at the table waiting for you, right here next to your brothers. Join us and say your piece. We make room on the inside even for the outsider.'"

Question 318

Out of the four sons, who deserves the most attention?

The Hebrew prophets were most upset at those who failed to ask, "Where is God?"[38] – their wrath especially reserved for Torah teachers, *kohanim*, etc., who pretended that they already knew all the answers. "I made myself available to those who did not inquire," complains Yirmiyahu, "I said, 'Here I am,' to a nation that did not call My name!"[39] The child who doesn't know how to ask merits the most attention. The Haggada's goal is to nudge each child towards the boundaries of their understanding, and help them overcome these limitations by posing questions. The wise son is defined as such not because he possesses such great wisdom, but because he realizes that he still has a long way to go, and is willing to question *within* the framework of Jewish law.

Question 319

What's the father's role in the scenario of the four sons?

What is often overlooked is that there may be multiple sons, but usually only *one* father. That there be one respondent, one learned role-model within the family structure who can answer all of the questions is critical when the "four sons" saga is seen in the context of pure pedagogic directives (*chinuch*). The Jewish

---

38. *Yishayahu* 2:6, 8.
39. Ibid., 65:1.

continuity represented by the Seder desperately depends on a father who can simultaneously field the microquestions from his "wise" son as efficiently as dealing with his quarrelsome "wicked" son, simplistic "simple" son, and from the son who does not know to ask. In the art of outreach, there is no one "right" answer to every question. In fact, not all Torah responses are eternal; the Haggada cautions against using the four sons as Exhibit A, emphasizing that answers must be fashioned according to the background and attitude of the seeker, whether wise beyond his years or a complete ignoramus, a simple simpleton or one who knows everything – except how to ask.

And more! By advising the father to start thinking of Pesach a few weeks earlier ("We ask about and discuss the laws of Pesach for thirty days before Pesach"),[40] the Haggada recognizes the need to be prepared (this is why the response to the wicked son, "It is for this that God acted for me," doesn't come from the same Torah portion, but from another section, the knowledge of which requiring preparation). Ad-hoc replies are too dangerous, the Torah warns, which is why it words the verse, "When your son asks you *tomorrow* [not *today!*]." In other words, be prepared!

Question 320

Who wrote the Haggada?

I don't know. This classic composition of the history of the Jews was verbally transmitted until around 300 BCE, when the Men of the Great Assembly reduced it to writing. Thus we know

40. *Pesachim* 6a.

that basic parts of it (the context of a parent-child dialogue) already existed during the Second Temple times. However, it has been lengthened and added to and expanded to such a great extent over the years that it's now impossible to credit it to any one person.

The rabbis of the Mishna, who refer to it as *aggadeta*, because of its multiple homiletic sayings and Midrashim (*aggadot*), were the first to compile content and a framework of instructions to the "order" (*seder*) of the Seder.[41] These Sages, who lived around 100 BCE (around the time of Hillel) to 200 CE, were called *Tannaim* ("teachers"), plural for *Tanna*, from the Aramaic verb "to study" or "repeat." These scholars, including such high-powered names as Rabbis Yochanan Ben Zakkai, Shimon Bar Yochai, Akiva, and especially Yehudah HaNassi ("Judah the Prince"), were *the* recognized authorities of the "Oral Law" which preceded the "Written Law" by forty years (and is about fifty times larger). The Haggada format began in fluidity, and continued in that way until the "Great Rabbis" (*Geonim*) of the ninth- and tenth-century CE Babylonian yeshivot of Sura and Pumbedita decided that a more "stable" Haggada text was essential.

The first complete Haggada appears in the tenth-century *Saadia Gaon Siddur* of the Sura rosh yeshiva ("borrowing" heavily from the *Mechilta*, a rabbinic commentary on the Book of Exodus, and the *Sifre*, a similar commentary on Numbers and Deuteronomy). An earlier, incomplete Haggada can be found in the *Seder of Amram Gaon*, a top ninth-century Torah scholar in Sura, whose manuscript is the oldest order of Jewish prayers in existence.

---

41.   *Pesachim* 10; 116.

How does Rav Amram's Haggada differ from today's? Significantly! It's a relatively petite "after-dinner-type" liturgy. So when did it expand? The former grew considerably after the horrifying European Crusades; its format during the time of the Rambam's[42] *Mishneh Torah* is basically the same as it is today, although a lot of the songs were "tacked on" later by German-Polish Jews during medieval times. The Haggada, always part of the *siddur* or *machzor* (as in the twelfth-century *machzor* of Rabbi Simcha of Vitri, a pupil of Rashi) came out on its own merit in the thirteenth century replete with beautiful illustrations.

Question 321

Why does *Leshana Haba b'Yerushalayim,* "Next year in Jerusalem" seem to be tacked on to the end of the Haggada?

Because it was. Originally, the Seder was a festive banquet held in the holy land when the first and second Temples stood in Jerusalem. Their theme was simply to recall the Exodus and give thanks to God. However, after the Romans decided that the destruction of Jerusalem and the Second Temple[43] was some kind of noble act, the Pesach Seder theme shifted, its focus of prayer and hope expanding to not just redemption, but also a "return" redemption to the land of Israel. Thus *Leshana Haba b'Yerushalayim* was added as an annual reminder of the centrality of Jerusalem to Jewish thought.

---

42.   1135–1204.
43.   70 CE.

So why do those in Jerusalem say it? Because Jerusalem refers not just to a geographic location, but to a spiritual ideal. Remember: the Torah ends with the Jews still in the desert, still wandering, still seeking the ultimate spiritual home, Jerusalem. (This is the genesis of the custom to leave a corner of the Jewish home unpainted, a reminder that our permanent "home" is still coming; in fact, the nineteenth-century *mussar* movement saw dozens of Jews in "voluntary exile," bizarrely wandering across Europe, stressing the elusiveness of "home.")

Question 322

What do herbs, shank bone and roasted eggs symbolize?

Herbs, consisting of either romaine lettuce or horseradish, commemorate the harsh conditions of slavery (because of their sharp, bitter taste). Since the time of the destruction of the Second Temple in Jerusalem in 70 CE by the Romans, the slaughtering of a paschal lamb was replaced by the roasting of a hard-boiled egg and the shank bone, which are two of the symbolic foods on the Passover Seder plate. (Samaritans in Nablus still slaughter lambs on Mount Gerizim on the 14th of Nissan. However this is halachically unacceptable.) The shank bone stands for the sacrificial lamb (*zeroa*).

In my home we eat hard-boiled eggs right at the beginning of the Pesach Seder meal. Why? I don't know. The egg is a religious symbol in nearly every culture (because of its oval, round circular shape, which symbolizes life and eternity); the Talmud even has a tractate called *Beitza* ("egg"), which deals with the use of eggs laid on Jewish festivals (perhaps it's a symbol of the festival offering, *chagiga*). The size of an egg is often used as a halachic guide to measures (e.g., the *kiddush* cup must have the capacity of one and a half eggs). When my mother would shop in pre-war Poland she would search for a *"beitza,"* an egg-size of oil. Abudarham, a fourteenth-century expert on the *siddur*, thought the roasted egg custom derived from its Aramaic translation, *be'ah*, which resembles *ba'a*, "desire," in that God was desirous of redeeming Israel. Others link it to the mourner's practice of eating eggs after a funeral; still others claim it's simply a leftover of the typical *hors d'oeuvre* in Roman banquets.

Question 323

What's the purpose of *Koso shel Eliyahu*, the "Fifth Cup"?

Chronologically, this invisible seventh-century BCE prophet, Elijah (*Eliyahu HaNavi*), has nothing to do with the Exodus, since he lived some 600 years after the time of Moses. What then does he have to do with Pesach? The Talmud was at an impasse. The rabbis couldn't agree if Jews should drink four or five cups of wine, so they decided to pour a fifth cup and *not* drink from it – thus deferring the answer until, according to tradition, Elijah makes his pre-Messianic return to answer all of history's open-ended Judaic disputes, stalemates, problems and inconsistencies. Whenever these "hard questions" appear, the Torah text concludes with the word *teyku*, derived from the Hebrew root *kum*, which denotes, "let it stand," or from *tik*, a "file." Thus the term *teyku* suggests, "File it away!" Jewish mystics see *teyku* as the synonym of *Tishbi y'taretz kushiyot veba'ayot*, "Elijah the Tishbite will resolve all problems and difficulties" (Tishbite referring to Elijah's birthplace, the village of Tishbe in Gil'ad, north of the River Yabbok).[44]

That is why so many Yiddish folksongs have been composed in his honor as the harbinger of unity, salvation and consolation, expressing love and longing, sung when the Pesach doors are flung open or at the closing of the Shabbat. That hope springs eternal in the human breast is why Elijah's annual comings and goings left in their wake a contagious symbol of enthusiasm and expectation for a better world, for the light of liberty, for an indomitable Judaic optimism.

Question 324

Am I allowed to ask a question to which there's no answer, or is this blasphemy?

No, it's not irreverent to ask. During *Havdala* we sing, "There is no one like our God" but then continue on with, "*Who* is like our God?" The sequence is critical. First comes a declaration of faith, immediately followed by a line of questioning. It was the same "order" (*seder*) at Sinai: *Na'aseh venishma* was a cry to "do" first, "hear" later. Hear what? The answers to our questions on faith. For in a religion that requires challenge and response, and frowns on intellectual complacency, blind faith is an anomaly. To hear is to understand, to understand is to triumph over all doubt. Judaism recognizes "eternal questions" (*she'elot hanetzach*)

---

44. 1 Kings 17:1.

that have no final, definitive answers. In fact, the texts are full of
partial answers, deductions, guesses and speculation.

Does this mean, as that Yiddish adage goes, *M'darf nicht
fregen*, "we shouldn't even ask?" Absolutely not! There is a long
accepted tradition to search for *ta'amei hamitzvot*, "reasons for
the commandments." Even the greatest of minds still grapple
with "eternity" which, by its very definition, is eternal. The
Torah contemplated this conundrum and created an internal
mechanism for all the "too-hard-to-solve" problems. Elijah, the
experienced prophet-Sage who ascended bodily into Heaven,
was given a timeless job. To return at the time of Redemption
(preferably during the Seder itself) to answer all of history's
unanswerable questions,[45] in order "to bring agreement where
there is dispute [to ensure harmony and] peace in the world."[46]
That is why, when Talmudic debates are left open-ended, the text
concludes with the word *teyku*, an acronym for *Tishbi y'taretz
kush'yot veba'ayot*, "Elijah the Tishbite will resolve all problems
and difficulties."

Question 325

Is the Seder meal the most important "mitzva meal" of the year?

Jewish law insists that every Shabbat, chag, erev Yom Kippur and
erev Tisha b'Av[47] has a *seudat mitzva*; however it is the Pesach
Seder that is the ultimate halachic, and communal-fellowship,

---

45.   11 Kings 2:11.
46.   *Eduyot* 8:7; *Malachi* 4:5.
47.   Rambam, *Hilchot Yom Tov*, 6:16–18.

meal *par excellence.* This meal is the only one that comes with a specific interrelated text (Haggada); it has basic rules (e.g., one must "provide for the stranger, orphan, widow, needy" – not just to get a good meal, but to help each Jew fulfill the mitzva of "seeing himself as if he personally went out of Egypt," an impossible feat if you're not sitting at a table nibbling on the "bread of affliction"). The Jew who "locks his door and eats alone with his family," writes the Rambam (noting how man is the only creature that can "sit down" and eat), "has no *simcha* of mitzva, only *simcha* of his stomach!"

Question 326

Is Aggada and Haggada one and the same?

The latter means "to tell," whilst the former is a body of rabbinic "legends," based on our Sage's insights into the Torah. *Aggada* fills in the missing parts of the Torah (e.g., Abraham's childhood), implicit but not stated, a flowing storyteller format, which was continued by the Midrash (especially the eighth-twelfth-century CE *Pirkei deRabbi Eliezer,* the thirteenth-fifteenth-century CE *Sefer Hayashar,* and the fascinating *Yalkut Shimoni,* a thirteenth-century twenty-four-book rich anthology edited by Rabbi Simeon of Frankfurt that delves into the character of the Patriarchs), Jewish mystics, the folkloric yiddish style of the Middle Ages and Chassidut.

The exegetical form was so enticing and mesmerizing that it was "borrowed" by secular Jewish writers (S.Y. Agnon, I.L.

Peretz, I.B. Singer, M.J. Berditchevsky) who created a body of non-Torah work from its genre.

Question 327

What was so important about the "Amsterdam" Haggada?

When it came out in 1695, this was the first illustrated Haggada to use copper-plated engravings to draw all "four sons" in order. Although of historic interest, the medieval images are not very "Jewish" since the artist, a convert from Christianity (Abraham ben Jacob), copied the imagery from the paintings of Matthaeus Merian, a Swiss-Christian artist. The result? The wise kid is not your typical sweet-looking *yiddishe kindt* wearing a *yarmulke* and clutching a *chumash*, but Hannibal, "wise" general of Carthage, as he swears to conquer Rome. It thus flows, from an artist's un-Jewish perspective, that the wicked child is…a Roman soldier! And the simple child? At least ben Jacob included something *Jewish* here: Merian's King Saul, depicted as a shy young guy about to be anointed by Samuel the prophet. But his choice for the youngest child was just another version of Hannibal. And worse! None of the "sons" are shown as "young," but as fully formed adults.

Question 328

Is there a time limit to the Seder or are we supposed to go on all night in the style of the Bnei Brak Sages?

There is only one "drop-dead" time: the *afikomen* must be eaten before midnight, which brings the basic Haggadah to an end, but you can continue singing and storytelling (Storah-telling) as long as you have the *koach* (energy) and can stay awake (although there's a dispute whether this post-midnight "telling" is considered part of the *Maggid* mitzva). Does midnight also apply to the second Seder? No. And remember, midnight is not necessarily 12:00 a.m. In Jewish law, midnight is exactly halfway between sunset and sunrise.

Question 329

Can I sing any song I want at the Seder?

It's better to stick to the script; but if you feel the need to add songs, make sure they're appropriate for Pesach (i.e., happy 'n praiseful).

Question 330

What were the ten plagues of Pesach?[48]

1) **Blood** – the Nile turned into blood for seven days, causing fish to die and leaving the population with undrinkable water;

2) **Frogs** – a swarm of frogs arose out of the Nile and covered the land of Egypt;

3) **Lice** – a plague of lice descended on the Egyptians and their animals;

4) **Flies** – a swarm attached themselves to Egyptian eyelids;

5) **Murrain** – a deadly cattle virus;

6) **Boils** – a painful plague that made it difficult for the populace just to stand or walk;

7) **Hail** – a hailstorm that destroyed people and animals, and devastated the agricultural economy;

8) **Locusts** – clouds of locusts, so dense that the sky was darkened;

9) **Darkness** – it was so dark for three days, one could feel it;

10) And finally the **death of the firstborn son of every Egyptian family**, especially the firstborn son in the Pharaoh's family.

Were the plagues singular in nature? It's still being debated in mystical terms. Rabbis Eliezer and Akiva argue that there were four plagues in each plague; Rabbi Yose Haglili says that each

---

48.   Exodus 7:14–11:10.

plague was only one. What is the basis of this multiple plague-within-a-plague theory? It flows from the notion of God's intent. Why plagues? In order to break the impurity of Egypt, which was so all-consuming, the plague's penetration had to be deep in order to be effective. Rabbi Eliezer is convinced that the unfortunate "beneficiary" of each strike was so overwhelmed that even its elementary four elements (fire, water, air, earth) were also pervaded. Rabbi Akiva believes his colleague doesn't go far enough, and claims that plagues reached an entire new (fifth) dimension (*hiyuli*) that so permeated their "recipient" that it collapsed back into its pre-Creation shapeless core, adding a fifth plague dimension to Rabbi Eliezer's four basic elements. Rabbi Yose Haglili, more optimistic in nature, was content in simply calling a plague a plague, one that only affected its target externally.

Question 331

Why do we not lean when we eat maror?

Leaning is a sign of freedom: the maror represents the exact opposite – slavery.

Question 332

What's a *Bird's Head Haggada*?

It is the dream of every Judaica collector in the world to own one! The thirteenth-century *Bird's Head Haggada* from Franconia,

Bavaria, is the earliest illuminated Haggada to have survived as a separate book. Why the strange title? Because it's a strange Haggada! What could be stranger than people with bird heads and long beaks conducting a Seder? Talk about weird! Some are shown with short, pointed animal ears; others have distorted blank faces, bulbous noses, and all wear the degrading conical compulsory "Jew's Hat" (decreed by the anti-Semitic Lateran Council in 1215). Why bird heads? Some *meshuggene* illustrator decided that this was the loophole against the Torah's injunction against graven human images. Later, it was decided that image reality was OK, on the basis that the Haggadah was not as sacred as the Torah.

Question 333

How do I place the items on the Seder plate? Must they be in a specific order?

Yes. Going clockwise, and starting at the bottom, the order never changes: *chazeret* (lettuce), *karpas* (vegetable), *beitza* (roasted egg), *zeroa* (roasted bone), *charoset* (nuts and dates). And in the center? *Maror* (bitter herbs). What's the rationale for this *seder* ("order")? It follows the chronology of the Haggada events, and is faithful to a rabbinic concept known as *Ain ma'avirin al hamitzvot*, not to "pass over" one present-and-clear mitzva for a future one.

So how many items are on the Seder plate? Six. How many actual mitzvot are there at the *Seder tisch*? Seven. Two are derived straight from the Torah (eating matza, telling the Exodus story), and the other five are rabbinical (maror, *afikomen*, saying *Hallel*, drinking four cups of wine, reclining on pillows as a display of free aristocracy).

Question 334

Who's the most important participant at the Seder?

The Jewish child. In fact, the entire night of "retelling" is centered around one concept: "When *your child* will ask...you shall tell *your child.*" Jewish boys and girls are the VIPS at the table; and everything said and done is said and done to involve them.

Question 335

Are all the socially and politically correct Haggadot acceptable?

Yes and no. It is true, as Rebbe Naftali Ropshitzer noted, that each year the Haggadah has new classical commentaries without altering a word. When asked, "why then do we continue to print new ones every year?" the Rebbe replied, "No doubt, last year's wayward son of the Haggada's four sons has repented, so we need a new edition with a new *rasha* to take his place." The Haggadah may be an "open book," but tradition and custom remain the key.

It is true that Jews are encouraged to talk, eat and talk some more. However, in certain circles the Seder has been hijacked as a metaphoric Rorschach test for personal agendas, a perfect tool to vent on other private issues whilst lamely trying to link one's own moral agenda to a custom-free Pesach. And so we are bombarded with a new phenomenon: the Seder as a platform for social campaign, ranging from union Seders to anti-war Seders to feminist, gay-rights, political agendas ("Let My people go" needs to be stretched to cover, for example, the black civil-rights movement) and freedom Seders (workers need liberation from their bondage of employer capitalism).

Question 336

What's the right way to spell "Haggada"?

I haven't got a clue! Any will do: try Hagadah, Hagada, Haggada, hagaddah, haggaddah, hagadda, haggadda, etc. How do you say it in plural? Haggadot. What does it mean? It's Hebrew for "narration, telling, recital," derived from *vehigadeta levincha*, which literally means, "And you shall tell your child." This translation, argues Rabbi David Avudraham, is incomplete: he claims that when the term *higadeti* is used elsewhere in the Torah, it does not mean, "I shall tell" but "I shall praise"[49] (which is how the *Hallel* came to be incorporated into the *Maggid*, "telling").

---

49.   Deuteronomy 26:3.

Question 337

If the Haggada's Rabban Gamliel tells us to mention "Pesach, matza and maror," why do we only point to the latter and not to the Pesach?

Despite being on the Seder table, the bone symbol of the Pesach (paschal lamb) is not the real McCoy (i.e., actually sacrificed in accordance with the Torah).[50] However, in contrast, the matza and maror (bitter herbs) are very "real" and thus we point to them – and eat them.

Question 338

I don't see the distinction between "telling (*sippur*)" and "remembering (*zechira*)"? How can you do one without the other?

The once-a-year mitzva to tell the Exodus story (*sippur yetziat Mitzrayim*) is a distinct Torah order ("And you shall tell your son on that day, saying....."),[51] an overlay on the nightly mitzva to "remember" the Exodus (*zechirat yetziat Mitzrayim*) which is also a "*mitzva min haTorah*"[52] – despite the fact that the Rambam excludes it from his 613 *minyan hamitzvot* in both his

---

50. Exodus 12.
51. *Pesachim* 116b; Exodus 13:8.
52. Deuteronomy 16:3; Rambam *Hilchot Keri'at Shema* 1:3, *Berachot* 21a.

Sefer Hamitzvot and in *Yad Hachazaka*,[53] including it within the concept of *kabalat ol malchut Shamayim* under the mitzva of saying the nightly *Shema*. Remembering, states Rav Chaim of Brisk,[54] is an individual act; telling is a community act, putting a story into words in order to share it with others. Remembering is academic; telling requires a personal involvement, whereby you can't help but feel the pain (of enslavement) and the joy (at liberation). And more! Having remembered via the vehicle of telling, one instinctively wants to praise God for miracles and deliverances (remember to tell this to your friends: the Haggada verse *harei zeh meshubach*, "The more one tells of the going out from Egypt, the more he is praised," can also be translated as, "the more *He* is praised!").

Rav Yitzchak Zev Soloveitchik (Griz) thought the differences between "telling" and "remembering" were rather obvious: the former requires a question-answer interaction with another person (*derech she'eila u'teshuva*), a specific preamble (*genut*, our initial shame in Jewish history), and a precise ending (*shevach*, emphasizing the triumphs of our history) – all accompanied by certain rituals (Pesach, matza, maror), specific study (the laws relevant to *yetziat Mitzrayim* and *korban pesach*),[55] and a formula of identity.[56] None of these idiosyncratic, all-encompassing prerequisites apply to the nightly "remembering" of the Exodus, which can be done alone, silently, in private and in

---

53.   *Minchat Chinuch, Mitzva* 21.
54.   Rav C. Brisker, *Chiddushei HaGrach al Hashas.*
55.   *Haggada Mibeit Levi; Pesachim* 10:8; *Tur Orach Chayim,* 481; Rabbi J.B. Soloveitchik, *Shiurim Lezecher Abba Mori,* Vol. 11, *Mesorah Torah Journal,* Vol. 3, Nissan 5750, Vol. 5, Adar 5751.
56.   *Haggada Mibeit Levi; Hilchot Chametz veMatza* 7:1; *Shulchan Aruch, Orach Chayim* 472:1.

passing (*hirhur*), with no accompanying fanfare of reminiscing rites and rituals, no learning (*Talmud Torah*), no singing nor praising (*Hallel*), no innovation (on "retelling" Pesach, even *talmidei chachamim* must come up with original thoughts), no attempt to reconstruct, revive and relive the Exodus experience personally – and finally, no presence of Jewish children.[57]

Question 339

Is there any connection between matza and inviting the poor to the Seder?

According to Lamentations,[58] the tribe of Judah was exiled from the holy land because of *"ani,"* the mitzva of giving tzedaka to the poor. The Midrash links *ani* to *oni* from *lechem oni*, the mitzva of matza, which led the Chida to conclude that the two are linked on Pesach.

Question 340

Aren't the Pesach symbols confusing and contradictory?

Although not to the same extent as Purim, which is *purposefully* a chag of opposites (*Venahafoch hu*), the Seder also barrages us with conflicting images: one minute we're celebrating freedom, the next minute we're recalling the bitterness and cruelty of being

---

57. *Ramban al haTorah*, Exodus 20:8; Rambam *Hilchot Chametz veMatza* 7:6.
58. Lamentations 1:3.

slaves; we recline and drink wine to demonstrate our nobility as free people, but then dip food in saltwater and eat bitter *charoset* so as not to forget the tears and hardships of our ancestors. Jewish mystics summarize the differences in one statement: "Light is only *fully* recognized when emerging from darkness"; and thus appreciation and praise at the Seder requires the full understanding of what has transpired, including detailing all the glory – *and* gory!

Question 341

I don't have the patience for a long Seder. Any (legal) shortcut tips?

OK, but the Haggadah recommends the exact opposite ("The *more* one expands on the story, the more commendable," which is why you must read it in a language you understand). But if you must "shortcut" your way through the Haggadah, here are the priorities (but remember the Rambam caveat: no matter what you do, you must "make a change in the routine of that night" in order to actively engage everybody, especially the children, in a genuine search for the meaning and understanding behind the Exodus saga).

It is preferable, but not halachically mandatory, to say every paragraph in the Haggada; in fact, it is possible to say every single word and *not* have fulfilled the mitzva of Seder (e.g., singing *Ma Nishtana* alone is insufficient; Jewish children must inquire, not just recite; just singing *Avadim Hayinu*, "We were slaves,"[59] is inadequate if not followed by a story carefully scripted to the

---

59.   Deuteronomy 6:21.

intellectual level of those present, etc.). The minimum requirements (not necessarily universally accepted) are candle-lighting,
*kiddush, Shehechiyanu, Urchatz, Karpas, Yachatz, Halachma Anya,
Ma Nishtana, Avadim Hayinu, Mitchila, Arami Oved Avi* (which
includes the ten plagues), Rabban Gamliel's *Pesach, matza,
maror; Bechol Dor Vador, Hallel,* washing hands, eating matza,
maror and *korech, afikomen, Birkat Hamazon, Shefoch Chamatcha,*
and, of course, drinking four cups of wine (remember: *sefirat
haomer* is obligatory on the second Seder night). In this witty
observation, Rabbi Nachman of Breslov brilliantly captures
the theme of the Seder, which can be summarized as, "Hang in
there. It's worth the wait!"

> Dan, a homeless person, turns to Bob, also homeless,
> and says, "Hey, do you know what tonight is? It's
> Pesach. That's when the Jews have their Seder feast,
> with fine food and delicious wine. Last year I went to
> a Seder and it was incredible!"
>
> "How do we get invited?" Bob asks.
>
> "It's real simple. All we have to do is go to the
> synagogue tonight, and when the services are over,
> someone will invite us to their home."
>
> And sure enough, that night in shul, they each
> get invited to separate homes for the Seder. "Good
> luck," says Dan, "you're gonna love it."
>
> At the Seder, Bob is really excited. He's hungry
> and hasn't had a home-cooked meal in months. He
> can already smell the delicious food wafting from
> the kitchen. He sits patiently as the family reads in a
> language he doesn't understand. He's getting hungrier,
> but finally he sees a plate of food being passed around.

But it's only little pieces of celery. After this, they go back to reading from the book. An hour goes by and Bob is really hungry now. He's willing to eat anything. Finally they pass around some matza and Bob takes a big piece. Then they serve a bowl of some white vegetable and Bob heaps a big pile on his plate. He stuffs his mouth full with it and…FIRE!!! The horseradish burns Bob's mouth and stomach, and he runs out of the house screaming and cursing.

Later that night, he yells at Dan, "I can't believe you did that to me! The Seder was terrible!"

"What do you mean? At the house I went to, they had incredible fish, soup, chicken, kugel and dessert! All you had to do was hang in there and you'd have gotten yours, too!"

Question 342

If one of the four sons was so "wise," why is he making such undemanding inquiries?

Aha! You just grasped the entire purpose of the Seder *tisch*; the rabbinic determination to make everything so different as to stimulate curiosity, arouse the intellect, and challenge average Jewish children to ask, ask, ask! And so a wise son asks superficial questions (such as, "What is the meaning of the statutes and laws that God has commanded you to do?"). Think about it: how did he become wise in the first place if *not* by asking simple questions?

Question 343

What motivated illustrators to illustrate the Haggada more than any other Torah book?

Illiteracy. The illustrations (*scriptoria*) were supposed to literally "shed light" on their related texts (which is why they used exquisite bright colors and precious metals that "glittered" like gold) for those who couldn't read. Sometimes sophisticated miniature pictures were drawn into the text's letters themselves. Another custom in the Middle Ages developed: drawings of the author, so in the thirteenth century we see decorative likenesses of King David, Solomon, Joshua, and, in the introduction of *Sefer Isaiah*, a bizarre sketch of the prophet being sawn in half (supposedly a nod to the fact that he died, yet lived). During the Middle Ages, artists were suddenly in demand, and their creativity became more extravagant. Why? Because wealthy Jews decided to create one Haggada for each member of the household, with some of the artistry being especially eye-catching in order to provoke the curiosity of the children.

Question 344

Why do we lean "left" on pillows?

Reclining on pillows and cushions (*heseiba*) was the natural position for kings and queens, aristocratic free men and women; slaves, on the other hand, were hunched over, crunched, bent and deformed (who could afford a pillow on a slave wage?).

The Greek nobility would stretch out (a living room in Greek is *triclinium*, "three beds or couches"), sip wine (*symposium* means "drinking together"), dip vegetables in appetizing sauces, discuss a topic, usually pedagogic, innovative and philosophic for "persons worthy of culture" (e.g., the nature of life or love or war – as in Plato's *Symposium*), and then join in a sing-along of praises (replace Homer with Torah and philosophy with the mitzva of *vehigadeta* – and you get a Seder!).

The Rashbam and *Mishna Berura* offer a much more pragmatic reason for why we lean on the left: we lean on the left because the right hand is needed for eating. Does that mean a left-handed person can lean on the right? Yes, but it would be better that one lean left when eating, whether left- or right-handed ("Reclining on one's right side," writes the Rambam, "does not constitute reclining").[60] And then we have the medical reason: doctors claim that leaning and eating on the right can cause epiglottis, a form of choking (caused by the windpipe receiving the food before the esophagus), which will obviously serve as an obstacle to conducting a healthy Seder *tisch*!

According to the Jewish mystics, leaning on the "left side," which is associated with darkness and death, shows that even these qualities can be elevated by Pesach (the same reasoning is used to explain why the *menora* is lit on the left side of the door and *tefillin* are worn on the left arm). Reclining during all four cups, reminds the Steipler Rav,[61] is a compromise: some rabbis of the Talmud argued that Jews need only recline whilst drinking the first two cups of wine (this is the beginning of telling the tale of freedom): others argued to the contrary, that

---

60.   Rambam, *Pesachim* 108a; *Mishna Berura* 472:10, 11.
61.   *Kehillat Yaakov, Brachot* 1.

Jews should not recline until after freedom is firmly established (i.e., reclining only with the final two cups).

Question 345

How did the Haggada arrive at "four sons" as the right educational vehicle to teach Torah?

The *arba'a banim* ("four sons") seems to be a magnet for debate and discussion: in other words, the Haggada succeeded in its desire to create an educational context (*keneged arba'a banim divrei Torah*). But why *four* sons? Reasons abound. The Torah itself directs us to teach the Exodus in four different places at four different times, and suggests that there are four different father-son teaching methods. The first time is, "And it shall come to pass, when your children shall say to you, 'What do you mean by this *avoda?*' Then you shall say, 'It is the sacrifice of God's Passover, Who passed over the houses of the people of Israel in Egypt, when He struck the Egyptians, and saved our houses...'"

The second instruction appears about thirty verses later ("And you shall tell your son on that day, saying, 'This [seven-day feast of matzot] is done because of that which God did to me when I came forth out of Egypt'").

It then recurs a few verses later ("And it shall be when your son asks you in time to come, saying, 'What is this [the laws of sanctity for firstborn animals and humans]'? Then you shall say to him, 'By strength of hand, God brought us out from Egypt, from the house of slavery'").

And then we have the fourth and final instruction ("And when your son asks you in time to come, saying, 'What do the testimonies and the statutes and the judgments mean which God has commanded you?' Then you shall say to your son, 'We were Pharaoh's slaves in Egypt; and God brought us out of Egypt with a mighty hand...'").[62]

Look closely at the pedagogic context. The first instruction is preceded by a question to the father (which is why the answer is more detailed); the second interaction is absent of any question, it's one-sided, the son is mute (which is why the answer is generic and vague). The third interactive instruction is a merger of the first two, general yet detailed (its question, "What is this?" is less direct). The last instruction in Deuteronomy is a "repeat," but brings God's instruction manual up to four questions.

Question 346

Is it my imagination or do the words "heavy" and "hard" appear often in the Haggada?

You're right. The root in Hebrew for "heavy, hard" is *k, b, d*; and, ironically, the two adversaries, Moses and the King of Egypt, are both described as being "heavy." Moses describes himself as being *kaved peh ukaved lashon*, "heavy of speech and of a heavy tongue," when claiming to be unfit to carry out God's task;[63] while Pharaoh is *kaved lev*, "hard-hearted." During the plagues of frogs, gnats and pestilence, he is "hardened" by God while

---

62. Exodus 12, 12:25–27, 13:8, 14; Deuteronomy 6:20–25.
63. Exodus 4:10.

the hailstorm not only "hardened (*vayachbed*)" his heart, but also that of "his servants."

The Hebrew root appears again in Pharoah's vocabulary when his response to the demand, "Let my people go," is, "Let heavier work (*tichbad ha'avoda*) be laid on the men, that they may labor in it!"[64] Pharaoh "hardens" (*mechazek*) his heart repeatedly, yet it is not until a time "of heaviness (*kevedut*)" at the Red Sea ("God looked to the Egyptian camp through the pillar of fire and of the cloud, and brought confusion into the Egyptian camp. And He took off their chariot wheels, that they drove heavily, *bichvedut*)"[65] that the Egyptians realize the battle has been lost.

According to Jewish tradition, this is a perfect example of the concept of *midda keneged midda*, the enemy suffering the same fate that they planned to impose on the Jews: "Rabbi Yehuda says, 'The same way that they meted out, You meted out to them.' They said, 'Let heavier work (*tichbad ha'avoda*) be laid on them,' and You paid them back in the same way; therefore it is written: 'And they drove heavily (*bichvedut*)!'"[66]

Question 347

How popular is the Haggada?

Not surprisingly, the Haggada's commercial demand seems inexhaustible, its audience unlimited. It is by far the Number One bestseller, and it's easy to see why – God's presence in history is

---

64. Ibid., 5:9.
65. Ibid., 14:25.
66. *Mechilta.*

felt right at the Seder table. It is also, by far, the most illustrated of all Jewish books (Joel ben Simeon's 1454 Rhineland Haggada is the epitome of *hiddur mitzva*, "beautifying a commandment," with its magnificent and elaborate drawings). In fact, more Torah commentaries exist on the Haggada, a book read only one night in Israel (two nights everywhere else) a year, than on any other Jewish text, *including* the Bible!

From the day it made its first appearance (1482) in Italy's Reggio di Calabria, Judaica collectors have amassed more than 3,000 separate editions. Consider this: during the entire sixteenth century, only twenty-five Haggadot were printed; by the nineteenth century, publishers were churning out 1269 Haggadot a year…and this record was broken in just the first *half* of the twentieth century! Its scholarly lure is underlined by a startling fact: in comparison to the oldest-known thirteenth- or fourteenth-century Haggada manuscript (currently in Russia's Leningrad Library), which consists of only four leaves (eight pages), the early-twentieth-century *Otzar Peirushim Vetziyyurim*, "Treasury of Commentaries and Illustrations," compiled by J.D. Eisenstein, is bursting with *over* three hundred pages, and *growing*!

Question 348

When did the first printed Haggada come out?

As any Judaica collector knows, the first Haggada was printed in Guadalajara, Spain (1482) and then in Italy (1505). What's the oldest surviving illustrated Haggadah? The one printed in

Prague by Gershom Cohen in 1526, which was so popular that a facsimile version came out in 1560 in Mantua, Italy. The oldest illuminated Sephardic Haggada is the 1320 "Golden Haggada" from Barcelona. What's the most popular version? The Venice layout, published repeatedly (in 1599, 1601, 1603 and 1604), and it continues to be the prototype for Spanish-Italian Jews, while Ashkenaz Jews embraced the "Amsterdam" edition.

What's the difference? Not much. The latter simply has more illustrations that looked better because they were on copper.

Question 349

How many purely symbolic foods are there at the Seder *tisch*?

Seven. *Matza* (symbolizing the haste of the Jews fleeing Egypt); *charoset* (symbolizing the mortar of Jewish slaves); *beitza* (a roasted hard-boiled egg which symbolizes the first lamb sacrificed, the *korban Pesach*); *saltwater* (symbolizing the tears of oppression); *maror* (bitter horseradish, symbolizing the hardships of slavery); *karpas* (a symbol of the undernourishment of Jewish slaves); and *zeroa* (shank bone, a reminder of the paschal lamb).

Question 350

When did the practice of "adding" to the Haggada cease?

The metamorphosis of the Haggada ended in the late Middle

Ages. Why? Because the rise of the printing press put an end to any further ad-hocs. If you compare today's Haggada with, for example, Rashi's,[67] you'll discover that his follows that of Rav Amram, Babylonian rosh yeshiva of Sura,[68] and includes *Dayenu* but not *Chad Gadya*, and his Seder finishes immediately after the fourth cup of wine. When his *talmid*, Rav Simcha of Vitri, brought out the influential and reliable *Machzor Vitri*, it included sections of the Haggada that are also missing in today's version.

Thirteenth-century Italian Rabbi Tzidkayah HaRofei (*Shibolei Haleket*) solidified the prevailing *minhag* of adding *piyutim*, "poetic prayers," because they added "words of praise and thanksgiving." These included *Chasal siddur Pesach kehilchato* (penned by Rav Yosef Tur-Elam 1),[69] *Az Rov Nissim* (written by Yannai, ninth-century teacher of Eliezer Hakalir; later the Maharil added *Vayehi bechatzi halayla*), *Ometz gevuratecha* (by the seventh-century Eliezer Hakalir; again the Maharil added the words, *U'vechein ve'amartem zevach Pesach*), *Ki lo naeh, ki lo yaeh* (from the anonymous *Adir B'Melucha*), and the unknown authors of *Adir hu yivneh beito bekarov, Echad Mi Yodeiya?* and *Chad Gadya* (*Chad Gadya* made its first appearance in *Sefer Rokeach*;[70] the Vilna Gaon[71] was so enamored by it that he wrote no less than ten explanations outlining its importance).

---

67. 1040–1105.
68. 856–876 CE.
69. Died 1040 CE.
70. 1160–1238.
71. 1730–1798.

Question 351

I can't help but keep eyeing the *zeroa*. Can I eat it during the Seder?

No, but you can, according to the Magen Avraham, eat the roasted shank bone at a meal on the following day. Why? Because the nighttime eating may suggest that this lamb is being eaten in the absence of a Temple (which it is obviously not, and is a punishable offense). However, there are no such associations on the following day.[72]

Just to be on the safe side and avoid temptation, the Lubavitcher Rebbe, Yosef Yitzchak Schneerson, would remove almost all the meat from the *zeroa* before putting it on his Seder plate.

Question 352

How can simply eating a green vegetable be considered a step towards freedom?

You miss the point. Putting aside the symbolism of *karpas*, the very notion of gratitude as an attitude is liberating. This is especially true for the small things in life, which is why the Talmud defines "Who is a rich person?" as "one satisfied with what he has." Since this concept requires a constant reminder, Jews are urged to say 100 blessings daily. The popular slang, "don't bite the

---

72. *Pesachim* 53a, *Mishna*; *Pri Chadash, Orach Chayim* 473; Magen Avraham 473:8.

hand that feeds you," is a direct hand-me-down of the Talmud's, "Do not throw stones into the well that you drank from!" This is a tangible expression of appreciation known as *hakarot hatov*, the purpose of which, according to Rav Eliyahu E. Dessler, is not just for the benefactor, but also for the recipient.

In fact, to "give thanks" is the very genesis of the term "Jew," whose Hebrew counterpart (*Yehuda*) is derived from *hoda'a* (thankfulness), the name chosen by Leah for her fourth child from Jacob. Why was the matriarch so grateful? Because this was the child that tipped the balance in her favor, contributing the largest number of children to the twelve tribes of Israel. And the reverse is also true! *Toda*, Hebrew for "thanks," notes Rav Yitzhack Hutner, a leading Torah scholar of the past decade, also means "to confess," thus linking the expression of gratitude to confessing that we are often ungrateful (*kafui tov*) to those who assist us in life.

Question 353

Why don't I have to wash for *karpas*?

There is a general principle that if you dip food in liquid it requires washing (*netilat yedayim*),[73] however many scholars (Tosafot) say that this principle was no longer applicable after the destruction of the Temple. As a compromise, in order to "remember" the past sanctity of the Temple rituals (*zecher lemikdash*), only the father or head of the Seder washes for *karpas*, but without a blessing.[74] (J.B. Soloveitchik, basing his opinion

---

73.   *Pesachim* 115a; Rav J.B. Soloveitchik, *Hilchot Chametz Umatza* 8:1.
74.   *Mechaber, Shulchan Aruch, Orach Chayim* 473:6.

on the Rambam and the custom in Brisk, thought one should wash with a *bracha*.)[75]

Question 354

Does everyone present have to say the *al achilat matza* blessing or just the head of the household?

Just the head of the household, but with certain caveats (*berov am*). According to the Vilna Gaon, this *bracha*, known as *birkat hamitzva* because it is an immediate occurrence, must be *inclusive* – that is to say that everyone present should have the intention that he (their *shaliach*) has them in mind, and all must listen attentively (*shome'a ke'oneh*) and reply *amen*. The participants of the Seder can eat the matza without having to recite the blessing.[76] The Chatam Sofer took no chances: at his large Seder, everyone said *al achilat matza* together in unison.

Question 355

What is the significance of the number "thirteen" in the "Who Knows One?" Pesach ditty?

Who knows 13? I know 13. Thirteen are God's attri-

---

75. Rav J.B. Soloveitchik, *Hilchot Chametz Umatza* 8:1.
76. HaGra's Glosses, *Orach Chayim* 8:12; *Chayyei Adam, Klal* 5:17; *Mishna Berura, Orach Chayim* 8:13.

butes, 12 are the tribes in Israel, 11 are the stars (in Joseph's dream), 10 are the 10 Commandments, 9 are the months of pregnancy, 8 are the days of circumcision, 7 are the days of the week, 6 are the Mishna sections, 5 are the books of the Torah, 4 are the Matriarchs, 3 are the Patriarchs, 2 are the Tablets of the Covenant, our God is One, in Heaven and on earth.

These thirteen refer to the merits, listed in order of importance, as a result of which the Jewish folk deserved to be liberated from Egypt.

Question 356

What does the word *Haggada* mean?

The catalyst of Pesach cheer is a marvelously enticing work known as the Haggada, a separate "stand-alone" Hebrew manuscript, an ancient piece of narrative pedagogy that, according to Rashi, "captivates the heart" of a daring drama. Literally, it means "thanks," but it is more than that. It is a symphony of gratitude, a chorus of appreciation, composed from the verse, "I acknowledge [*higadeti*] today to God." This is a salute to the Mishna's *aggadeta*, a multi-compilation of midrashic sayings and homiletic stories designed to fulfill a direct Torah command: "You shall tell [*vehigadeta*] your son on that day."[77]

---

77.   Exodus 13:14; Deuteronomy 6:20.

Question 357

Why is there an open-door policy after the meal on Seder night?

Originally, the door was opened at the beginning of the meal to invite all who were hungry to participate. Rabbi Matityahu, ninth-century Gaon, inspired by the thought of imminent redemption, made a point of *not* closing his doors the entire night; but this custom was abandoned during the Middle Ages because of Easter-inspired Christian pogroms, and the door was only opened after *bensching* during "the night of guardianship" (a night "set aside [*meshumar*] from Creation")[78] for *Shefoch*, an act of hope that the Messiah (or at least Elijah) would come and redeem them from their oppressors.

Why after *bensching*? The reason is very prosaic. Several families would often gather in one home to hear the Haggada, and then left to eat their meals in their own homes (the streets were also full of learned persons who went from house to house to read the Haggada for those who couldn't, and then they returned to their homes to eat the Pesach meal with their family). By the time they ventured out for the second section of the Seder after eating, the streets were filling up with gentiles riled up from their Easter sermons, so Jews opened their doors in the hope that God would protect them on their way back home, murmuring, "Pour out Your anger upon the heathen who know You not."[79]

---

78. *Rosh Hashana* 11.
79. Psalms 79:6.

Question 358

What is the best way to get my kids' attention on Pesach night?

The Seder is purposely designed to start with a series of unusual, and hopefully interesting, steps. For example: the head of the household drinks the kiddush wine *sitting*, arranges pillows in order to *"recline,"* washes his hands *without* a blessing and *without* leaving the table, and dips (an *unconventional* table etiquette) assorted vegetables into saltwater. To attract the attention of fidgety and impatient children isn't as easy as it sounds. The Jews who lived in the Ksurs (forts) of the Sahara desert, known as the "heretics of Wargla," got their kids' attention by leaving their homes and marching off into the desert.[80] Some Chassidic communities in Hungary dramatized the miraculous dividing of the Red Sea by jumping over a pitcher of water until the water spilled on the floor, followed by singing and dancing.[81]

A rare fifteenth-century Haggada suggests, by way of drawings, the following technique: suspend a curtain across the room, hold it up in two places from behind, letting it hang in three festoons, each at a different level. to indicate openings to solve the "mystery" of Pesach on the other side of the curtain. Did this work? I don't know. Rabbi Akiva had a better idea: he would hand out candies in *shul* to keep the kids in good spirits. He even sent his entire *Beit Hamidrash* staff home early with the advice, "Now is not the time to review another Halacha, but to

---

80.   N. Slouschz, *Travels in North Africa*, JPS, 1927.
81.   A. Scheiber, *"Ikvot Kramatizatzia beTekese haPesach beHungaria,"* Yeda-Am, May 1951.

attend to your child, so that he or she will participate actively in the Seder."[82]

Rabbenu Manoah, a medieval commentator, was more aggressive. He got his kids' attention by starting the meal backwards; the sight of desserts as an opening was a definite success – that is, until they ran out desserts. A custom amongst Afghanistan Jews was for each Seder participant to strike the person he or she was sitting next to with a green onion stalk during the singing of *Dayenu*, which means "enough, already!" This must have appealed to aggressive children. Yemenite Jews perform a symbolic reenactment of the Exodus as the family head throws a knapsack over his back containing the *afikomen*, walks around the room leaning on a cane, and begins to reminisce on how he has just come out of Egypt. The Talmud's Rabba offers his own suggestion: that of *akzrat hashulchan*, which required removing the fully set table from the room. Apparently this worked for his nephew (Abbaye) who asks, "Why are you removing my table? We haven't eaten yet!"[83]

In Iraq and Kurdistan, Jews began their Seder with a dramatic dialogue. One of the children went outside, knocked on the door, and then answered a series of questions from the head of the household.

> Where have you come from?
> Egypt.
> Where are you going?
> To Jerusalem.
> What are your supplies?

---

82. *Pesachim* 109a; *Rashbam*.
83. *Pesachim* 115b.

The child's final answer is the recitation of the *Ma Nishta-na.*

Question 359

Is the mitzva of the four cups in the drinking or reciting?

The primary mitzva is "recitation *(amira al hakos)*," not just drinking. This is done in four stages: *Kiddush, Haggada, Hallel,* and *Birkat Hamazon,* each an independent phase not just of *sippur yetziat Mitzrayim* but also of *pirsumei nisa,* " publicizing the miracle"[84] (some even suggest that one hold a cup of wine during the entire recitation of the Haggada, similar to *kiddush*).[85]

Question 360

What does *afikomen* mean?

I don't know, and neither did the Jews in third-century Babylon, however a Talmudic *Amora* describes *afikomen* loosely as some "kind of song."[86] According to Elijah Levita, famed sixteenth-century Hebrew grammarian, it is a Greek word that describes festive banquet games. Rab thought it was a code-worded abbreviation of *apiku manaihu,* "remove your vessels," as in, "Let's finish and go join another Seder" (in his day it was a crime for

---

84.   Ibid., 108a; Rav J.B. Soloveitchik, *Siach haGrid.*
85.   *Brachot* 51a; Rambam, *Hilchot Shabbat,* 29:7; *Shulchan Aruch, Orach Chayim,* 183:4.
86.   *Pesachim* 119b.

Jews to "mingle"). Samuel thought it stood for *aphiku man*, "remove the food," as in, "Let's move on to dessert and delicacies!"

The Ashkenaz custom for children to "steal and hide" the *afikomen* comes from the Talmud's "One quickly eats up [*choftin*] matza erev Pesach so that the young children will not sleep" (*choftin* can also mean "to grab").[87] The "hiding" custom introduced the term *zafun* ("conceal") into the Haggada; some Torah linguists associate it with the lyrics of David, "How great is thy goodness which thou hast laid up (i.e., concealed) for them that fear thee!"[88]

Rabbi Yaakov Emden would wrap the *afikomen* in a napkin and carry it on his back for at least six feet before hiding it, to re-enact the verse, "The people took their dough before it rose, their kneading troughs bound up in their clothes on their backs."[89] In the Aden Haggada, there is a description of Jews "walking back and forth with the *afikomen* strapped to their backs." Moroccan Jews at the end of the meal take the *afikomen*, put on their shoes, put a belt on, take a staff, place the *afikomen* on their back, and say, "So shall you eat it: your loins girded, your shoes on your feet, your staff in your hand, and you shall eat in haste" – before eating the *afikomen*.[90] In some oriental communities, the *afikomen* was a symbol of hope and redemption, so they bored a hole in part of it and hung it near the front door, as if it was an amulet, for protection. If it was still there the following Pesach, it was replaced with the next year's *afikomen*.

---

87. Ibid., 109a.
88. Psalms 31:20.
89. Exodus 12:34; Y. Emden, *Beis Yaakov Siddur*.
90. Exodus 12:11.

310 AND YOU THOUGHT THERE WERE ONLY FOUR

Question 361

Does the Haggada lend itself, like Purim, to parody?

And how! Take, for example, this ditty from Levi Reuben Simlin (sung to the tune of *Ma Nishtana*), from his famous parody *Order of the Hagadah for Teachers*, penned in an effort to improve the lot of Yiddish teachers...

Why is the teaching profession different from all other professions in the world?

> Why do all other professions enrich and their practitioners eat, drink and rejoice all the days of the year, but teachers whine and are distressed even on this night?...
>
> We were slaves to the householders and to their children who ruled us with a mighty hand. Even if all the householders were well versed in Torah, we would have been compelled to reply also to their questions.
>
> And if all of us were wise, all of us were intelligent, all of us were authors, and even if all of us were miserable, all of us were poor, it would be our duty to emancipate ourselves from the suffering of teaching, and whoever hastens to liberate himself before he reaches the gates of death, behold he is praiseworthy...
>
> Next year may I be a householder! (*Repeat three times*)

Question 362

Do my wife and daughter also have to recline during the Seder?

It depends: the Talmud obligates an "important woman" (*isha chashuva*) sitting next to her husband to recline;[91] a non-important woman need not. So the question is: who's an *isha chashuva* and who's not? The answer is not so easy, so in order not to make distinctions between women in this way, Tosafot and Rama state that all women must recline at the Seder table. That is not to say that scholars have not tried to define an "important woman." Rav Yosef Karo defines an "important woman" as one who is either the (unmarried) head of the household, one with *yichus* (good genes) combined with *yirat Hashem* (fear of God), or a rich Jewess who can sit and relax because she has maids and servants to do the work.[92] One of the early *gaonim*, the *Sheiltos d'Rav Achai*, was opposed to a woman reclining in public, deeming it to be immodest.

Question 363

Is there any difference between *epikomios* and *afikomen*?

No. They're one and the same. The word *afikomen* comes from the Greek *epikomios*, an "after-meal festival of desserts, songs,

---

91. *Pesachim* 108a.
92. *Shulchan Aruch Orach Chayim* 472:4; *Kesef Mishna* on the Rambam's *Hilchot Chametz Umatza* 7:8.

entertainment…going from one group to another,"[93] a custom of revelry, which the early rabbis frowned upon. But the "game" was popular, so the rabbinate tolerated it but gave it a different rationale: "We snatch away the matza from children, so they should not stuff themselves with it and become drowsy and then no questions will be forthcoming from them."[94]

Question 364

I read that the occurrence of the plagues was not miraculous in nature, but can actually be attributed to ecology and Mother Nature. Is this true?

Torah skeptics believe they can "prove" that the the plagues against Egypt were all natural ecological occurrences. Such classical Torah scholars as Abravanel agree that the first nine plagues could be seen as natural phenomena, but argues that it was the timing of the plagues that was miraculous, forcing Pharaoh's capitulation. Rav Hertz analyzes the plague of desert locusts and finds nothing miraculous in the plague itself; after all locusts (and hailstones) have been a destructive scourge since the beginning of history. (In 1951–52, locusts devastated hundreds and thousands of square miles of greenery in Iran, Iraq, Jordan and Saudi Arabia; over five hundred million locusts ate up everything "green" in their path transforming a green landscape into a desert!).

---

93.   *Pesachim* 119b.
94.   *Tosafot Megilla* 21a; *Pesachim* 109a; 119b.

Question 365

So what was miraculous about the plagues then?

The miracle lies elsewhere: neither scientists, meteorologists nor biologists have been able to predict when and where a swarm of locusts will appear. They seem to simply show up, without warning. However, the Torah tells Pharaoh with conviction and certainty they will come *"tomorrow!"*[95] Josephus says the parting was caused by God "or by accident"; a Jewish Hellenistic historian (Artapanus) from the second century BCE claims that Moses was a clever tour guide who simply knew the wilderness better than anybody, and thus knew exactly where and when the tides of the Nile would be low. Others link the sea parting to the aftereffects of a volcanic eruption on a tidal wave in an obscure island in the Mediterranean. Some speculate it was all just a mirage, while some scientists, using computer stimulations, use the Torah's "strong east wind" to suggest that a sustained wind simply lowered the water level so that Jews could walk over an exposed ridge.

Try to follow this argument: the plague of blood was a result of red microscopic organisms in the Nile River that caused photosynthesis which made the water recede, thus a breeding ground for frogs (the second plague) was formed, who were then killed by the Egyptians, however their decomposing bodies bred lice and caused an ecological imbalance that attracted swarms of wild animals, cattle diseases, and, finally, clouds of locusts whose solid mass caused the darkness plague. And the

---

95. Exodus 12:12.

tenth plague? The "guessing" game suddenly stops here. Why? Because the killing of the firstborn cannot be explained through an ecological lens.

Goodbye reason, hello faith! And what does our faith tell us? Even as they walked between two towers of crystallized water, the needs of the Jews were taken care of ("whatever their hearts desired"). If they were thirsty, there was even sweet water to drink; if a child cried, the mother only had to stretch out her hand and pluck an apple or a pomegranate to feed her child.[96] And not just the Red Sea parted, "but all the water in Heaven and earth, in cisterns, in wells, in caves, in casks, in pitchers, in drinking cups, and in glasses, and none of these waters returned to their former state until Israel had passed through the sea on dry land." The waters were "piled up 1600 miles, so they could be seen by all the nations of the earth."[97] Pharaoh was the sole survivor ("Not one man remained alive"),[98] granted eternal life so that he could stand at the gates of hell, the ultimate defeated oppressor of Israel, and rebuke each Jew-hater who shows up with the words, "You should have learnt from my example!"

Question 366

Why don't we say the traditional "l'chaim" before we drink the four cups of wine?

Our rabbis knew from experience all the advantages of wine:

96. *Exodus Rabba.*
97. Midrash, *Mekilta Bashalla.*
98. Exodus 14:28.

it "gladdens the human heart,"[99] it's an aid to health,[100] and it deadens the senses ("Give strong drink to him that is about to perish [be executed]).[101] But they also knew about its adverse effects: the Zohar identifies Adam's "forbidden fruit" as grapes, the Torah links Noah's sin directly to wine,[102] and all Torah scholars agree that there is a direct correlation between drinking and indecency (e.g., *lashon hara* – "When wine comes in, discretion leaves!").[103] Thus the custom to shout out *l'chaim* ("to life!") before a drink was a loud self-reminder to speak and act properly despite the beverage.

However, the Seder table is already infused with sanctity and spirituality, so no such reminder is necessary (although it's not forbidden!).

Question 367

Pesach's expensive! What if I can't afford to make the Seder?

Two of the first three orders of the Seder in the Mishna (*Arvei Pesachim*) make it clear that poverty is not to be used as an excuse to avoid certain Pesach obligations; even "the poor among Israel" must "recline" and drink four cups of wine.[104] It was a premier mitzva before chag to donate to the communal charity, known as *ma'ot chittim* (in Aramaic, *kimcha d'pischa*, "flour for

---

99. Psalms 104:15.
100. *Shabbat* 67b.
101. Proverbs 31:6; *Sanhedrin* 43a.
102. Genesis 9:21.
103. *Eruvin* 65a; Proverbs 23:29.
104. *Pesachim* 112a.

Passover"), in order to ensure the anonymity of the giver and the recipient. Their job was to make sure that every *ani* ("poor person") has enough money to buy wine for Pesach. (Anybody who lived in the city for at least twelve months had to contribute to this "Passover Fund."[105] In those days, when the power of the local rabbinate was absolute, Jews were forced to participate and help.)

One day Rabbi Eizel Harif, the rav of Slonim, saw a rich Jew, known for his stinginess, shaking all the chametz out of his pockets on erev Pesach. "You are not required by Halacha to do that," he tells the man. "Why not?" Asked the man. "Because," replied the rav of Slonim, "the Halacha requires a person to check 'as far as the hand reaches,' and your hand does not reach into your pockets." The Chafetz Chaim would visit booksellers in his town as Pesach approached and ask them to stop selling Jewish books (except the Haggada) until after chag. He was concerned that Jews would spend their money on *sefarim* instead of meat and fish for chag, presents for their wife, or new clothes for the children (he called the booksellers who ignored his advice collaborators of "evil urges!"). When a poor man knocked on the door of Rabbi David of Lelov asking for money, the only thing Rav Dovid had in his home was *shemura matza*. He didn't hesitate and, to the shock of his family, gave away all his specially-prepared matza, explaining, "We use *shemura matza* at the Seder because it has been guarded against spoiling by fermentation [*himutz*, which means "missing"]. Should I then, because of the commandment of eating *shemura matza*, miss the fulfillment of the mitzva to give charity, a special commandment

---

105. *Baba Batra* 1:6.

[in Hebrew, *mitzva shemura*] for gaining entry into *Olam Haba* [the World to Come]?"

When Rabbi Naftali of Ropshitz finished his *Shabbat Hagadol* sermon, he told his family, "In my *dvar Torah* today, I managed to go halfway. I persuaded the poor of the town to be willing to accept charity from the Pesach Fund. Now all I have to do is to persuade the rich to open their clenched fists and contribute!"

Question 368

Is the *Ma Nishtana* of today the same as in ancient times?

No. The version in the Mishna, and old manuscripts that have been discovered, only contain three questions,[106] all culinary-directed, rotating around maror, chametz and matza (*tibbulim*), and cooked and roasted meat (*korban Pesach*) – in other words, the *Ma Nishtana* focused on what we eat and why we eat it.

Question 369

What does *Yachatz* mean?

This refers to the breaking of the middle matza into two pieces. In Hebrew, *Yachatz* means "dividing." The Seder plate has three compartments to hold the three matzot. Why three? Some say each matza symbolizes one of the three patriarchs (Abraham,

---

106. D. Goldschmidt, *Haggada shel Pesach Vetoldotecha.*

Isaac, Jacob), or the three affiliations of the Jews (*Kohanim, Leviim, Yisraelim*).

Question 370

I still don't get it! How does biting into a piece of tasteless, visually displeasing cracker remind me of anything?

Everything we do at the Seder is for one reason only: to re-experience the plight that befell our enslaved, oppressed folk from Egypt over three thousand years ago. The most effective way to be Jewish is to never forget what it meant to be a slave in the shadows of the Pyramids and, through this vehicle of remembrance and memory, to continue displaying thanks and gratitude to God for the lesson of freedom, consummated in the light of Sinai. The matza (your "cracker") is symbolic of the "bread of affliction" (*lechem oni*); the dough was flattened because when it came time to leave, in the middle of the night, the Jews did so in such a rush that they did not even wait for the most life-sustaining food product (bread) to be ready.

Question 371

Do the five Sages in Bnei Brak have anything in common?

Apart from reclining at the same time? Yes. All of them (except for Rabbi Akiva, the child of a convert) came from the Tribe of Levi, a tribe that had been exempted from slavery by Joseph in order to continue learning Torah. Thus none of their ancestors were ever enslaved,[107] and yet they (Rabbis Eliezer, Yehoshua, Elazar Ben Azaryah, Akiva and Tarfon) still stayed up all night discussing the Exodus from Egypt.

Question 372

It is hard enough for me to stay awake for one Seder night, so how am I supposed to manage for two nights?

If you look deep into Kabbalah, you'll discover that due to the Diaspora's lower level of spirituality, it takes two days to absorb the spiritual energy that Jews in the holy land can soak up in one day. If you ask Tevye of *Fiddler* fame, he'll give (or sing) you the right answer: Tradition, tradition!

Question 373

What is the purpose of a Seder *tisch*?

The Seder provides food for the mind and refreshment for the spirit. As they inhale the aroma of chicken soup and *kneidlach*, grandparents interact with young children to discuss the whys and hows of Jewish destiny, a partnership that affectionately bridges space and time, past and present, ignoring the age barriers within families and injecting harmony into the home. as The Jewish family unite in the dining room to recite the Haggada,

---

107. *Simchat Haregel.*

declaring the same proclamations of faith ("Once we were slaves, Now we shall be free!"), eating the same foods, singing the same songs (*Dayenu, Chad Gadya*), and drinking wine in anticipation of the arrival of the same guest (Eliyahu). No other event in the Jewish calendar holds such magnetism, power, fascination.

The Seder is an encounter with history; it reflects our struggle with tyranny and freedom, and provides a glimpse at the mirror of our past and the reflective fate of our future. Pesach's roller coaster ride takes place at the Seder *tisch*, a festively laid-out table on the first two nights of Pesach. This is the single most important meal in the entire Jewish calendar; even more than the three Shabbat meals.

Question 374

Why so much fuss over the Sarajevo Haggada?

This elegant fourteenth-century 109-page Haggada, produced in northern Spain, happens to be, by far, the best-known Hebrew illuminated document extant. It is a lavish masterpiece, one of the most precious and priceless Jewish manuscripts in the world; its style, replete with full-page miniatures, relates to the Gothic school prevailing in fourteenth-century Catalonia.

What does Sarajevo have to do with it? The Haggada was brought to Bosnia via Salonika in the sixteenth century by Jewish-Spanish refugees and for many centuries belonged to the local Koen family. It resurfaced in 1894 when a little Jewish boy tried to sell it at school after he had been left penniless by the death of his father. It then became the property of the Sarajevo

National Museum. During World War II, it was smuggled to safety in a mountain village by a Muslim professor, resurfacing in 1995 when Bosnia's president produced it to "prove" it was undamaged as a result of Sarajevo's four-year siege.

Where is it now? In an underground bank vault in the heart of Bosnia's capital.

Question 375

Is there a famous "runner-up"?

Yes: the rare, richly decorated fifteenth-century *First Nuremberg Haggada*, handwritten in Ashkenaz Hebrew script in sepia ink. It is one of the few works of Jewish art by a Jewish-European artisan (Joel ben Simeon, aka Feibush Ashkenazi, "the Leonardi da Vinci of Jewish illustrators") that survived the late Middle Ages, having been dedicated to a "Rabbi Nathan ben Solomon."

Question 376

Is eight an important number?

More so than it is given credit. Rabbi Samson Raphael Hirsch considered the number eight to symbolize the spiritual – just as the *brit* of a male infant when he is eight days old symbolizes his spiritual birth. That is why our rabbis answer the Haggada song, "Who Knows Eight?" with "eight days of mila."

Question 377

What's the difference between the Karaite Haggada and the traditional Haggada?

Unlike the traditional version, with its Mishna and Midrashic inserts, the Karaite Haggadah doesn't believe in a "fixed" *seder* ("order"), and uses only direct quotes from the Torah with short explanations. There are in fact two versions of the Karaite Haggada, which developed in the two centers of late Karaism: the smaller "Egyptian" version (from Cairo), and the more expanded "Russian" version (from Crimea). In the Egyptian version, the *Birkat Hamazon* occupies about a third of the entire Haggada, while in the Russian version, it occupies about twenty-five percent.

Question 378

I don't get it! In the popular *Chad Gadya*, it might be OK for God to "smite the Angel of Death," but wasn't it clearly wrong for the cat to eat the little goat in the first place?

Rabbi Noson Adler once observed a few Jews intervening in an argument between some other people. He approached them, and said...

In the song *Chad Gadya*, it was clearly wrong for

the cat to eat the little goat. Therefore the dog was apparently justified in biting the cat. If so, the stick should not have beaten the dog. Therefore the fire was justified in burning the stick. If so, the water should not have extinguished the fire. Therefore the ox was justified in drinking the water. If so, the slaughterer should not have slaughtered the ox. Therefore the angel was justified in slaying the slaughterer. If so, then God should not have smote the angel. So how could God have done such a thing?! Because, while it was certainly wrong for the cat to eat the little goat, it was also wrong for the dog to get involved in an outside dispute. It only made things worse. Thus, the dog deserved to get beaten. But the stick had no right getting involved! And so on… Therefore, at the end of the line, God was justified in punishing the angel, which similarly had no business getting involved in the dispute of others!

Question 379

Is *Chad Gadya* just a children's song or does it have any additional meaning?

As the Seder's concluding number, *Chad Gadya* is a paradox: it's a simple children's song but it has enough complicated allegorical meat on it to keep Torah scholars intrigued. Based on a German folksong, the song unfolds in ten stanzas, starting with a father who buys a young goat for two coins and ends with the Angel of Death striking down the butcher and, in return, being struck down by the Heavens.

When the song first appeared in 1590, the Haggada commentators immediately assigned importance to *Chad Gadya*. Some interpreted it to be an allegory about Jewish history (the Jews are goats, victims of generations of enemies, until God comes to the rescue).

Question 380

Can we extract any messages from the style of art of *Chad Gadya*?

The art illustrates the ambivalence towards the complexity of the song and its allegorical content. Eighteenth-century Jewish artisans, in their early attempt to resuscitate the lost art of Judaic manuscript illumination, took to *Chad Gadya* like a magnet. In his charming 1739 Copenhagen Haggada, Uri Pheibush Segal gave it a simple, uncomplicated folk-art rendition (the goat is a goat, the Angel of Death appears as a skeleton, God's arm descending from a cloud, sword in hand). But by the time El Lissitzky illustrated the song in 1919, using lithographs, the art had become politicized, Communist hybrid-style. Lissitzky, a Russian-Communist avant-garde Jew, decided to use his talents to proselytize for the Russian Revolution. And so the Angel of Death wears the Tsar's crown; burning sticks become burning synagogues; God's extended arm from the sky is painted red. In 1979, Tel Aviv's Frank Stella's artistic pull turned the innocent and simple *Chad Gadya* into a modern abstract work of colorful geometric shapes, splashes, swirls (the goat is nothing more than a mass of yellow-brown squiggles). Sophisticated yet liberal-minded Israeli artists, like Seymour Chwast, are uncomfortable with death so they show the butcher dying of natural causes as the Angel of Death, a fiendish ghost with fiery wings, waits patiently outside.

Question 381

What is meant by "The Fifth Son?"

It was an expression used by Rabbi Menachem Mendel Schneerson, seventh Rebbe of Chabad, in the following letter:

> During the Seder service, we read in the Passover Haggada that the Torah speaks of four sons, "one wise, one wicked, one simple, and one who does not even know how to ask a question." The Passover Haggada then proceeds to tell us the questions posed by each of these sons, and the reply which we are to give to each of them.
>
> While the Four Sons differ from one another in their reaction to the Seder, they have one thing in common: they are all present at the Seder. Even the "Wicked" son is there, taking an active, though rebellious, interest in what is going on in Jewish life around him. This, at least, justifies the hope that some day also the "Wicked" one will become wise, and all Jewish children attending the Seder will become conscientious, observant Jews.
>
> Unfortunately, in our time of confusion and

spiritual bankruptcy, there is another kind of a Jewish child – a "fifth son," who is conspicuous by his absence from the Seder; the one who has no interest whatsoever in Torah and Mitzvot, laws and customs; who is not even aware of the *Seder-shel-Pesach*, of the Exodus from Egypt and the subsequent Revelation at Sinai.

A challenging and pertinent question is: What brought about this regrettably all-too-common phenomenon of the "fifth son"?

The "Fifth Son" is the result of an erroneous psychology and misguided policy on the part of some immigrants arriving in a new and strange environment. Finding themselves a small minority, and encountering social and economic difficulties, some parents had the mistaken notion, which they transmitted to their children, that the way to overcome these difficulties is to become quickly assimilated into the new environment by discarding the heritage of their forefathers and abandoning the Jewish way of life. Finding that this process leads to the discomfort of inner spiritual conflict, some parents resolved to spare their children this conflict altogether. They simply gave their children no Jewish education or training.

To justify the desertion of their religion and appease their stricken conscience, it was necessary for them to devise some rationale. They persuaded themselves, and in turn their children, that the Jewish way of life, with the observance of the Torah and Mitzvot, was incompatible with their new surroundings. They sought, and therefore also found, faults with the true Jewish way of life; while in the non-Jewish environment everything seemed to them only good and attractive.

By this attitude, these parents hoped to assure their children's existence and survival in the new environment. But what kind of existence is it if everything spiritual and holy is traded for the material? What kind of survival is it if it means the sacrifice of the soul for the amenities of the body?

The tragic consequence of this utterly false approach was that thousands upon thousands of Jews have been severed from their fountain of life, from their true faith, and from their fellow Jews. Deprived of spiritual life, there has risen a generation of children who no longer belong to the "Four Sons" of the Passover Haggadah, not even to the category of the "Wicked" one. They are almost a total loss to their fellow Jews and to true Yiddishkeit.

The Exodus from Egypt and the festival of Pesach are forceful reminders that an attempt to emulate the environment does not lead to survival, deliverance and freedom. These come from staunch loyalty to our traditions and the Torah way of life. Our ancestors in Egypt were a small minority, and lived in the most difficult circumstances. Yet they preserved their identity and with pride and dignity tenaciously clung to their own way of life, traditions and uniqueness. Precisely in this way was their existence assured, and eventually their deliverance from every slavery, both physical and spiritual.

Question 382

Shouldn't drinking several cups of wine be mentioned in the *Ma Nishtana* as being "different from other nights"?

No. Drinking wine is not an unusual activity at a Jewish table, especially on Shabbat and Jewish festivals. And, if you look closely at the *Ma Nishtana* context, you will see that it deals in sharp contrasts (e.g., slavery vs. freedom, chametz vs. matza, etc.).

Question 383

Why do we dip a "finger" into a cup of wine, and then drop the substance on the side when recalling the ten plagues (*D'tzach, Adash, Ve'achav*)?

Despite our awe at the miracles that destroyed our enemies, we do not automatically rejoice – thus, our cup does not remain full when talking about another's suffering. We use our fingers symbolically, since the magicians of Egypt, unable to copy the plague of vermin, were forced to publicly admit, "This is the finger of God."[108] *D'tzach, Adash* and *Ve'achav* are the traditional acronymic abbreviations of the ten plagues, grouped in three by Rabbi Yehuda with their initials.

---

108. Exodus 8:15.

Question 384

During the rest of the year, it's OK for any person who ate to lead the *bensching*. Why is it, then, at the seder, according to some *minhagim* the head of the household leads the Grace after Meals?

The head of the home is being honored with the *bensching* because he is the one who has invited the hungry, poor and needy to join in (this custom is linked to Proverbs: "He who has a bountiful eye shall be blessed, for he gives of his bread to the poor").[109]

Question 385

What is *Tzafun*?

This is the eleventh step of the Seder, the eating of the *afikomen* at the end of the meal (which must conclude with matza). The word *Tzafun* means "the hidden thing," a reference to the half-matza hidden at the beginning of the Seder. Why "put aside" half a matza? To emphasize that until we eat the *afikomen*, we've only heard "half" the story (an effective ploy to keep Jewish children awake).

---

109. Proverbs 22:9.

Question 386

What is the "Rainbow Haggadah"?

In March 1945, whilst fighting in Germany, a young Jewish chaplain (Eli A. Bohnen), part of the famed 42nd (Rainbow) Infantry Division, arranged for a slim, unbound, untranslated and unillustrated Haggada to be used on Seder night. It was printed by photo-offset on a press that American soldiers cleaned down with Nazi flags. This became known as "the Rainbow Haggadah," and was the first Hebrew text printed in Germany since the end of 1939. More importantly, it was the first modest book of Torah – used by Jewish GI's on German soil to recall the festival of freedom – that was printed after Adolf committed suicide, proof positive that the evil moustached German mass murderer failed in his mission to rid the world of Jews and Judaism ("for not just one enemy has arisen to destroy us; rather in every generation there are those who seek our destruction, but the Holy One, praised be He, saves us from their hands").[110]

Question 387

What is the purpose of singing *Adir Hu*?

This song (*Adir Hu* means "acceptance, conclusion") is sung during *Nirtza*, towards the end of the Seder, and praises God in a unique repetitive literary style, with different alphabetically arranged adjectives that include every single letter in the Hebrew alphabet (known as an acrostic). It calls for Messianic

---

110.   Haggada.

days, the rebuilding of the Temple, and reiterates the dream of going to Israel ("Next year in Jerusalem"). With the exception of *Adir Hu*, which stands alone as an introduction, there are twenty-one adjectives, a number with Judaic relevance because it is a multiple of the mystical number seven.

Question 388

Why don't we open the door at *Halachma Anya* instead of at *Shefoch Chamatcha*?

At first glance you are right: *Kol dichfin yaitai v'yechol*, an invitation to all who are hungry to join us, surely requires opening the door for them! However, the Strikover Rebbe saw this expression as not only an invitation to those who were in need physically, but also an invitation to the Seder participants, who were perhaps spiritually impoverished, to be introspective and reflect on God's greatness.

This idea echoes the Talmudic adage that the essence of Pesach is not merely physical freedom and relief (*geulat haguf*) from Egypt, but also the unshackling of the spirit (*geulat hanefesh*) from a prison of pure paganism.

Question 389

Isn't giving a prize for finding the *afikomen* sending a message to children that it is acceptable to steal and blackmail?

No, it's a harmless game designed to maintain a child's curiosity until the end of the meal.

Question 390

Why isn't the structure of the Haggada more like the Talmud?

If you look closely, it is. Mark Twain thought Jews had an "aggressive and inquisitive mind." He was right: the basic linguistic structure of the Talmud is *shakla v'tarya*, the reciprocity of questions and answers, which is the raison d'etre of the entire Pesach festival. The singular image of Pesach is that of a young Jewish child getting up on a chair in front of his proud family and asking *"Ma Nishtana?"* The Haggada is infused with questions from asking "What do the wise and wicked say?" to "Who knows one? Who knows two? three? four? etc." What if there's only one person at the Seder? Then he has to ask himself the questions, and answer himself!

Question 391

What does Elijah's Cup symbolize?

One Pesach night, Rabbi Menachem Mendel of Kotzk sent one of his followers to open the door after filling Elijah's Cup. But the Jew was frozen to the spot and couldn't do it. When asked why, he replied that he was scared stiff in his certainty that Elijah the Prophet was on the other side of the door. "You're wrong!" Reb Menachem Mendel answered, "Elijah the Prophet enters through the heart, not the door!"

Why Elijah? Pesach is the time of Redemption and Elijah is historically known as the Angel of Redemption, his cup brimming over with optimism, honored with being the figure in history who will herald the coming of the Messiah. The Talmud relates how a certain rabbi bumped into Elijah and asked him when the *Mashiach* would come. Elijah replied, "Immediately." When he didn't materialize, the rabbi became upset and agitated, sought out Elijah and berated him for giving him false hope. In defense, Elijah responded that he had been correct: the Messiah was enthusiastic and ready to come but the rabbi wasn't ready to receive him.

Question 392

How can we reconcile being told to answer the Four Sons, including the wicked one, and the instruction in Proverbs: "Do not answer the fool according to his foolishness, lest you become equal to him. Answer the fool according to his foolishness, lest he be wise in his own eyes."[111]

This may seem like a contradiction but it is not. Judaism recognizes two types of fools: one who already knows everything, who, in his arrogance, will never admit a fault as he scoffs at the Torah. The other fool is aware of his limitations, and thus deserves a response. The Haggada's message is that we have a primary responsibility to engage this type of fool in dialogue, even in his "wickedness," for one simple reason: he's at least present at the Seder – and thus not irretrievably lost.

Question 393

When did the first Seder in history take place?

After a full year in the desert, the Jews celebrated the Pesach festival. But to whom did they tell the story? Weren't they all still witnesses to the fresh events? Yes, but the children of at least

---

111.   Proverbs 26:4, 5.

one Jew were not present and were therefore the first recipients of the tale told by firsthand witnesses: Gershom and Eliezer, the sons of Moses who were in Midian at the time of the Exodus. Moses thus was the first to inaugurate *sippur yetziat Mitzrayim,* the "telling of the going out of Egypt."

Question 394

Isn't there a chronological error in the Haggada? Shouldn't the paragraph *Avadim Hayinu,* "We were slaves unto Pharaoh in Egypt," come after the announcement *Mitchila Ovdei Avoda Zara Hayu Avotenu,* "At first our fathers were idol worshipers"?

That would be true if the Torah were a chronological historic document. But it is not. The Torah, as well as all the other scriptural-rabbinic texts, centers around ethics.

Question 395

Why are so many new Haggadot printed every year?

Rabbi Naftali Ropshitzer has a good explanation: because those whom the author of the Haggada considered wicked last year are called righteous today. (See question 335.)

Question 396

There seems to be a discrepancy as to "when to stop" teaching the laws of Pesach. Am I right?

Yes: the cause is a printing error. An old Shas in the Strashun Library reads, "Explain to him [the wise son] all the laws of the Pesach [*beHilchot haPesach*, and not *keHilchot haPesach*] until one may not eat after the *korban Pesach*." The key word here is "until" – in other words, one should be teaching the laws of Pesach from the beginning, up *until* the last chapter in the Mishna[112] (which begins with, "One may not eat until after the *korban Pesach*").

Question 397

Shouldn't the order of matza and maror be reversed?

The Brisker Rav (Yoshe Ber) points out that although the "bitterness" of slavery (as represented by the maror) came first ("They embittered their lives"),[113] human nature requires the context of contrast (i.e., freedom, as symbolized by the matza).

---

112.   *Pesachim* 10, 8.
113.   Exodus 1, 14.

Question 398

Why did Rabbis Tarfun and Akiva differ over the blessing of redemption?

Rabbi Tarfun preferred the shorter version of *past* redemptions ("Who redeemed us and redeemed our fathers from Egypt") because he opposed the rebellion against the Romans and didn't want to include any unnecessary provocations.[114] In contrast, Rabbi Akiva fully supported Bar Kochba's actions, and saw the night of Pesach as the prime time to agitate for *future* redemption, so he added a lengthy sentence: "So also our God and God of our fathers bring us to other festivals and holidays that come our way in peace, rejoicing in the building of Your city and joyful in your service...Blessed are You, God, Who redeemed Israel."

Question 399

When did the *afikomen* enter the Seder?

Before the destruction of the Temple, the *afikomen* was the paschal lamb ("Please pass the Paschal!"), which was eaten on erev Pesach by Jews who came to Jerusalem with lambs in tow. A small portion of lamb was burnt on the altar; the rest was eaten at the end of the Seder. After the Romans destroyed the Temple, no more sacrifices were offered. Instead, the paschal lamb was replaced with a piece of matza, a symbol of oppression (this is

---

114. *Pesachim* 116b.

why the *afikomen* is broken in half, a reminder that we have yet to become "whole").

Question 400

Is the message of *Dayenu* restricted to the Exodus story?

No, even though that would have been enough! The Talmud tells of a father who carries his son on his shoulders, day and night, and feeds him by simply stretching his arm upwards, taking care of his boy's every need. One day they pass a traveler and the child yells out, "Hey, have you seen my father?" Thus the Haggada, aware of how easy it is to become so complacent and accustomed that we no longer recognize nor appreciate God's help, expands the fifteen "gift" stanzas of *Dayenu* past the provincial Egyptian experience as a tool of repetition of the positive consequences of aligning with the Jewish God. Its first five "Thank-you's" center around the Exodus (i.e., escaping enslavement, "executing justice upon the Egyptians and their gods"), the next five describe miracles (i.e., how God changes nature by "splitting the sea for us, providing manna in the wilderness"), whilst the last five hone in on the closeness to God ("He gave us Shabbat, the Torah, the land of Israel, the Temple to atone for all our mistakes").

Leshana Haba b'Yerushalayim